The Roots and Flowers of Evil
in Baudelaire,
Nietzsche, and Hitler

The Roots and Flowers of Evil in Baudelaire, Nietzsche, and Hitler

CLAIRE ORTIZ HILL

OPEN COURT
Chicago and La Salle, Illinois

To order books from Open Court, call 1-800-815-2280 or visit
www.opencourtbooks.com.

Cover drawing: *Rose de Jéricho* by Jacqueline Wegmann

Open Court Publishing Company is a division of Carus Publishing Company.

© 2006 by Carus Publishing Company

First printing 2006

Printed and bound in the United States of America.

Library of Congress Cataloging-in-Publication Data

Hill, Claire Ortiz.
    The roots and flowers of evil in Baudelaire, Nietzsche, and Hitler / Claire
Ortiz Hill.
      p. cm.
    Includes bibliographical references and index.
    ISBN-13: 978-0-8126-9586-1 (trade pbk. : alk. paper)
    ISBN-10: 0-8126-9586-0 (trade pbk. : alk. paper)
    1. Good and evil. 2. Baudelaire, Charles, 1821-1867. 3. Nietzsche,
Friedrich Wilhelm, 1844-1900. 4. Hitler, Adolf, 1889-1945. I. Title.
BJ1401.H55 2006
170—dc22
                                       2005036612

This book is dedicated to Jacques Sommet, s.j.,
Philosopher, priest, and survivor of Dachau,
and to his cousins,
André, Yves, Georges, and Jacques Montel,
victims of Buchenwald-Dora

What if a much of a which of a wind
Gives truth to summer's lie;
Bloodies with dizzying leaves the sun
And yanks immortal stars awry?

  . . .

What if a dawn of a doom of a dream
Bites this universe in two,
Peels forever out of his grave
And sprinkles nowhere with me and you?

e. e. cummings

Contents

Acknowledgments

The path leading to the writing of this book started in September 1967, when I was sixteen years old. My German I teacher at Redlands High School, Ingeborg Schuler, suggested that I study German at the university level. My across the street neighbors, Frank and Harriet Blume helped me to do just that. Frank's father, a German professor, had been forced out of Nazi Germany in the 1930s on the grounds that he was a decadent intellectual and writer. Frank's maternal grandparents perished after deportation to Theresienstadt. Harriet is a Quaker.

Frank was chairman of the Social Sciences Division at San Bernardino Valley College. He intervened with the dean on my behalf and suggested that, if I would like to study Philosophy in addition, he had a friend who was an excellent teacher. I didn't know what philosophy was, but the idea appealed to me. The friend was Roger Schmidt, who changed me from a foreign language major into a philosophy major. Most importantly, he imparted to me a way of conceiving of the philosophical task that has never left me and has weathered many a storm. Roger is the only teacher I have ever had with whom there has ever been ongoing communication.

When I was seventeen I transferred to my local campus of the University of California. There I specialized in German philosophy under Bernd Magnus, a child of the Holocaust and founder of the North American Nietzsche Society. He recommended that I pursue studies in Comparative Literature. So, I did a Master's Degree in Comparative Literature with a specialty in French Literature and Philosophy. Some years later it was through Bernd Magnus's advice that I came to specialize in the Austro-German roots of twentieth-century philosophy.

Since 1989, Father Jacques Sommet, a Jesuit political philosopher, a former member of the French Resistance, and a survivor of Dachau has been my spiritual director. When he began studying philosophy in the 1930s, his goal was to understand his century, which had been my initial

reason for studying philosophy. Father Sommet is the honorary president
of an organization of deportees of which he was long the president. Owing
to him, I find myself in the thought-provoking situation of knowing much,
much more about what became of the victims of Nazi concentration camps
than I do about the fate of my high school and, above all, university class-
mates. It is to him and to four of his cousins, victims of Buchenwald-Dora,
that this book is dedicated.

During the years that I was working on this book, I had two excep-
tionally reliable and competent assistants, Emiko Ima Ray and Aurelia
Valero Pie. In addition, I owe much to the support and encouragement of
colleagues like Manuel Alvarez Perez, Jairo da Silva, Paul Gochet, Ivor
Grattan-Guinness, Jaakko Hintikka, Ruth Barcan Marcus, Judy Miles,
Barry Smith, Dallas Willard, and to my friends for their fidelity.

Once again I must thank Jacqueline Wegmann for the opportunity to
use her art work on the covers of my books. She calls the drawing on the
cover of this book *Rose of Jericho*. Roses of Jericho are plants that look
dead, but come to life in water. My cousin Anthony DiSalvo took the picture of me that is on the cover. I am still indebted to the erudite booksellers at my nearby philosophy bookstore, Le Chemin des philosophes
(specialists in old, modern, rare, and out of print books, 1 rue des
Feuillantines, 75005, Paris, www.chemin-des-philosophes.com) for all the
ways in which they help me and others. My other local booksellers were
admirably understanding about my search for books on the disturbing subjects treated in this book.

For a long time I have wanted to find a way to thank certain people
who have meant a lot to me and I think that a book that, in part, deals with
the question of cleansing society of "useless" lives is a good place to do so.
When I was a counter girl, an elderly man, impeccably dressed in a suit and
tie, used to come every morning and order a coffee and a doughnut for
nineteen cents and leave me a twenty-five cent tip. Later, when I was a student, he used to send me a card every month with five dollars in it to help
me financially. This was John Schuster. He was in his late seventies. He was
a retired farm laborer living on Social Security. He had been orphaned at
an early age. At the orphanage his brother had fallen off of a haystack and
died and another brother had died when he fell down the stairs at the
orphanage while carrying acid. John was ultimately adopted by farmers
who soon died as well. He never married and had no family. One day he
had a heart attack while crossing the street in downtown Los Angeles. The
last time I saw him he was lying unconscious and paralyzed by a stroke in
a home where the old people were lined up in wheelchairs drugged and
crying. By that time I was living in faraway France. From the California
Death Index on the internet, I learned that he died a year later.

The second person is Hazel, an elderly widow who was going blind who "adopted" me when I was a church social worker in the Washington D.C. inner city during the Ronald Reagan presidency. With her orphaned, mentally retarded niece and grandnephew, she lived right in the heart of the 14th St. ghetto, about a block from the site of the 1968 riots. Hazel used to prepare the most delicious meals for me and was so generous that at times I had to borrow her grandnephew's wagon in order to take home everything she gave me.

The last person that I want to thank is a widow who is now in her eighties. Her parents suffered from syphilis and because of that she was born with impaired vision and hearing. She was orphaned at a young age and only able to attend school for a few years. At times, in her childhood the only thing that there was to eat were snails that the children went out collecting. For over fifty years she has lived in a seventh floor walk up apartment. She is one of the most well informed people I know and one of the people upon whom I most rely for advice. She always gives me what I really need. Once she told me that she was obliged to help me because I did not have anything.

Anyone who has ever shared the life of the disadvantaged knows that it is a one-way street, for one receives from them far more, even materially, than one could ever give them or repay. I shall never forget my debt of gratitude towards them.

Claire Ortiz Hill
Martin Luther King Day, 2006
Paris, France

Au Lecteur

This book is composed of small, fairly independent chapters on themes common to the works of the poet Charles Baudelaire (1821–1867), the philosopher Friedrich Nietzsche (1844–1900) and the politician Adolf Hitler (1889–1945), who are not such very odd bedfellows as some might at first consider.

Their writings are rich in insights, images, ideas, and facts about evil. From them I have gleaned pieces of the puzzle of evil, which I have endeavored, to borrow an image from Hitler's *Mein Kampf*, to piece together like the pebbles of a mosaic. Where the ideas of one begin to blur, I have used the thoughts of the two others as a corrective or as a complement to enhance the correctness or the clarity of the picture (Hitler, 35–36). I hope that in so arranging the insights of this poet, this philosopher, and this politician I have been able to form a picture of evil that proves insightful because it is greater than the sum of the disparate parts used to compose it.

To give my argumentation form I have adopted a methodology inspired by *Mein Kampf*. There Hitler wrote of how the world picture and philosophy that became the unshakeable basis of his action for the rest of his life had taken shape within him (Hitler, 22). He tells of how the experience of life during the difficult days of his youth in Vienna had played a determinant role in inspiring him to undertake an in-depth theoretical study of social issues. He explains how in those days he had read extensively and observed life, alternatively using theoretical studies to verify what he had learned from reality and using reality to test his theories. This was how, he said, he had kept both from drying up his mind with purely theoretical considerations and from holding too fast to superficial realities.

Minds whose intellectual ballast is not ordered in terms of real life, but merely in terms of the series of books that they have read, he observed in *Mein Kampf*, are doomed to grow more and more removed from reality until, not infrequently, they end up in a sanitarium or going into politics (Hitler, 34–37).

It was through this method of using theoretical studies to verify what he had learned from reality and using reality to test his theories that Hitler says that he had, for example, come to understand the importance of physical terror toward the individual and the masses, which was something to be precisely calculated and learned from life, not books. Inspired by the experience of daily life, "by balancing the theoretical truth and nonsense" of Marxism "with the reality of the phenomenon," he said he had also gradually obtained a clear picture of the hidden motivations of Marxist social movements, the deep inner reasons behind their success, and had been "able to picture the consequences" (Hitler, 42–44, 50, 63).

So, Part One of this book is called "From Theory. . . ." It is principally based on analyses of ideas about evil conveyed: in *The Flowers of Evil* and *Spleen of Paris*, by Baudelaire; in *Daybreak, Thoughts on the Prejudices of Morality, Beyond Good and Evil*, and *On the Genealogy of Morals*, by Nietzsche; and in *Mein Kampf* by Hitler. All these are works in which evil was depicted, beautified, glamorized, justified by people working calmly at their desks to lay bare its roots and romanticize its horrors.

Baudelaire, Nietzsche, and Hitler were most lucid, most frank, and most eloquent about painting evil and presenting it in glorified garb. These three specialists of the human soul understood that the rawest evil could be presented in attractive trappings and they proved to be exceptionally perceptive about the seductiveness of evil. Underlying any appearances of contradiction, in their writings one finds uncanny insight there into the human nature lying behind human masks, hypocrisy, and conventions.

Charles Baudelaire, the author of the *Flowers of Evil*, labored to "extract beauty from evil" and to express this in poetic form. In him, evil found a master poet. Baudelaire's language, while poetic, is, as one cannot help but notice, direct, clear, and unambiguous. He worked and reworked his poems to polish and perfect them. In 1857, he wrote to the French Empress that with *Flowers of Evil* he believed that he had created a "beautiful and great work, above all a clear work" (Pichois and Ziegler, 344–46; 367). The great difficulty for a translator lies in doing justice to his exquisite poetry, not his ideas, which are conveyed in the clearest of terms.

Like Baudelaire, Friedrich Nietzsche dared to say things about evil that others would never have said, and did so in impassioned, jolting, even inebriating language. Hitler did that too, all the while suggesting in the most specific, concrete terms how that knowledge might be used to the advantage of his political movement. Moreover, with the help of bureaucrats working in the calm and safety of their offices, he largely succeeded in translating the evil theories that he had consigned to paper in *Mein Kampf* into reality. And he succeeded on a scale that keeps imaginations reeling today. How many perpetrators, or would-be perpetrators, of evil deeds throughout the world today still trace their inspiration to him!

My principal aim in dealing with Baudelaire, Nietzsche, and Hitler as thinkers in Part One is to set up a contrast between their ideas as set to paper and concrete realizations of such ideas. It is just too convenient and misleading to speak of evil in purely abstract terms. No blood, suffering, or anguish stains ideas as long as they stay on paper. And in philosophizing about evil we are by no means obliged to restrict ourselves to thoughts expressed in words. We can appeal to real life and real events. It is easy to find samples of real evil that upon inspection tear us away from the carrion comfort of pure theorizing.

Evil is too often glorified in myriad ways that foster a blurring of the differences between fiction, fantasy, and reality. By proceeding from ideas about evil consigned to paper to real, flesh-and-blood instances of evil, and then back from those evil realities to theoretical conclusions, one can show how what is charming, persuasive, and seductive in words may distract people from the real implications of theories which transformed into concrete realities can have unacceptably horrible consequences. This can help explain how certain kinds of evil come about, who is responsible for that, and what can be done about it.

So the discussions of Part Two, entitled ". . . to Reality" are to a large extent inspired by actual events. There I move from the world of theories of Part One, where action is still a sister of dreams, to the real world where people use the sword and perish by the sword (Baudelaire 1857, CXVII), where rape, poison, the dagger, and fire really embroider their designs on the stories of people's destinies (Baudelaire 1857, "Au lecteur"). I make the transition from the world of poetry or theories in which one kills without daggers or guns, from the "greedy, lewd, hard and grasping tyrant; slave of the slave and rivulet in the sewer; the torturer who is enjoying himself, the martyr who is sobbing" of Baudelaire's poem (Baudelaire 1857, CXXVI) . . . to the actual world of executioners and tyrants with real daggers, guns, and of victims who obviously suffer the consequences of real deeds.

In decrying evil, it is such concrete phenomena that people most often have in mind. The majority of people do not seem to believe in the existence of evil in any purely abstract sense. And, as soon as one begins thinking about evil, one finds oneself before the perfectly concrete, unmysterious fact that most of the evil that disturbs, revolts, moves and challenges consciences is performed by actual people who could have done otherwise. The most horrific instances of inhumanity of human beings to fellow human beings is voluntary, desired, and often pursued with a determination that would destroy any who would stand in the way.

These things do not take place in the dark, but in the plain light of day. Direct experience of the most horrible forms of evil has become a normal, unavoidable feature of everyday life throughout the entire world. Everyday the mass media provides a spectacle of horrors whose images echo in our consciences and are as concrete as anything there is: violence, torture, murder, cruelty, war, extermination, racism, hatred, terrorism, massacres. Ghastly instances of evil are photographed, recorded, and replayed over and over. Given the graphic portrayal of evil that is so pervasive and relentless nowadays, it is no wonder that many are disturbed by the ancient philosophical problem of evil and in search of responses and explanations.

Counterpoised to the evil witnessed in the twentieth century has been the development of successful nonviolent movements in which certain people have espoused what most people think of as derisory, even laughably naive and weak approaches to redressing, vanquishing, or escaping evil. And seemingly against all odds, these movements have often achieved their goals. Their efforts have also often been accompanied by a genuine *philosophy* of nonviolence whose seemingly inexplicable, but nonetheless impressive triumphs can serve to loose minds from any too superficial appraisal of their potential effectiveness. They call for an explanation. Finding an explanation for such an apparently incongruous way of attacking evil promises to crack open some of evil's secrets.

So it is that in Part Three, entitled "And from Reality to Theory," I use the reality and successes of such movements to wrest people from superficial ideas about the ultimate power of evil and to show how a philosophical argument can be developed in favor of nonviolent responses to certain forms of evil. I endeavor to show how nonviolent responses to evil that might superficially look unattractive, naive, and all too idealistic in theory are more solidly grounded in human realities than at first appears. For, despite superficial appearances, there is a deep core of realism in nonviolent responses to evil. Evil bears within itself its own contradictions and in them the seeds of its own destruction.

It is in fact just too easy to talk about some mystery of evil, about some incomprehensible, complicated phenomenon shrouded in an aura of ineffability, a sort of festering sore that produces a tangle of thorny problems that do not seem amenable to any rational solution or explanation and before which one might silence one's conscience and grow resigned. And, it is wise to remember that evil wants it that way. It thrives in a darkness that would diffract light and blur vision. It thrives in hypocrisy and conspiracies of silence. Perhaps more than anything else, it would be unforeseeable beforehand, unseen at the time, and unspeakable afterwards. And numerous factors conspire to have things just that way. Evil often comes often veiled in denial, repression, and silence, not only on the part of evil-doers haunted by shame, remorse, or fear of discovery, but also on the part of victims so overwhelmed by what they have undergone as to need to withhold the truth and facts both from themselves and others.

However, while there are surely dimensions of evil that promise ever to elude analyses powerless to capture the nuances of an all too vast problem that seems beyond any rational, coherent use of language, the evil that appears utterly irrational, incomprehensible, and unfathomable is not always so. One can cut oneself a chunk for examination, say a chunk laid bare by nonviolent responses to evil. One can expose its workings and limit its chances of survival. There are ways of removing the veils that people use to screen evil, of bringing to light what would rather go unperceived. One can remove coats of lies, strip away the varnish, expose hypocrisy. There are ways of saying what would rather be unspeakable. May this book be a step in that direction.

PART ONE

From Theory . . .

Baudelaire, Nietzsche, Hitler, and Theories

At first it may seem surprising to find Charles Baudelaire, Friedrich Nietzsche, and Adolf Hitler studied side by side in the same book, and it is certainly even more astonishing to find all three of them being treated together as theorizers.

It is, however, not so very hard to persuade doubters that Baudelaire, Nietzsche, and Hitler might well belong together in a book on the subject of evil.[1] For as perverse or incongruous as the idea may at first sight seem to some, there are quite good reasons why philosophers seeking to plumb the depths of evil, understood as that which is intentionally morally bad or injurious, or causes suffering, misfortune, or disaster, might well want to study the writings of this poet, this philologist turned philosopher, and this painter turned politician.

Baudelaire's greatest masterpiece was entitled *The Flowers of Evil* (Baudelaire 1857), and evil was the subject of the main works of Nietzsche's mature period, *Beyond Good and Evil* (Nietzsche 1886) and the *On the Genealogy of Morals* (Nietzsche 1887). As for the beguiling Adolf Hitler, he is frequently portrayed as having been evil incarnate. After giving the matter a little thought it is, in fact, relatively easily to come to the conclusion that Baudelaire, Nietzsche, and Hitler, each in his distinctive way, were actually undeniably great experts on the problem of evil, as well as three of the history's most eloquent and alluring disseminators of ideas about evil. So those wishing to get to the roots of the evil problem potentially have much to gain from harvesting for philosophy something of what these remarkable manipulators of words, ideas, and people sowed into society.

But an eloquent disseminator of ideas is not necessarily a theoretician. So, it will surely take considerably more effort to convince skeptics that there may be any point in treating any of these three as systematic thinkers. And that is not exactly what I am going to try to do. Although, I look at Nietzsche's and Hitler's explicit defenses of the coherence and consistency of their ideas, there are perfectly good arguments for believing rather strongly that neither was a perfectly coherent and consistent thinker. As for Baudelaire, he was a poet. Poets are not systematic thinkers, and system-

---

[1] It is probably wise to say right from the start that this book is not an attempt to equate Nietzsche's and Hitler's ideas. There is, however, ample material in it to show how the Nazi movement might have been inspired by Nietzsche's thought in a perverse way. See, Golomb and Wistrich, eds., *Nietzsche, Godfather of Fascism? On the Uses and Abuses of a Philosophy*, 2002; Golomb, *Nietzsche and Jewish Culture*, 1997; Aschheim, *The Nietzsche Legacy in Germany 1890–1990*, 1992; Strong, "Nietzsche's Political Misappropriation," *The Cambridge Companion to Nietzsche*, 1996.

atic thought is so inherently different from poetry that any attempt to lend poetic insights a didactic form always constitutes a grave and serious threat to the art. And Baudelaire was the first to insist upon this. Poetry, he once wrote, "cannot, under pain of death or of failure, become assimilated to science or to morality; it does not have Truth as its goal. It only has itself. The methods of demonstrating truth are elsewhere. . . . Cold, calm, impassive, the demonstrating temperament thrusts aside the diamonds and the flowers of the muse; it is therefore absolutely the inverse of the poetical temperament (Baudelaire 1859, 498; Baudelaire 1855-57, 598). The "artifices involved in rhythm are an insurmountable obstacle to that meticulous development of thoughts and expressions whose goal is the *truth*" (Baudelaire 1855-57, 596).

So I have to ask the forgiveness of poetry lovers everywhere that, for the sake of this study, I have translated Baudelaire's ideas at the expense of his exquisite lyricism, sacrificed his beautiful poetry at the altar of his profound ideas. Baudelaire was, though, a very philosophical poet, but one who wrote that "poetry is essentially philosophical; but as it is above *fatal*, it must be involuntarily philosophical" (Baudelaire 1846, 444).

In the case of Nietzsche, an avid reader of Baudelaire's writings (Gilman, 163), both detractors and apologists hasten to underscore the paradoxical, contradictory, and ambiguous nature of his writings in general. And they seem all the more prone to do this as soon as anything as sticky as his ideas on evil comes up. Moreover, Nietzsche sympathizers are always eager to lay responsibility for some of his most embarrassing and shocking pronouncements on his sister's shoulders who, after his major works had already been published and republished under his supervision, really did deform his thought once he had sunk into insanity—while otherwise burnishing his reputation.[2]

Still others would dismiss Nietzsche's writings as the overheated rhetoric and ranting of a rebellious preacher's son, as a clever and thought-provoking conceit set to paper by a gifted fellow who had grown fed up with the overblown piety of a parsonage and who, like a number of the most ardent atheists of the twentieth century, Bertrand Russell, Albert Camus, Jean-Paul Sartre, for example, had lost his father at a tender age and was raised by a bunch of women.

However, one should never be too hasty about denouncing, dismissing, or excusing Nietzsche's ideas as being paradoxical, ambiguous, and con-

---

2 See, Aschheim 1992, *The Nietzsche Legacy in Germany 1890–1990*, 45–48; Santaniello 1997, "A Post-Holocaust Re-Examination of Nietzsche and the Jews *Vis-à-vis* Christendom and Nazism," 22–23; Hollingdale 1996, "The Hero as Outsider," 86–87; Holub 2002, "The Elisabeth Legend: The Cleansing of Nietzsche and the Sullying of His Sister"; Wistrich 2002, "Between the Cross and the Swastika: A Nietzschean Perspective."

tradictory. For might it not be, at least as concerns the subject of evil, that Nietzsche, as Ida Overbeck once observed, was "very logical . . . but he felt pressed into unbearable formulations"? (Gilman, 143). Nietzsche himself insisted on the importance of preserving the unity of his thoughts. In the preface to *On the Genealogy of Morals*, he himself specifically addressed the matter of the importance of being consistent. Philosophers, he underscored there, do not have the right to be piecemeal at any point. "We may neither err in piecemeal fashion, nor encounter truth piecemeal. Rather our thoughts, our values, our yeses and nos, and ifs and whethers, grow out of us with the same necessity that a tree bears its fruit—related and interconnected all together with one another, and are witnesses to *a single* design, *a single* healthiness, *a single* soil, *a single* sun" (Nietzsche 1887, Foreword §2).

But Hitler as philosopher? In approaching Nietzsche as a philosopher one already courts controversy. In Arthur Danto's words, it has "seemed to many that Nietzsche had been manhandled into the history of philosophy for want of an obvious alternative space to store him in" (Danto, 9). But isn't it just going too far to approach Hitler as a philosopher, to try show, in adapting a bit of Danto's approach to Nietzsche, that Hitler thought systematically and deeply about a traditional question of philosophy and that he gave serious, original and coherent answers to it? (Danto, 9). For many it would even constitute a dangerous form of travesty or perverseness to grant, or merely to suggest, that there was any rime or reason in what Hitler said, to conclude that *Mein Kampf*, was a "serious work" that revealed something about Hitler "that few took seriously before the war and even after: 'a powerful, horrible message which he had thought out, a *philosophy*,' that he obviously took very seriously. . . . "[3]

Yet as perverse or offensive as that may sound to some, that is what I am going to try to do because I do not think that people are ever going to be able to "explain" Hitler unless more work is done along those lines. It is just too common and too easy to dismiss him as a madman given to empty raving who owed his success to a genius for appealing to the irrational instincts of masses of people. For one thing, isn't *it precisely the rational, systematic, methodical, and cold-blooded manner in which his cruelest and most ruthless designs were carried out that is one of the main things about his legacy that inspires the greatest revulsion and incomprehension and raises the greatest number of questions about evil?*

In "Nietzsche's Political Misappropriation," Tracy Strong notes that "of all important political movements since the French Revolution, National Socialism appears to be the least philosophically legitimated.

---

[3] Of Trevor-Roper's estimation of *Mein Kampf* in Rosenbaum, *Explaining Hitler: The Search for the Origins of his Evil*, 70.

There is, it would appear, little or no political theory of any value associated with the movement. Indeed, some have argued that rational legitimation was incompatible with the very nature of the National Socialist project." Yet Strong acknowledges that it "has become increasingly difficult to maintain this position in recent years. The (renewed) revelations about the involvement of Martin Heidegger in the practice and ideological arguments of National Socialism make it clear that a thinker of indisputable stature nevertheless perceived an 'inner truth and greatness to this movement' . . ." (Strong, 130).

In this regard it is worthwhile to cite this statement published in 1924 by two Nobel prize-winning German physicists, Philipp Lenard and Johannes Stark. They wrote:

> As recognized natural scientists we should like herewith to announce in conformity with our innermost feeling that in Hitler and his comrades we discern the same spirit which we always looked for, strove toward, developed out of ourselves in our work that it might be deep going and successful; the spirit of clarity without residue, of honesty toward the outer world, and simultaneously of inner unity, the spirit which hates any compromise work because of its insincerity. This, however, is exactly the spirit which we early recognized and advanced in the great scholars of the past, in Galileo, Kepler, Newton, Faraday. We admire and adore it likewise in Hitler, Ludendorf, Pöhner and their comrades; we recognize in them our nearest relatives in spirit. . . . It is clear, complete personalities . . . that we wish to have, just as Hitler has. He and his comrades in struggle appear to us like God's gifts out of a time that has long passed, in which races still were purer, men were still greater, minds less deceived. (cited Weinrich, 12)

In the wake of World War II, Max Weinrich thoroughly documented his claims that German scholars "supplied nazism with the ideological weapons which any movement, but particularly a German movement, needs for its success," that it was not a matter of mere "second-rate writers or sham scholars," but of "mounting numbers of people of regular academic standing, some of them scholars of note," and "that nothing is gained by calling the perpetrators and accomplices madmen and their deeds 'collective madness.' There was too much method in this madness, too much premeditation and planning" (Weinrich, 239–40). As Christian Pross points out in his introduction to *Cleansing the Fatherland: Nazi Medicine and Racial Hygiene* (Aly, Chroust, and Pross 1994), ideas of cleansing the German people of everything sick, alien, and disturbing was a dream that Hitler shared with many, including the cream of German medicine, university professors, outstanding scientists and researchers (Pross, 5, 15). Gitta Sereny has noted that most people would now like to forget the time:

when American expatriate writer Gertrude Stein thought Hitler should get the
Nobel Peace Prize; George Bernard Shaw passionately defended him; the
Swedish explorer Sven Hedin lauded his 'indomitable passion for justice,
breadth of political vision, unerring foresight and a genuine solicitude for the
welfare of his fellow citizens;' and Britons such as Lord Halifax (in reports to
the Foreign Office) and David Lloyd George conferred their stamp of approval.
'Hitler is a born leader of men, a dynamic personality with resolute will and a
dauntless heart, who is trusted by the old and idolized by the young', wrote
Lloyd George in the *Daily Express* after attending the 1936 Olympics . . . 'Yes,
indeed, *'Heil Hitler,'* he replied. 'A great man'." (Sereny 1995, 179)

There is no doubt both that Hitler himself intended to set forth a rational doctrine and that his designs have been judged to be quintessentially
evil ones. Through *Mein Kampf,* he endeavored to impose his logic on his
readers. Does he not say in the preface to the book that his intent in writing it was to set down basic elements of his doctrine for all time, for that
was what was needed "for a doctrine to be disseminated uniformly and
coherently?" On the concluding page of the book, he further predicted
that, if led and organized by the principles that he had preached there, his
National Socialist Workers' Party would "with almost mathematical certainty some day emerge victorious from its struggle" and that one of the
reasons that it had found itself stronger than ever in November 1926 was
precisely owing to the "correctness of its ideas."

However, the mere fact that Hitler considered what he had written to
be coherent does not make it so. In fact, thinking that what one has said
is coherent when it manifestly is not can well be a sign of madness or of
incipient madness. For those scratching their heads and wringing their
hands trying to "explain" Hitler, I suggest that what is really hard, and
embarrassing, to explain is not Hitler himself, for the world is full of hard-
to-explain people and phenomena. What is more challenging to explain is
his success in persuading so many people to acquiesce to his extraordinarily evil designs.

So, I am arguing, what may at first appear contradictory, inexplicable,
purely emotional, or poetical might not always prove to be as much so
upon closer examination. As fragmentary, disparate, contradictory, irrational, or unconnected as the ideas of Baudelaire, Nietzsche, and Hitler
may variously be considered to be, upon inspection their approaches to the
problem of evil actually prove more consistent and kindred than one might
at first expect. One would be grievously remiss to pass up the opportunity
to cull the utterly remarkable insights into evil that appear in their writings,
as disparate, unconnected and incoherent as these insights may look.

So I intend to do just that, and then, to borrow the image from *Mein
Kampf* already mentioned in the preface, to take what might otherwise be
considered a disparate mixture of ideas and fit them together, like the

pebbles in a mosaic, to create a picture of evil that can help form a clearer general picture of this difficult matter in the mind of the reader (Hitler, 35). In Nietzsche's case, to obviate any charges that his sister, that notorious plastic surgeon of his ideas, unduly distorted the ideas I use, my pebbles are almost exclusively drawn from writings whose publication, and republication, Nietzsche himself oversaw.

"From a Common Root . . ."

If any one of our three writers on evil has been recognized to be a philosopher and a theoretician, it has been Friedrich Nietzsche. In addition to that, as pointed out in the last section, he himself even went so far as to maintain that as a philosopher he did not have the right to be inconsistent, a claim which, coming from a thinker so notorious for contradicting himself, calls for examination. So given the aims and orientation of the present work, in biting into Nietzsche's ideas about evil, we need to take a closer look at the specific claims that he himself explicitly made about the internal consistency of the ideas that, to use his metaphor, he had initially planted and later brought to fruition. For it is essential to confront the specter of contradiction so often conjured up to spook people trying to get a taste of what he really meant.

Nietzsche's two most important books on the problem of evil, *Beyond Good and Evil* and *On the Genealogy of Morals*, were the fruit of the mature period of his thought and were published and republished by him. The latter book, as the author states on the title page, was intended as a complement and elucidation of the former book. In the foreword to *On the Genealogy of Morals* (Nietzsche 1887, Foreword §§2–4, 6–7), Nietzsche writes eloquently of the consistency of his own ideas on the origins of our notions of our moral prejudices that he committed to paper in that book. He particularly invites readers to look at what he had written in *The Wanderer and his Shadow* (Nietzsche 1880), *Human, All Too Human* (Nietzsche 1878, II), and *Daybreak* (Nietzsche 1881) on the origin of justice as a compromise between more or less equal forces (balance being the basis of any contract and consequently of any right). Finally, he asks readers to look at what he had said in *The Wanderer and his Shadow* about the origin of punishment, where the intention to inspire terror was neither essential nor primordial.

In the foreword to *On the Genealogy of Morals*, Nietzsche traced his reflections on good and evil back to older ideas first tentatively and charily committed to paper in *Human, All Too Human* (Nietzsche 1878) during the winter of 1876-77. It was then, he writes, that he had had an opportunity "to stop as a traveler does to survey the vast and dangerous land" through which his "mind had until then roamed." He further expresses his hope that during the intervening years his ideas had grown "riper, brighter, more vigorous and more perfect." The fact that he "still held fast to them and that they, in the meantime, had themselves held ever more tightly one to the other, had even grown into one another and grown together," had, he confides, fortified in him the "glad assurance" that from the beginning they had wanted to spring from him, "not in a piecemeal fashion, not arbitrarily, or sporadically, but rather from a common root, from some profoundly compelling, basic design of knowledge, speaking ever more precisely and insistently" (Nietzsche 1887, Foreword §2).

It was in 1877, he confides, that he had made what he considered to be his first awkward attempts to divulge the hypotheses about the origin of morality to which that book was devoted. It was then that he had begun to write down his thoughts in *Human, All Too Human* about the origins of good and evil as concerned the aristocracy or the slaves, the value and the origin of ascetic morality; the "morality of morals," a more ancient, more primitive sort of morality that is utterly different from the altruistic value system (Nietzsche 1887, Foreword §4, concerning for example, Nietzsche 1878, I §§45, 92, 96). The particular ideas in question, he explained, were the fruit of certain only reluctantly acknowledged reservations that he had long entertained concerning everything fêted on earth as being moral up until his time. Those reservations, he recounted, had sprung up in him so unbidden and so irresistibly at such an early age, and in such perfect contradiction with his surroundings, age, example, and origins that he considered that he almost had the right to call them his "*A priori.*" It had been inevitable, he said, that in good time his curiosity and suspicion would take him so far as to inquire into what it was that was actually at the origin of what we call good and evil (Nietzsche 1887, Foreword §3).

At the tender age of thirteen, he recalls, he had devoted his first written philosophical exercise to that problem. And of the solution that he had proposed at the time, he says: "I gave, as is only fair, glory to God and made him the *father* of evil. Was it precisely this that my '*A priori*' wanted of me? that new unmoral, at the very least immoral '*A priori*,' and that, ah, so anti-Kantian, so puzzling 'categorical imperative' proclaimed by it to which I have in the meantime increasingly lent my ear, and not only my ear?" (Nietzsche 1887, Foreword §3).

Upon learning to divorce theological prejudices from moral ones, Nietzsche says, he ceased to look for the origin of evil somewhere *behind* the world. In little time, a certain schooling in history and philology, plus an inborn, scrupulousness with respect to psychological questions in general, transformed his problem into one of determining the conditions under which people had forged those value judgments regarding good and evil and what value those value judgments themselves had. That had brought him to ask whether this had impeded or promoted human growth, whether these were a sign of distress, impoverishment, of degeneracy of life, or the opposite, whether they were the fullness, the power, the will of life, its courage, its confidence, its future betrayed in them (Nietzsche 1887, Foreword §3).

Nietzsche recalls having found and ventured sundry answers to his questions. He came to distinguish eras, peoples, ranks. He sharpened his understanding of the problem. From his answers, he confides, sprang new questions, inquiries, hypotheses, probabilities, until finally he "had his own land, his own soil, a whole hidden, growing, flourishing world, secret gardens, as it were, about which no one might suspect anything" (Nietzsche 1887, Foreword §4).

What he was especially intent upon investigating, he said, was the *value* of morality, and the value of compassion and the morality of compassion in particular. And it was precisely in so doing that he had had the dizzying experience of finding new, vast horizons opening up around him, something that was the occasion of all sorts of suspicions and of fears and shook all his faith in any morality, ultimately calling for a critique of moral values beginning with the questioning of the very value of these values, a critique that presumed knowledge of the conditions and circumstances of their birth, growth, and their modification, a kind of critique that not only had not existed up until then, but had not even been desired (Nietzsche 1887, Foreword §§5–6). Once he had adopted this radically new way of looking at morality, he wanted to join with others to discover that vast and far-off land of morality, which remained so hidden, but had really existed, really been experienced (Nietzsche 1887, Foreword §7).

The Roots of Moral Values for Nietzsche

To understand Nietzsche's claim that his ideas on evil had sprung from a common root, one must study his bold investigations into the roots of moral values, for as Ida Overbeck once observed, "Nietzsche's introduction to morality contains personal thoughts that give occasion to call him inconsistent and arbitrary, unless we remain at every moment aware of his foundation of morality . . ." (Gilman, 105).

In *On the Genealogy of Morals*, Nietzsche wrote of the need to question the very value of moral values in a way that presumed knowledge about the conditions and circumstances of their coming into being, their development, and the modifications they had undergone. This was necessary, he argued, because people had always thought of the value of these values as being something given, real, and beyond question. The cause of the birth of something, however, he stressed, was *toto coelo* different from its use, from its actual application and its classification within a system of goals (Nietzsche 1887, II §12).

A philologist by training, in Part I of *On the Genealogy of Morals* entitled "Good and Evil," "Good and Bad," Nietzsche investigated the etymological roots of the words associated with morality for insight into the conditions and circumstances under which moral values had actually come into being, developed, and undergone modification. Doing so led him to conclude that the study of the etymological roots of the words used to designate what was good in the different languages all led back to the same transformation of concepts (Nietzsche 1887, I §4).

For example, tracing the roots of the words he was studying back to Latin words for war, dissension, and discord taught Nietzsche to interpret the Latin word '*bonus*' as the warrior and the German word for good as meaning godly and identifiable with the Goths. He further concluded that it was an obvious fact that the judgment good had not come from those towards whom goodness had been displayed, but had rather come from good people themselves, by which he meant aristocratic, noble, powerful, higher-ranking, high-minded people, who themselves felt and judged their deeds to be good in comparison to all that was lowly, low-minded, common, plebian. Confronted with this dramatic disparity, they had taken it upon themselves to create values and to give those values a name free of any notion of utility or unselfishness (Nietzsche 1887, I §§4–5).

Nietzsche suggested that in Latin the word '*malus*' could be used to characterize both common people and dark-skinned people, and dark-haired people especially, when the pre-Aryan inhabitants of Italian soil stood out most clearly in color from the blonde, Aryan race of conquerors who became their masters. He thought that the Gaelic language had supplied him with a perfect example in the word '*fin*' indicating nobility, ultimately the good, noble, pure, and originally the blonde, in contrast to the original dark-haired, inhabitants (Nietzsche 1887, I §5).

Nietzsche's study of the kinds of considerations that he fancied underlie the contrast between good and bad led him to conclude that there was not any *a priori*, necessary link between the word 'good' and unselfish acts, and he set out to show what a terrible error it was to search for the origins of the good in the praise lavished on unselfish deeds by those for whom those actions had been performed and were useful. Such deeds, he maintained, had wrongly come to be considered good because it had become customary to praise them as such, as if they were inherently so. He even suggested that people who took moral, unselfish, and disinterested to be equivalent concepts might be sick in the head. It was only when aristocratic value judgments were in decline, he was convinced, that the notorious contrast between selfish and unselfish came to exercise a hold on the human mind. People, he complained, had forgotten who it was who had been doing the praising (Nietzsche 1887, I §2).

Nietzsche said that he was even prepared to run the risk of offending innocent ears by suggesting that selfishness was part of the essence of the noble mind. By selfishness he said he meant that unshakable belief that by nature beings "like ourselves" must subjugate other beings and have them offer themselves as sacrifices to them (Nietzsche 1885, §265), a theory echoed by Zarathustra when he said that to understand his message concerning good and evil, one had to understand his message concerning life and the nature of all the living. Wherever he had found the living, he said, he had found the nature of being to be that whatever lives, obeys and that those who cannot obey are themselves commanded (Nietzsche 1883-85, 226).

To offset the damage done by those who had denigrated selfish acts, Nietzsche aspired to restore the good reputation and value of deeds having acquired the bad reputation of being selfish. The condemnation of selfishness being so prevalent, this would be a quite significant step in robbing people of their bad consciences and in removing "the *evil appearance* from the whole scene of deeds and life." The outcome would be very important, he enthused, for: "When people no longer consider themselves evil, they cease to be so!" (Nietzsche 1881, §148).

Nietzsche's understanding of the difference between master morality and slave morality was crucial to the formulation of his theories of the origins of ideas about good, bad, and evil. In *Beyond Good and Evil*, he told of how by taking a look at the many refined and crude moralities that had at one time held sway upon the earth, he had discovered the distinction between these two basic types. (He hastened to add that attempts at mediation between them, and more often confusing and mutually misunderstanding them, appeared in all higher, mixed civilizations and that both moralities sometimes coexisted in the same person, in one soul) (Nietzsche 1886, §260).

Nietzsche imagined that in master morality, superior, proud frames of mind were felt to be distinctive and to determine the basis of the hierarchy. Noble people, he believed, see themselves as those who set values. They do not need to seek approval. They judge what is detrimental to them to be detrimental in itself. They are the creators of values. They esteem everything they find in themselves. Their morality is a morality of self-glorification. They give preeminence to feelings of abundance, superfluous power ready to overflow, the happiness of high expectations, the consciousness of wealth, the readiness to give and to part with what they have. They respect their own power and self-mastery. The strong understand what respect is. They have deep respect for old age, their forebears, and tradition (Nietzsche 1886, §260).

According to Nietzsche, noble, brave people could not be farther from the morality that sees compassion or unselfishness as characteristic of morality. Noble people also help the unfortunate, but not, or almost not, out of compassion, but out of an urge brought on by an excess of strength. They are proud to have not been made to inspire pity. Belief in oneself, self-pride, a basic ironic animosity towards unselfishness, as well as a disparaging and cautious attitude towards compassion and being warmhearted are traits definitely belonging to noble morality, Nietzsche thought (Nietzsche 1886, §260).

When masters determine the notion of good, Nietzsche believed, the contrast between good and bad becomes that between noble and worthy of contempt. Nietzsche found the talent and duty to display protracted gratitude and vindictiveness only towards one's peers, finesse in retaliation, a refined sense of friendship, a certain need to have enemies to drain off feelings of jealousy, quarrelsomeness, high spirits, basically the ability to be a good friend, all to be typical characteristics of noble morality. He imagined that noble people cut themselves off from people who display opposite feelings, that they feel contempt for cowardly, fearful, petty individuals, for those thinking in narrow terms of utility, as well as suspicious people with guarded looks, those who humble themselves, doggish people, who allow themselves to be mistreated, supplicating flatterers, and, above all, liars. Nietzsche considered it to be a fundamental belief of all aristocrats that the common people were deceitful (Nietzsche 1886, §260).

To Nietzsche's mind, those who are noble conceive of the basic concept "good" beforehand and spontaneously from their own standpoint and create from this their own idea of "bad" (*schlecht*) in exactly the opposite way that the members of the slave class do. He stressed the difference between the "bad" (*schlecht*) of noble origin and the "evil" (*böse*) brewed in unsated hatred, both apparently the opposite of the same concept "good." For him, the former was a secondary creation, an accessory, a complementary color, the latter the original, genuine act in the conception of a slave morality (Nietzsche 1887, I §11).

To the question as to who was genuinely "evil" in the sense of the morality of resentment, Nietzsche's answer was that strictly speaking it was precisely the "good" person of the other morality, precisely the noble, powerful ruler lent a new meaning by the poisoned eyes of resentment. Those who had only known these "good" people as enemies had known nothing else but evil enemies and these were the same people (Nietzsche 1887, I §11). "The evil of strong people," for Nietzsche in *Daybreak*, "hurts others without thinking about it—it *must* have a release; the evil of weak people *wants* to hurt and see the signs of the suffering" (Nietzsche 1881, §371). "Strange madness of moral judgments!" Nietzsche cried, "When human beings have a sensation of power, then they feel and call themselves good: and straight away then the others upon whom they have to release his power experience and call them evil" (Nietzsche 1881, §189). To the descendants of those trampled upon, robbed, abused, uprooted, sold, noble people seem hard, cold, cruel, heartless, unconscionable, seem to dash everything to pieces and coat everything in blood (Nietzsche 1887, I §11).

Of the origin of the concept of the good as seen by resentful people, Nietzsche wrote that it was not at all astonishing to find lambs cross with big birds of prey, but that there was no reason to blame big birds of prey for going after little lambs. If the lambs said among themselves that those birds of prey were evil, and those who were good were as little like a bird of prey as possible, there would be no problem in making that into an ideal, just that the birds of prey would view it a bit sarcastically and might say to themselves that they were not at all cross with the good lambs, that they even loved them, for nothing was more delicious than a tender lamb (Nietzsche 1887, I §13).

According to Nietzsche's theories, when out of the vengeful cunning of powerlessness the oppressed, the downtrodden, victims of violence resolve to be different from evil people, to be good people who are nonviolent, do not hurt, attack, retaliate, but place vengeance in God's hands, keep themselves hidden, steer clear of evil, expect little from life, are patient, meek, just, to the impartial and unbiased, they are proclaiming their weakness and that it is good for them not do anything they are not strong enough to do. Nietzsche calls this an unpleasant state of affairs, a display of a low level of intelligence that even insects have when, owing to the self-deception of powerlessness clothed in the pompous splendor of resigned, quiet, cautious virtue, they play dead in order to not to overexert themselves in times of great danger, as if the weakness of the weak were itself commendable (Nietzsche 1887, I §13). According to Nietzsche, priests were the most evil of enemies because they were the most powerless. Owing to their powerlessness, he maintained, a monstrous, sinister hatred of the most spiritual and most poisonous type thrives in them (Nietzsche 1887, I §§4–5, 7).

In *Human, All Too Human*, Nietzsche contended that the revolting injustice that may be attributed to the powerful was not at all as great as it appeared. According to him, the inherited feeling of being a superior being with superior rights already made one rather callous and gave one an easy conscience. When the difference between ourselves and another being is very great, he said, we hardly feel any sense of injustice and kill a gnat, for example, without any compunction. So it was not a sign of wickedness for Xerxes, depicted by all Greeks as eminently noble, to take a father's son from him and eliminate him like an annoying insect by having him chopped into little pieces. He was too inferior to be allowed to arouse any distressing feelings in the rulers of the world for long (Nietzsche 1878, I §81). Nietzsche acknowledged that it was in holding fast to the principle that one's only duty is towards one's peers, that towards beings of lower rank, towards all that is foreign one may act at one's own discretion, as one's heart desires, and any rate "beyond good and evil" that master morality was most foreign and distressing to modern sensibilities (Nietzsche 1886, §260).

Beyond Good and Evil

In the foreword to *On the Genealogy of Morals*, Nietzsche confided that hypothesizing about the origins of morality was only one of the things that he had on his mind as he developed his ideas on good and evil. Of greater importance to him were questions that the "the passion and hidden contradiction" of *Human, All Too Human* had addressed concerning the value of morality and Schopenhauer's ideas about the value of unselfishness, instincts of compassion, self-abnegation, and self-sacrifice that Nietzsche believed had led Schopenhauer to say no to life and to himself (Nietzsche 1887, §§2, 3, 5).

It was precisely there that Nietzsche said that he saw the greatest danger for humanity, its most sublime enticement and temptation to nothingness, the beginning of the end, the coming to a standstill, the backward-looking weariness, the will against life, the final illness tenderly and mournfully revealing its presence. He considered the increasingly spreading morality of compassion that he saw afflicting and sickening philosophers to be the most disturbing symptom of disturbed European civilization, and perhaps its roundabout route to a new Buddhism. Those considerations, he maintained, had brought him to ask whether that had impeded or promoted human growth, whether it was a matter of signs of distress, impoverishment, degeneracy of life, or the opposite, of the fullness, power, will of life, its courage, its confidence, its future betrayed itself in them (Nietzsche 1887, §§2, 3, 5).

Nietzsche says that those endowed like himself with some mysterious curiosity who had given thorough thought to Schopenhauerian pessimism and had really looked into and beneath the most world-denying of all ways of thinking, had set their sights beyond good and evil, and no longer like Buddha and Schopenhauer on the charms and illusions of morality, had perhaps in so doing, without really wanting to, opened their eyes to the opposite ideal, to the ideal of the most high-spirited (*übermütigsten*), most lively, most world-affirming people (Nietzsche 1886, §56).

In *Beyond Good and Evil*, Nietzsche had affirmed his conviction that traditional morality in the sense of a morality of intentions had been a hasty prejudice and perhaps provisional, along the lines of astrology or alchemy, but in any case something that had to be overcome, through "long, secret work" on the part of "the finest, most honest, the most malevolent consciences (*boshaftesten Gewissen*)" of his day. He asked whether he and his contemporaries might not at that time be on the threshold of a time that it would be suitable to call outside morality, an age in which immoralists were coming to suspect that "the essential value of an action dwelt precisely its being *unintentional*" (Nietzsche 1886, §32). He closed the first paragraph of the 1886 Foreword to the then decade-old *Human, All Too Human* with the affirmation that he himself was still alive and already beginning again to do what as an old immoralist he had always done, "speak unmorally (*unmoralisch*), outside morality (*aussermoralisch*), 'beyond good and evil'" (Nietzsche 1878, I §1).

In *Beyond Good and Evil*, Nietzsche affirmed that just as any genuine physio-psychological theory that derives all good instincts from bad ones meets with unconscious resistance from robust consciences already prone to be troubled and disgusted by subtle immorality perceived in affirmations of the mutual interdependency of "good" and "bad" instincts, so anyone who would go so far as to entertain the idea that the impulses of hatred, jealousy, greed, lust for power were fundamentally and essentially necessary in life, that they must be augmented if one was to have still more life, would suffer from something akin to seasickness. And yet, he suggested that

> that hypothesis is by no means the most painful and the strangest one in this immense almost still new realm of dangerous knowledge—and there are actually a hundred good reasons why anyone who *can* stays away from it. On the other hand, if one's ship is some time driven off course there, then let's clench our teeth, open our eyes, and hold fast to the helm, because in traveling and venturing there we are journeying directly beyond morality; we are therewith crushing to death, pulverizing perhaps, our own remnant of morality. Never yet has a deeper world of insight been opened up to daring voyagers and adventurers. (Nietzsche 1886, §23)

Nietzsche considered that the "dangerous formula 'beyond good and evil'" that he used spared him and other free spirits from being confused with freethinkers who, to his mind, were actually slaves of democratic ideas who, in the name of equal rights, sympathy for all who suffer, and the abolition of suffering, strove to assure security, safety, protection, and an easy life for the herd. He placed himself in the opposite camp of free *spirits*, whom he considered to be the heralds and forerunners of philosophers of the future who would be *very* free spirits and something better, higher, greater, and fundamentally different. He saw free spirits like himself as having been at home, or at least guests in many realms of the mind, as ever escaping stifling, pleasant nooks, into which some special predilection or special hatred, youth, lineage, accident of people and books, or even weariness of wandering seemed to lure them. He depicted free spirits as being full of wickedness regarding the lure of dependency lying hidden in honors, money, or official positions, or sensual delights, as being grateful for perils and the vicissitudes of illness because this always extricated them from some rule and its partiality, as grateful to the god, devil, sheep, and worm in them, curious to the point of vice, seekers to the point of cruelty, unhesitatingly reaching for the ungraspable, having teeth and stomachs for what is hardest to digest, ready for any task calling for a sharp mind and keen senses, ready for any risk, grateful for an excess of free will, with a soul up front and a soul in the wings whose ultimate intentions no one easily sees, with motives up front and ulterior, unfathomable motives cloaked beneath a mantle of light . . . (Nietzsche 1886, §44).

Nietzsche contended that those who had opened their eyes and minds know where and how the human "plant" had grown tall and robust were of the opinion that harshness, violence, slavery, danger, secrecy, stoicism, the art of temptation, and all sorts of deviltry, that everything evil, terrible, tyrannical in people, predatory, and snaky serves to raise up the human species as much as its opposite (Nietzsche 1886, §44). According to his theories, extending principles of mutually abstaining from being violent from harming, exploiting one another, equating one's will to that of others to make that a *basic principle of society* would immediately reveal itself for what it is: the will to the negation of life, principle of decomposition and decay. Getting to the root of the matter, he maintained, one is obliged to recognize that life is *essentially* usurpation, hurting, subjugating what is foreign and weaker, oppression, toughness, forcing one's own model, annexation, at the least, at the most lenient, exploitation. Exploitation, he stressed, was not unique to a vicious society or an imperfect, primitive society. It was inherent to life whose primordial function it constitutes. It flows out of the will to power, which is the will to life (Nietzsche 1886, §§257, 259).

Nietzsche made Zarathustra an eloquent spokesman on the subject of the "old illusion, which is called good and evil," the wheel of which has so far "revolved around soothsayers and stargazers." According to Zarathustra, there have "been only illusions so far, not knowledge, about good and evil," "all things have been baptized in the well of eternity and are beyond good and evil; and good and evil themselves are but intervening shadows and damp depressions and drifting clouds" (Nietzsche 1883-85, 277–78, 313–14). Zarathustra taught that "it is with man as it is with the tree. The more he aspires to the height and light, the more strongly his roots strive earthward, downward, into the dark, the deep—into evil" (Nietzsche 1883-85, 154).

On Blonde Beasts and *Übermenschen*

Stressing the need to be in contact with the periods of history that had really proved decisive for conventional morality and had determined the character of humanity, in *Beyond Good and Evil*, Nietzsche set out what he thought of as an innovative theory based on what he called the ultimate fact of all history and he challenged readers to be honest enough to acknowledge it without indulging in any sentimental weakness. So it was that he asked readers to take a hard, unprettified look at how any higher civilization had *begun* upon this earth (Nietzsche 1886, §257).

In the beginning, according to Nietzsche's theory, the superior caste had always been the barbarian caste. People still in a natural state, barbarians in any awful sense of the word, predators still in possession of unbroken strength of will and lust for power, originally cast themselves upon weaker, more moral, more peaceful races, or upon old, worn out civilizations in which the last sparks of vitality were flickering out in a glittering fireworks display of spirit and decay (Nietzsche 1886, §257).

At the bottom of all the noble races, Nietzsche fancied, were unmistakably predatory animals, magnificent "blonde beasts"[4] roaming about lusting after prey and conquest. This latent, underlying reality needing a release from time to time, the animal had to come out again, had to go back into the wild where, in Nietzsche's words, "it reverts back to the innocence of the conscience of predatory animals, as triumphant monsters who perhaps leave behind a horrible series of murder, fires, rape, torture, in high spirits and emotionally well-balanced, as if just having performed a student's prank, convinced that the poets will once again have something to sing about and glorify for a long time to come" (Nietzsche 1887, I §11).

Nietzsche professed to believe that the "State" obviously came into being when such a pack of blond beasts of prey, a powerfully militarily organized race of conquerors and master race, unhesitatingly laid its terrible claws on a still formless, still itinerant people perhaps far greater in number (Nietzsche 1887, II §17). When writing of the work of the blonde beasts in *On the Genealogy of Morals*, Nietzsche quoted a passage from *Daybreak* idealizing "that time when everywhere suffering was considered to be a virtue, cruelty a virtue, dishonesty a virtue, vengeance a virtue, imperviousness to reason a virtue, well-being a danger, intellectual curiosity a danger, peace a danger, compassion a danger, being an object of commiseration an insult, work an insult, madness a kind of godliness, change something immoral and fraught with disastrous consequences (Nietzsche 1887, III §9; Nietzsche 1881, I §18).

---

[4] Nietzsche put "Roman, Arab, German, Japanese nobles, Homeric heroes and Scandinavian Vikings" into the category of blonde beasts (Nietzsche 1887, I §11).

Nietzsche acknowledged that people might well be justified in not letting go of their fear, and remaining on their guard, concerning the blonde beasts at the basis of all noble races, for he believed that it was a hundred times more preferable to live in fear and admiration, than not to be afraid, but unable to flee the disgusting sight of misfits, enfeebled, stunted, infected people that was the fate of his contemporaries. It was obvious to him that his contemporaries suffered, not feared, people. Rather than living in fear, he said, the vermin people were crawling around in the forefront. Domesticated, dreadfully mediocre, uninspiring people had learned to feel they were the goal and culmination, the meaning of history, that they were superior people, and even that they had a certain right to feel so inasmuch as they set themselves apart from the surplus of misfits, of sickly, worn out, decrepit people beginning to stink up Europe. Nowadays, said Nietzsche, people believed that civilization had to extract the beast from people and tame it into a domestic animal, so that all the reactionary instincts and resentment that end up humiliating and dominating the aristocratic races and their ideals become the genuine instruments of civilization. Nietzsche saw the people having these instincts of vengeance, the descendants of all the slaves of Europe and pre-Aryan peoples, as being the most backward of humanity (Nietzsche 1887, I §11).

To free people's natural tendencies, Nietzsche looked to a completely different kind of mind, one fortified by wars and victories for whom conquest, adventure, danger, pain had become a need. Robust health was a must and a sublime form of wickedness, that supreme maliciousness of knowledge aware of itself that comes with robust health. A redeemer of great love and of great contempt would have to come who could free people from the curse of accepted ideals, a creative spirit of impulsive strength, for whom solitude was a way of plunging, digging, going deeply into reality to bring redemption, an anti-Christ and anti-nihilist, a conqueror of God and nothingness . . . (Nietzsche 1887, II §§24–25).

To teach people the future of human beings, Nietzsche placed his hopes in minds robust and primitive enough to revalue, reform "eternal values." He envisioned a new sort of philosophers, commanders, in comparison with which all the hidden, terrible, benevolent minds that had been on earth would seem pallid, dwarfed. Free spirits like himself were to use, or to create, the circumstances ripe for the emergence of such leaders, were to explore, to test the manners and means by which minds were likely to grow to the appropriate heights and acquire the strength to feel compelled to undertake the needed revaluation of values. Such free spirits were to resort to new hammers and anvils by which a conscience of steel might be forged, a heart transformed into brass to bear the weight of such a responsibility . . . (Nietzsche 1886, §203).

Nietzsche had his hermit Zarathustra preach the *Übermensch*, a conception of the superior people of the future largely expressed in lyrical, metaphorical terms that have captured many an imagination, but out of which no really clear picture emerges of what exactly these future people will be like and how they can be coherently connected with the other superior people of Nietzsche's writings.

Zarathustra claimed that he was the first, and only, person to ask how people were to be overcome and he claimed the *Übermensch* as his "first and only concern—and not man: not the neighbor, not the poorest, not the most ailing, not the best" (Nietzsche 1883-85, 399). He told of how he had "picked up the word *Übermensch*... and that man is something that must be overcome—that man is a bridge and no end" when his "wise longing" swept him "way and up and far" and he "flew, quivering, an arrow, through sun-drunken delight, away into distant futures which no dream had yet seen, into hotter souths than artists ever dreamed of, where gods in their dances are ashamed of all clothes—to speak in parables and to limp and stammer like poets" (Nietzsche 1883-85, 309–10). Zarathustra spoke of the *Übermensch* in these terms:

> Man is something that shall be overcome. . . . What is ape to man? A laughing-stock or a painful embarrassment. And man shall be just that for the *Übermensch.* . . . The *Übermensch* is the meaning of the earth. . . . a polluted stream is man. One must be a sea to be able to receive a polluted stream without becoming unclean. . . . The *Übermensch* is this sea. . . . Where is the lightning to lick you with its tongue? Where is the frenzy with which you should be inoculated? . . . the *Übermensch* . . . is this lightning, he is this frenzy. . . . Man is a rope, tied between beast and *Übermensch*—a rope over an abyss, a dangerous on-the-way, a dangerous looking-back, a dangerous shuddering and stopping. . . . I will teach men the meaning of their existence—the *Übermensch*, the lightning out of the dark cloud of man . . . . Bitterness lies in the cup of even the best love: thus it arouses longing for the *Übermensch.* . . . A shadow came to me— the stillest and lightest of all things once came to me. The beauty of the *Übermensch* came to me as a shadow. O my brothers what are the gods to me now? (Nietzsche 1883-85, 124–27, 132, 183, 200).

On the topic of *Übermenschen* and evil, however, Zarathustra was more specific. He said: "evil is man's best strength. Man must become better and more evil. . . . The greatest evil is necessary for the *Übermensch*'s best" (Nietzsche 1883-85, 400). To the question, "Who represents the greatest danger for all of man's future?" Zarathustra answered, "Is it not the good and the just? Break, break the good and the just!" (Nietzsche 1883-85, 324–25). "Behold the good and the just! Whom do they hate most? The man who breaks their tables of values, the breaker, the lawbreaker; yet he is the creator. . . . Fellow creators, the creator seeks —those who write new values on new tablets. . . . Destroyers they will be called, and despisers of good and evil . . . I shall join the creators. . . . I shall show them . . . all the steps to the *Übermensch*" (Nietzsche 1883-85, 135–36). "Verily," said Zarathustra, "you who are good and just, there is much about you that is laughable, and especially your fear of that which has hitherto been called devil. What is great is so alien to your souls. . . . you who are wise and knowing, you would flee from the burning sun of that wisdom in which the *Übermensch* joyously bathes his nakedness. You highest men whom my eyes have seen, this is my doubt concerning you and my secret laughter: I guess that you would call my *Übermensch*—the devil" (Nietzsche 1883-85, 256).

The Reversal of Values and the Specter of Contradiction

Fundamental to Nietzsche's conception of a new, extra-moral era beyond morality, to "that long, secret work" of the overcoming of morality reserved "for the finest, most honest, the most malevolent consciences" (Nietzsche 1886, §32), was his call for a reversal of values. "Should we not be concerned," he asked in *Beyond Good and Evil*, "about the need to resolve once again to bring about a reversal and fundamental shift of values, thanks to a renewed self-awareness and deeper understanding of human beings . . . ?" (Nietzsche 1886, §32). "Can not one turn around *all* values? And is good perhaps evil? And God only an invention and refined quality of the devil?" asked the free spirits of *Human, All Too Human* with "dangerous inquisitiveness" (Nietzsche 1878, I Foreword §3).

As Nietzsche saw it, up until his time, no one had even remotely doubted and hesitated about according higher value to a "good" person, than to an "evil" person when it came to the advancement, utility, prosperity of human beings in general. But, he wanted to know,

> was a symptom of decline, like a danger, an enticement, a poison, a narcotic by which the present were lived *at the expense of the future*. Perhaps more cosily, less dangerously, but also in a more trifling, inferior style? . . . so that it would be the fault of morality if *the highest degree of power and magnificence* of the human race were never attained? So that morality would be the dangers of dangers? (Nietzsche 1887, Foreword §6)

Society, Nietzsche considered, had wrongly come to glorify virtues like a sense of community, goodwill, being considerate, industriousness, temperance, moderation, leniency, compassion, in virtue of which members of the common herd were tame, peaceable beings, useful to the herd (Nietzsche 1886, §199). He thought that weak, unmanly, concepts of good and evil and the monstrous sway they have over body and soul had ultimately weakened all bodies and souls and shattered self-reliant, independent, unconstrained people who form the pillars of a strong civilization (Nietzsche 1881, §163). In his new world of transformed values, 'bettered,' for example, would be equivalent to 'domesticated,' 'weakened,' 'disheartened,' 'refined,' 'pampered,' 'emasculated,' 'impaired' (Nietzsche 1887, III §21).

According to Nietzsche's view of history, it was the Jews, a people "born to slavery," who were responsible for bringing about the amazing reversal of values that he so decried (Nietzsche 1886, §195).[5] With awe-inspiring consistency, he maintained, they had ventured to turn around the aristocratic equation of values. Armed with the most abysmal hatred, that of the powerless, they had held fast to the idea that the wretched were the only good people, that the poor, the powerless, the lowly were the only good people, that the suffering, the deprived, the sick, the ugly were the only pious, blessed people for whom alone there was bliss. In contrast, for them, noble, powerful people were wicked for all eternity, and the cruel, lascivious, ravenous, ungodly were unhappy, accursed, and damned forever (Nietzsche 1887, I §7).

Nietzsche pointed the finger at the Jewish prophets for fusing rich, godless, evil, violent, sensual, and for making *world* a dirty word for the first time. He claimed that "the meaning of the Jewish people," with whom the slave revolt in the moral order was to have begun, was to be found in that reversal of values for which the word for 'poor' was used synonymously with *holy* and *friend* (Nietzsche 1886, §195). He professed to believe that the dictum 'love your enemies' could only have been invented by the Jews, whom he called the best haters there had ever been (Nietzsche 1881, §377). Nothing done upon the earth against noble people, against powerful people, lords, rulers, he stressed, was worth mentioning compared to the act of intellectual revenge that that priestly people the Jews

---

[5] Nietzsche persisted in speaking of Jews in this pejorative way. However, this reflects more his hostility towards the impact of the Judeo-Christian tradition on European civilization than an aversion to Jews as a people. There is every reason to believe that he was not anti-Semitic and ample reason to believe that was a semitophile. See the essays anthologized in Golomb 1997. However, it is well worth noting that any number of people have been branded anti-Semitic for far less. In *Frege: Philosophy of Language* (xii), Dummett calls Gottlob Frege "a virulent racist, specifically an anti-semite" on the basis of remarks that he jotted in a diary kept for one month in 1924, not long before his death, at a particularly devastating moment in the history of the left-wing Weimar Republic in Germany (Frege 1924). According to Dummett, what Frege wrote shows him "to have been of extreme right-wing opinions, bitterly opposed to the parliamentary system, democrats, liberals, Catholics, the French and, above all, Jews, who he thought ought to be deprived of political rights and, preferably, expelled from Germany."

had perpetrated on them with their radical revaluation of values (Nietzsche 1887, I §7).

Zarathustra was doing his share to bring about the reversal of values in question when he preached that "whatever harm the evil may do, the harm done by the good is the most harmful harm . . ." (Nietzsche 1883-85, 324–25). He professed to have learned "that man needs what is most evil in him for what is best in him—that whatever is most evil is his best power. . . . that man must become better and more evil" (Nietzsche 1883-85, 330–31). His torture, he said, "was not that man is evil . . . but . . . that his greatest evil is so very small . . . that his best is so very small" (Nietzsche 1883-85, 331). He taught that

> good and evil that are not transitory, do not exist. Driven by themselves, they must overcome themselves again and again. With your values and words of good and evil you do violence when you value. . . . But a more violent force and a new overcoming grow out of your values and break egg and eggshell. And whoever must be a creator in good and evil, verily, he must first be an annihilator and break values. Thus the highest evil belongs to the highest goodness. . . . (Nietzsche 1883-85, 228)

When he came to people, Zarathustra said he had found "them sitting on an old conceit: the conceit that they have long known what is good and evil for man. All talk of virtue seemed an old and weary matter to man; and whoever wanted to sleep well still talked of good and evil before going to sleep." Zarathustra felt he disturbed this sleepiness by teaching that "what is good and evil no one knows yet, unless it be he who creates. He, however, creates man's goal and gives the earth its meaning and its future. That anything at all is good and evil—that is his creation" (Nietzsche 1883-85, 308).

In writing as he did of reversing the accepted meanings of words like *good* and *evil*, Nietzsche knew well that he courted contradiction and paradox. But it was his conviction that: "Life wants to build itself up into the heights with pillars and steps; it wants to look into vast distances and out toward stirring beauties: therefore it requires height. And because it requires height, it requires steps and contradiction among the steps and climbers. Life wants to climb and to overcome itself climbing" (Nietzsche 1883-85, 213).

He was keenly aware that his thoughts about morality had sprung up in perfect contradiction with his surroundings, age, example, and origins, but saw himself as one of those deep thinkers who feared more being understood than being misunderstood (Nietzsche 1886, §290). "Everything that is profound loves masks," Nietzsche noted in *Beyond Good and Evil*. "Every profound mind needs a mask, more than that, a mask continually accrues around every deep mind owing to the constantly false, flat interpretation of every word, of every step, of every sign of life there is" (Nietzsche 1886, §40).

Our finest insights, he noted in *Beyond Good and Evil*, must and should sound like foolishness, in certain cases like criminal offenses, when illicitly heard by people who are neither made nor foreordained for that (Nietzsche 1886, §30). As he saw it, what higher people found nourishing and refreshing was bound to be practically a poison for a very different and inferior kind of person. The virtues of common people were liable to be vices and weaknesses in a philosopher. Certain books took on an opposite value when it came to the minds and health of different classes of people. They could be dangerous for people with inferior minds, less vigorous people, cause them to crumble, become unraveled, and yet challenge superior, more powerful people, the bravest to *their* bravery (Nietzsche 1886, §30).

It was Nietzsche's ambition to contravene conventional ideas and to stretch the limits of morality beyond what society, as he saw it, was prepared to consider morally acceptable. So if much of what he says about good and evil runs counter to common intuitions about what is good and what is evil, that was exactly the way he wanted it. He was trying to shake his contemporaries out of their dogmatic slumber and his ideas contradicted the ideas that he wished to contradict. However, that does not mean that there were inner contradictions in what he had to say about evil. *At least for this one theme of evil,* if (to use Arthur Danto's words to my own ends) "one takes the trouble to eke his philosophy out, to chart the changes in signification that his words sustain in their shiftings from context to context and back, then Nietzsche emerges almost as a systematic . . . thinker" (Danto, 13). For him, moral judgment all depended on whether one looked from the top down or from the bottom up. He preached that what was commonly held to be good was actually evil and what was commonly held to be evil, say "what is intentionally morally bad or causes suffering, misfortune or disaster," was good when perpetrated by the strong against weak elements of society.

Baudelaire on Bludgeoning the Poor

Many of Baudelaire's, Nietzsche's, and Hitler's contemporaries were persuaded that enthusiasm for equality and democratic principles had been one of the blatant and dangerous errors sown by the French Revolution. Humanity, they believed, needed a hierarchy, could not do without an aristocracy. Many considered it only right to protest vociferously against theories that they saw as being manifestly in opposition to natural laws. Rife as well was a certain anti-Semitic sentiment born out of the conviction on the part of some that the French Revolution had been based on Jewish ideas and was the result of a Jewish-Masonic plot to impose, among other things, egalitarianism on people who passionately considered this to be a great error.[6]

Baudelaire took aim at the egalitarian ideas of his time in a colorful way that is perfectly compatible with what Nietzsche later preached about compassion and behavior toward the weak and infirm. In Baudelaire's poem "The Rebel," the poet declares that to the admonition "that one must love, without grimacing, the poor, the wretched, the misshapen, the idiot, so that with your charity you may roll out a triumphal carpet for Jesus, when he passes," the damned always reply, "I do not want to!" (Baudelaire 1857).

The narrator of Baudelaire's prose poem "Let's Bludgeon the Poor" (Baudelaire 1869, XLIX) tells of how for fifteen days he had confined himself to his room and surrounded himself with the currently fashionable, pedantic books about the art of making people happy, wise, and rich within twenty-four hours, books counseling all the poor to become slaves and others persuading them that they were all usurped kings.

Dizzied or stupefied by this, the poet recalled only having a sense of the infinitely vague and obscure seed of an idea superior to all the formulas he had just read. He went outside and as he was entering a cabaret, a beggar reached out his hat to him, "with one of those unforgettable looks fit to topple kings, if it were that the mind acted upon matter, and if the eyes of mesmerizers caused grapes to ripen."

At that very instant a familiar voice whispered in his ear. It was the voice of the "demon of action, the demon of combat, that good angel, or good demon," who accompanied the poet everywhere he went to advise, prompt, persuade him. The voice whispered: "Only he is equal to another who proves it, and he alone is worthy of freedom who knows how to conquer it."

At that point, the poet instantly jumped upon the beggar and with a single blow of the fist hit him in the eye, which in a second's time grew as big as a ball. The poet then broke one of the beggar's fingernails and two of his teeth. Not feeling strong enough to bludgeon the old man quickly, the poet grabbed him by the scruff of the neck with one hand and with the other went for his throat. Seeing no police in sight, the poet then set about banging the old man's head vigorously against the wall. The poet then gave this weakened man in his sixties a kick in the back energetic enough to throw him to the ground and break his shoulder blades. Grabbing a big branch, the poet commenced to beat the old man with the obstinate energy of a cook tenderizing a piece of steak.

---

[6] See, for example: Cohn 1996 or Poliakov 1987.

Then all of a sudden, inspiring in the poet what he called the pleasure of a philosopher confirming the excellence of a theory, the "antiquated carcass" that he had beaten turned over, stood up with more energy than the poet ever would have suspected to find "in a so singularly broken down machine," and with a look of hatred that seemed a good omen to the poet, that "decrepit brigand" threw himself upon his attacker, blackened both eyes, broke four teeth, and laid him flat.

The poet concluded that this strong medicine had given the old man back his pride and his life. Considering the discussion to be over, the satisfied poet told him: "Sir, *you are my equal!*" and, reminding him that, whenever their comrades ask them for alms, true philanthropists should apply the theory that the poet had suffered to try out on old man's back, invited him to do him the honor of sharing with him the contents of his pocketbook. The old man then swore he had understood the poet's theory and would follow the advice.

Born for Evil

Baudelaire lived amid the social upheaval wrought by the French Revolution. Once she had rid herself of her monarchy and aristocracy, France had cast herself into the arms of the Emperor Napoleon Bonaparte, then came the first restoration of the monarchy, then the return of Napoleon, next a second restoration of the monarchy, the revolution of July 1830, the 1848 uprising, the short-lived Second Republic, the Second Empire, the socialistic Commune, then the Third Republic that took her all the way to World War II.

Baudelaire complained that "the utopian, communistic, alchemistic turn" of all France's brains allowed "her only a single passion, that of social formulas." In France, he complained, "each person wants to resemble everyone, but on the condition that everyone resembles her or him. From this contradictory form of tyranny results a struggle that only applies to social forms, finally a level, a general similarity, whence the ruin and suppression of any originality of character" (Baudelaire 1859, 505).

Baudelaire vented his antidemocratic and antiegalitarian sentiments in a particularly explicit way in two essays on the American writer Edgar Allan Poe (Baudelaire 1855-57), whom Baudelaire thought of as an aristocrat who "wrote in full overflowing of democracy." "One would say," Baudelaire wrote, "that the impious love of freedom is born of a new tyranny of beasts, or zoocracy . . ." (Baudelaire 1855-57, 576). As he saw it,

Nature only makes monsters and the whole question is to agree upon the word *savages*. No philosopher will dare propose as models these unfortunate, rotten hordes, victims of the elements, fodder for beasts, who are as incapable of fabricating arms as of conceiving the idea of a supreme spiritual power. But if one wishes to compare modern human beings, civilized human beings, with savages, or rather a nation said to be civilized with a nation said to be savage, meaning deprived of all the ingenious inventions that dispense individuals from heroism, who could fail to see that all honor goes to the savages? By nature, out of very need, they. . . . skirt as close as possible the ideal. (Baudelaire 1855-57, 593)

One of the main planks of Baudelaire's antiegalitarian sentiment was his conviction that human beings were intrinsically evil, what he called their "perversity," and he saw Poe as "a soul in love with the everlasting fire"(Baudelaire 1855-57, 593) who "clearly saw, imperturbably affirmed, the natural wickedness of Man," who took into account that "great forgotten truth,—man's primordial perversity." He wrote of how Poe was someone who recognized that there is in people, "a mysterious force that modern philosophy does not want to take into account; and yet, without this unnamed force, without this primordial penchant, a mass of human actions would remain unexplained." According to Baudelaire's reading of Poe, such

actions are only attractive *because* they are evil, dangerous; they possess the attraction of the pit. This primitive, irresistible force is the natural Perversity that means that human beings are ceaselessly both homicidal and suicidal, assassin and executioner;—for, he adds, with remarkably satanic finesse, the impossibility of finding a sufficiently reasonable motive for certain evil and perilous actions could lead us to consider them the result of suggestions of the Devil, if experience and history did not teach us that God often extracts the establishment of order and the punishment of rascals from it;—*after having used those very rascals as accomplices*! (Baudelaire 1855-57, 591)

Baudelaire derived a certain satisfaction from seeing some explosion of old verities flying thus in the face of all those wrongheaded egalitarians, all those flatterers of humanity, coddlers, and cajolers repeating in every possible tone of voice: "I am born good, and you too, and all of us, we were born good!" and feigning to forget that we are all born for evil! (Baudelaire 1855-57, 592)

Poe's life was a "lamentable tragedy," Baudelaire judged. Everything that he had read, he said, had led him to the conviction that for Poe the United States was just one "vast prison that he traveled with the feverish agitation of a being created to breathe in a world more amoral —than a great barbarity lit by gaslight. . . ." Baudelaire considered that Poe's "inner, spiritual life as a poet, or even a drunkard, was but a perpetual effort to escape the influence of that antipathetic atmosphere." Baudelaire advised that one should implore neither "charity or indulgence, nor any

elasticity whatsoever" in the application of the laws of the "pitiless dicta-
torship . . . of opinion in democratic societies" to the numerous, complex
cases of moral life (Baudelaire 1855-57, 576).

For a Race of Masters and Conquerors

Nietzsche consistently voiced the antipathy he felt for democratic and egalitarian causes. For example, in *Beyond Good and Evil*, condemning "the
imbecilic naiveté and gullibility lying concealed in 'modern' ideas, and
even more in the whole Christian-European morality," he aligned himself
with those who viewed the democratic movement as representing, not
merely a degenerate form of political organization, but a manner of ruin-
ing, debasing, and degrading humanity; he made allusion to the incomparable anguish that the thought of it brought to those who were aware of
everything that could be done to promote human growth and knew well
that humanity had yet to realize its full potential. He said that the overall
lowering of the level of humanity down to the level of what those he called
"socialist boobies and blockheads" thought of as being the ideal people of
the future,—to the level of perfect herd animals, the members of a free
society, the level of beasts, of dwarfs with equal rights and entitlements,
was enough to nauseate anyone who had thought the matter through
(Nietzsche 1886, §203). He called the French Revolution a "sinister farce"
marking the beginning of the last great revolt of the slaves (Nietzsche
1886, §§38, 46).

In *On the Genealogy of Morals*, Nietzsche maintained that the insights
essential for an understanding of the genealogy of morals had only come
at such a late point in history because of the inhibiting impact of democratic ideas on the modern world (Nietzsche 1887, I §4). He characterized
what he called the destruction of Europe's last political nobility by popular instincts of resentment during the French revolution as being a triumph
for Judea (Nietzsche 1887, I §16). He said that any legal system conceived
of, not as a medium for fighting among power complexes, but as measures
against all fighting in general, say in compliance with the communistic
principle that any will has to consider any other will as equal, was hostile
to life, a destroyer and disintegrator of human beings, an attack on the
future of mankind, a sign of weariness, a devious route to nothingness
(Nietzsche 1887, II §11).

In *Thus Spoke Zarathustra*, Nietzsche had Zarathustra proclaim that
what was needed was a new nobility "to be the adversary of all rabble . . .
and to write anew upon new tablets the word 'noble'" (Nietzsche 1883-
85, 315). Zarathustra vowed to bring the secrets of the preachers of equality to light and laughed in their faces with his "laughter of the heights"

(Nietzsche 1883-85, 211). He announced unequivocally: "I do not wish to be mixed up and confused with these preachers of equality. For, to *me* justice speaks thus: 'Men are not equal.' Nor shall they become equal! What would my love of the *Übermensch* be if I spoke otherwise?" (Nietzsche 1883-85, 213).

As discussed in earlier sections, Nietzsche believed that one had to face hard truths and not indulge in any humanitarian illusions about how aristocratic societies had originated and the human race advanced. He attributed human progress to societies that believed in a long, hierarchical ladder with varying degrees of worth between people and needed slavery in some sense. He considered that, without the passion for maintaining one's distance that grows out of intractable differences between ranks, out of the ruling caste's constantly looking or looking down upon its subjects and tools, and out of the constant practice of obeying and ordering, holding down and at a distance, the advance of human race, the continuous overcoming of humans by themselves could not be realized (Nietzsche 1886, §257).

According to his theories, noble people employ two sets of standards. In the company of their peers, they operate within strict limits of morality, veneration, custom, gratitude, watching out for one another, jealousy, which is evident in their behavior towards one another in the respect, self-mastery, consideration, loyalty, pride, and friendship that they display (Nietzsche 1887, I §11). However, he believed that, provided it is living and not dying out, any body in the midst of which the individuals relate to one another as peers, as happens in any healthy aristocracy, must itself, perpetrate against other bodies everything that the individuals making it up refrain from in their relationships with one another (Nietzsche 1886, §259).

Outside their group, where what is alien to them begins, noble people are not much better than unleashed beasts of prey, Nietzsche thought. There they enjoy freedom from all social constraints. In the wild, by reverting back to being monsters jubilantly indulging in abominable acts of murder, rape, torture with all the innocence of predatory animals, they enjoy an opportunity to recoup from the strain of being pent up and fenced in in the peaceful company of their peers. Everywhere they have gone, their crazy, absurd, unexpected boldness, their lack of concern about and disdain for life, limb, safety, comfort, the horrible merriment and profound enjoyment they have found in destroying, in all the sensual pleasures of conquest and cruelty, have earned the noble races the title of barbarians, he says (Nietzsche 1887, I §11).

For Nietzsche, a healthy aristocracy had to be the will to power incarnate. It grows, spreads, wins over to its side, not out of some morality or immorality, but because it lives and life just is will to power (Nietzsche

1886, §259). According to his theories about life, to the extent that an organ grows in an appreciable way, its "meaning" changes. Sometimes its partial death, its reduction in size (for example, through the destruction of mediocre members) can be a sign of growth in strength and perfection. The fact of becoming partially useless, perishing, and deteriorating, of losing meaning and usefulness, in short, of dying can also be a condition of genuine progress, which always takes the form of will to greater power and is always achieved at the expense of a great number of lesser powers. The amount of progress can even be measured by how much it is necessary to sacrifice. A quantity of humanity sacrificed to the benefit of a single species of stronger people would result in progress (Nietzsche 1887, II §12).

Nietzsche worried that in almost all of Europe the subjugated races had essentially finally achieved ascendancy, in color, in smallness of cranium, and perhaps even in the area of social and intellectual instincts. He asked whether anyone would stand guarantee that modern democracy, and modern anarchism even more so, especially the inclination towards communes, that most primitive form of society, now common to all the socialists of Europe, did not on the whole represent a colossal counterblow and that the Aryans, that race of conquerors and master race, were not being overthrown, even physiologically (Nietzsche 1887, I §5). He deplored that fact that one no longer saw anything wanting to become greater. There was a foreboding, he said, that everything was going down, down, becoming leaner, more good natured, cleverer, more comfortable, more mediocre, more apathetic, more Chinese, more Christian. As he saw it, people were undoubtedly continually becoming "better," but in having ceased to fear people, Europe had forfeited her love for them, her awe before them, her hope in them (Nietzsche 1887, I §12).

As seen above, Nietzsche thought that the hard truth was that it was the blonde beast (a category that included "Roman, Arab, German, Japanese nobles, Homeric heroes and Scandinavian Vikings," Nietzsche 1887, I §11) that had formed the basis of the noble races. For Nietzsche, such masters were by nature violent in their deeds and not to be reckoned with. They come like destiny, for no reason, without reason, without respect, without excuses. They strike like lightning, too terrible, too sudden, too convincing, too "different" even to be hated. They are born organizers who do not know what guilt, responsibility, respect are. They only have that frightening selfishness of an artist with a steely gaze.

Nietzsche described the beginning of the "State" as obviously taking place when a horde of such blond beasts of prey laid its terrible claws on a still formless population body. The shaping of a formless, unrestrained population began, he maintained, with an act of violence and was only achieved through public acts of violence, and it was thus that the oldest "State" made its appearance as a frightful tyranny, a crushing, ruthless machinery that carried on its work until the half-human, half animal raw material was finally kneaded into submission and took on form. This phenomenon was not to be underrated just because it had always been ugly and painful, Nietzsche said (Nietzsche 1887, II §§17, 18).[7]

The Victory of the "Better and Stronger"

Hitler and his minions made no secret at all of their antidemocratic and antiegalitarian sentiment and, what is more, they actually set out to create a new hierarchized society that reflected those theories. Although it is extremely doubtful that Nietzsche would ever have espoused their ideology and politics, the Nazis did espouse Nietzsche, and it is not hard to see how some of his antiegalitarian and antidemocratic theories, for instance, could have been warped to serve the National Socialist cause. At times, Hitler almost seemed to be parroting some of Nietzsche's writings. For example, there is this passage of *Mein Kampf* in which he stated that his philosophy,

> by no means believes in an equality of the races, but along with their difference it recognizes their higher or lesser value and feels itself obligated, through this knowledge, to promote the victory of the better and stronger, and demand the subordination of the inferior and weaker in accordance with the eternal will that dominates this universe. Thus, in principle, it serves the basic aristocratic idea of nature and believes in the validity of this law down to

---

[7] For two contrasting American reactions to such ideas see Nietzsche apologist H. L. Mencken's 1908 book *The Philosophy of Friedrich Nietzsche*, according to which "Nietzsche opposed squarely both the demand for peace and the demand for equality. . . . he believed that war was not only necessary, but also beneficial, and that the natural system of castes was not only beneficent, but also inevitable. In the demand for universal peace he saw only the yearning of the weak and useless for protections against the righteous exploitation of the useful and strong. In the demand for equality he saw only the same thing" (Mencken, 162–63). Nietzsche's "ideal was an aristocracy which regarded the proletariat merely as a conglomeration of draft animals made to be driven, enslaved and exploited." According to Mencken's translation of *Beyond Good and Evil* §258: "A good and healthy aristocracy must acquiesce, with a good conscience, in the sacrifice of a legion of individuals, who, for its benefit, must be reduced to slaves and tools. The masses have no right to exist on their own account: their sole excuse for living lies in their usefulness as a sort of superstructure or scaffolding, upon which a more select race of beings may be elevated" (Mencken, 102). On the other side of the spectrum, Martin Luther King advised followers: "Many white men in the South see themselves as a fearful minority in an ocean of black men. They honestly believe with one side of their minds that Negroes are depraved and disease-ridden. They look upon any effort at equality as leading to 'mongrelization.' They are convinced that racial equality is a Communist idea and that those who ask for it are subversive. They believe that their caste system is the highest form of social organization" (King 1956, 11).

the last individuals. . . . it cannot grant the right to existence even to an ethical idea if this idea represents a danger for the racial life of the bearers of a
higher ethics; for in a bastardized and niggerized world all the concepts of the
humanly beautiful and sublime, as well as all ideas of an idealized future of our
humanity, would be lost forever. (Hitler, 383)

In *Mein Kampf*, Hitler also wrote of how the "idiotic bourgeoisie looks
with amazement at such miracles of education" that make a Negro into a
lawyer, teacher, or even a pastor, and how, "full of respect for this marvelous result of modern educational skill, the Jew shrewdly draws from it a
new proof for the soundness of his theory about the *equality of men* that
he is trying to funnel into the minds of the nations. It doesn't dawn on this
depraved bourgeois world," Hitler continues,

that this is positively a sin against all reason; that it is criminal lunacy to keep
on drilling a born half-ape until people think they have made a lawyer out of
him, while millions of members of the highest culture-race must remain in
entirely unworthy positions; that it is a sin against the will of the Eternal
Creator if His most gifted beings by the hundreds and hundreds of thousands
are allowed to degenerate in the present proletarian morass, while Hottentots
and Zulu Kaffirs are trained for intellectual professions. For this is training
exactly like that of the poodle. . . . (Hitler, 430)

As for ideas about actually putting such theories into practice, Martin
Bormann's *Table Talk 1941-44* records Hitler as having said, for example,
that nothing would be a worse mistake on Nazi Germany's part than to
seek to educate the masses in occupied Poland. They should stay illiterate,
Hitler was to have said, because it was in the Nazi's interest that the people should know just enough to recognize road signs. Instruction in geog-
raphy could be restricted to a single sentence: 'The Capital of the Reich is
Berlin.' Elementary instruction in reading and writing in German,
Arithmetic, and the like was quite unnecessary. Any opportunity for higher
education would merely plant the seeds of future opposition to Nazi rule.
The cities built for German settlers should be beautiful with wide streets,
parks, and all facilities for leisure activities. Such towns would normally be
off-limits, but as a special reward, groups of natives could be taken to visit
them to see how their masters live (Hitler, 1941-44, July 27, 1941, July
22, 1942).
        Such echoes of a morality beyond good and evil were reflected in the
ideas of Hitler's devoted minions. For example, in 1942 Himmler, spoke
to SS-men of a battle to the death between Aryan Germans and Soviets
whose "physique" is so mongrel-like "one can shoot them down without
pity and compassion. . . . When you fight you are carrying out the same
struggle against the same sub-human, the same inferior races that at one

time appeared under the name of Huns and still another time under the name of Genghis Khan and his Mongols" (cited Rosenbaum, 176); in 1943, he told the leaders of the Hitler Youth, "Whether nations live in prosperity or starve to death interests me only insofar as we need them as slaves for our culture, otherwise it is of no interest to me. Whether ten thousand Russian females drop from exhaustion while digging an anti-tank ditch or not interests me only insofar as the anti-tank ditch for Germans is completed" (cited Sereny 1995, 311). In early 1943 Erich Koch, Reichskommissar for the Ukraine told Nazi party members: "We are a master race, which must remember that the lowliest German worker is racially and biologically a thousand times more valuable than the population here" (Sereny 1995, 311).

Hitler viewed the Western democracy of his day as being "the forerunner of Marxism which without it would not be thinkable," for it provided that "world plague with the culture in which its germs can spread" (Hitler, 78). "A philosophy of life which endeavors to reject the democratic mass idea and give this earth to the best people—that is, the highest humanity— must logically obey the same aristocratic principle within this people and make sure that the leadership and the highest influence in this people fall to the best minds. Thus it builds not upon the idea of the majority, but upon the idea of personality" (Hitler, 443). For him, when "the parliamentary principle of majority rule wins over that of a single person and replaces the chief by the number and the masses, it goes against the aristocratic principle of nature" (Hitler, 81, 87).

Hitler claimed to have "always hated" Parliament; which he called it an "absurd" institution (Hitler, 79). He decried the "devastation" wrought by modern parliamentary rule (Hitler, 81), which he said in "its most extreme form . . . created a 'monstrosity of excrement and fire'" (Hitler, 78). "There is no principle," he said, "which objectively considered is as false as parliamentarianism" (Hitler, 84). He remembered the first times he set foot in the halls of the Austrian parliament to witness a "lamentable comedy" unfolding before his eyes, which was enough to move him to laughter:

> The intellectual content of what these men said was on a really depressing level, in so far as you could understand their babbling at all. . . . A wild gesticulating mass screaming all at once in every different key, presided over by a good-natured old uncle who was striving in the sweat of his brow to revive the dignity of the House by violently ringing his bell and alternating gentle reproofs with grave admonitions. . . . A few weeks later . . . everybody was asleep. A few deputies were in their places, yawning at one another. . . . (Hitler, 77)

From then on, he recalled, he went back whenever the slightest opportunity offered itself. So it was that he passed "a year of tranquil observation," quietly and attentively watched "whatever picture presented itself, listened to the speeches in so far as they were intelligible, studied the faces." For him, this was yet another instance in which "the visual instruction of practical reality" prevented him "from being stifled by a theory which at first sight seemed seductive to so many, but which none the less must be counted among the symptoms of human degeneration" (Hitler, 76–78).

Neither Marx . . .

Baudelaire, Nietzsche, and Hitler each explicitly rejected the Marxist ideas that were digging in roots while Baudelaire was calumniating democratic, egalitarian, and socialist movements of the nineteenth century. He took aim at both the republican ideals of the French Revolution and the socialist ideas of his contemporaries, both of which would ultimately go into the making of the left-wing Weimar Republic that Hitler so hated.

To the question as to whom he hated most among the rabble of his times, Nietzsche plainly answered that it was the socialist rabble "who undermine the instinct, the pleasure, worker's sense of satisfaction with his small existence—who make him envious, who teach him revenge. The source of wrong is never unequal rights," Nietzsche stressed, "but equal rights" (Nietzsche 1888, §57). In *Human, All Too Human*, he condemned the socialist longing to create prosperous lives for the greatest number possible. If the perfect State in their sense were really realized and long endured, he argued, the prosperity would destroy the ground, the powerful energy, in which great intellects, and in general, powerful individuals grow. Humanity would have grown too weak with the founding of this State to be able to go on producing genius. So, Nietzsche asked, should people not wish to see life preserve its violent character and that wild strength and energy be called forth and ever renewed? (Nietzsche 1878, I §235).

Nietzsche was surely potentially adding fuel to the fire of Marxist ideology when he asserted that the injustice of the powerful was not at all as great as it appeared to be, that the inherited feeling of being a superior being with superior rights already made one rather callous and gave one an easy conscience so that, to use his example, a rich person who took away a poor person's beloved could not empathize with the loss sustained by someone who had little because rich people were accustomed to having many possessions and did not have a sense of the worth of a single possession. The two live in different worlds, Nietzsche explained, and when the gap between ourselves and another being is very great, we hardly feel any sense of injustice. For example we kill a gnat without any qualms whatsoever (Nietzsche 1878, I §81).

As for Hitler, he reserved some of his most scathing attacks and colorful language for his attacks on Marxism. *Mein Kampf* tells of how he "dug into this doctrine of destruction," immersed himself "in the theoretical literature of this new world, attempting to achieve clarity concerning its possible effects, and then compared it with the actual phenomena and events it brings about in political, cultural, and economic life"(Hitler, 154). So it was that he discovered the "difference between the glittering phrases about freedom, beauty, and dignity in the theoretical literature, the delusive welter of words seemingly expressing the most profound and laborious wisdom, the loathsome humanitarian morality . . . and the brutal daily press, shunning no villainy, employing every means of slander, lying with a virtuosity that would bend iron beams, all in the name of this gospel of a new humanity" (Hitler, 41–42).

Slowly, Hitler recalls, he became an expert in Marxist doctrine and used it as a weapon in the struggle for his own deepest convictions. At one time, he says, he was still childish enough to try to make the madness of their doctrine clear to them. Thinking that he would inevitably succeed in convincing them how ruinous their Marxist madness was, he talked his "tongue sore" and his "throat hoarse," but he only found that whenever "you tried to attack one of these apostles, your hand closed on a jelly-like slime which divided up and poured through your fingers, but in the next moment collected again" (Hitler, 62).

Hitler particularly targeted the German Social Democratic Party that was in power as he wrote *Mein Kampf*. It was "by balancing the theoretical untruth and nonsense of this doctrine with the reality of the phenomenon," he said, that he "gradually obtained a clear picture of the intrinsic will" of Social Democracy and "was overcome by gloomy foreboding and malignant fear" as he saw before him "a doctrine, comprised of egotism and hate," which could "lead to victory pursuant to mathematical laws, but in so doing must put an end to humanity" (Hitler, 50–51).

He called Social Democracy "a pestilential whore, cloaking herself as social virtue and brotherly love" and expressed his hope that humanity would rid this earth of her "with the greatest dispatch, since otherwise the earth might well become rid of humanity" (Hitler, 38–39). He said that, with his "innermost soul," he wrestled with the "painful question" as to whether the Social Democrats were "human, worthy to belong to a great nation" (Hitler, 41). He recalls how at times he stood there thunderstruck, not knowing whether to be more amazed at the agility of their tongues or their virtuosity in lying. Gradually he began to hate "the diabolical craftiness of these seducers . . . race of dialectical liars, who twist the truth in your mouth . . ." (Hitler, 63). He was sure that the "original founders of this plague of the nations must have been veritable devils; for only in the brain of a monster—not that of a man—could the plan of an organization assume form and meaning, whose activity must ultimately result in the collapse of human civilization and the consequent devastation of the world" (Hitler, 63–64). The masses, he was sure, "absolutely fail to suspect the inner insanity of the whole doctrine" (Hitler, 40).

Inspired by the experience of daily life, Hitler said, he began to track down the sources of the Marxist doctrine. He said that it was only the knowledge of the Jewish question that enabled him to "draw a practical comparison between the reality and theoretical flim-flam of the founding fathers of Social Democracy" (Hitler, 64). In *Mein Kampf*, he tells how he learned to understand the connection between this doctrine of destruction and the "nature" of the Jews. "*Only a knowledge of the Jews provides the key with which to comprehend the inner, and consequently real, aims of Social Democracy*," Hitler maintained (his emphasis). For "the erroneous conceptions of the aim and meaning of this party fall from our eyes like veils, once we come to know this people, and from the fog and mist of social phrases rises the leering grimace of Marxism" (Hitler, 51). "Karl Marx was only the *one* among millions who, with the sure eye of the prophet, recognized in the morass of a slowly decomposing world the most essential poisons, extracted them, and like a wizard, prepared them into a concentrated solution for the swifter annihilation of the independent existence of free nations on this earth. And all this in the service of his race" (Hitler, 382).

As a foundation of the universe, the "Jewish doctrine of Marxism," Hitler found, "rejects the aristocratic principle of Nature and replaces the eternal privilege of power and strength by the mass of numbers and their dead weight." He was convinced, that as "a foundation of the universe," it would bring about the end of any conceivable order, that the application of such a law to human beings could only result in chaos and only mean destruction for the inhabitants of the planet. He warned that if, "with the help of his Marxist creed, the Jew is victorious over the other people of the world, his crown will be the funeral wreath of humanity and this planet will, as it did thousands of years ago, move through the ether devoid of men" (Hitler, 65).

In Soviet Bolshevism, Hitler saw a Jewish attempt to achieve world domination. More than a decade before he signed the nonaggression pact with the Soviet Union, he warned:

> Never forget that the rulers of present-day Russia are common blood-stained criminals; that they are the scum of humanity which, favored by circumstances, overran a great state in a tragic hour, slaughtered and wiped out thousands of her leading intelligentsia in wild blood lust, and now for almost ten years have been carrying on the most cruel and tyrannical régime of all time. Furthermore, do not forget that these rulers belong to a race which combines, in a rare mix-

ture, bestial cruelty and an inconceivable gift for lying, and which today more than ever is conscious of a mission to impose its bloody oppression on the whole world. . . . And you do not make pacts with people to whom no pact would be sacred, since they do not live in this world as representative of honor and sincerity, but as champions of deceit, lies, theft, plunder, and rapine. If a man believes that he can enter into profitable connections with parasites, he is like a tree trying to conclude for its own profit an agreement with a mistletoe. (Hitler, 660–61)

Hitler viewed the assumption of the equality of the races that becomes a platform for an analogous way of viewing peoples and finally individual men and hence international Marxism itself as "only the transference, by the Jew, Karl Marx, of a philosophical attitude and conception, which had actually long been in existence, into the form of a definite political creed. Without the subsoil of such generally existing poisoning the amazing success of this doctrine would never have been possible," he said (Hitler, 382).

. . . nor Jesus

Of our three specialists on evil, only Baudelaire, the son of a priest who defrocked himself during the French Revolution (Pichois and Ziegler, 19–29, 42–51), made any claim to being a Christian. He was fond of proclaiming, sometimes vociferously, that he was a Roman Catholic and some even thought he had something of a priestly look about him (Pichois and Ziegler, 428–29, 594).

However, Baudelaire was not a practicing Catholic and much that he did was in flagrant contradiction with Catholic teaching. The admiration openly professed for Satan, his exaltation of vices condemned by the Church, the plainly sacrilegious pronouncements made in many of his poems are enough to cast some doubt as to exactly how pious a Christian he could have been. He once warned his mother that the parish priest would think him damned, but would not dare to tell her so (Pichois and Ziegler, 428–29, 594).

The Ministry of the Interior report that recommended that Baudelaire's *Flowers of Evil* be brought before the courts called it "unwholesome, profoundly immoral." It found that among "these pieces and several others in which the immortality of the soul and the most cherished beliefs of Christianity are dismissed; there are others which are an expression of the most revolting lewdness: 'The Damned Women' is a song in honor of the shameful love of women for women; 'The Metamorphoses of the Vampire,' 'The Jewels' at every instant present the most licentious images with all the coarseness of expression" (Pichois and Ziegler, 352).

The report called Baudelaire's poems "The Denial of Saint Peter," "Abel and Cain," "The Litanies of Satan," "The Wine of the Assassin" "a string of blasphemies" (Pichois and Ziegler, 351).

The Mother Superior where Baudelaire was first hospitalized with his final illness considered that he was without religion. His mother was afraid that the sisters caring for him might torment him by speaking too much about the things of God. After he was removed from that establishment, it is said that the sisters fell to their knees, that with tears flowing abundantly from their eyes they sprinkled the place with holy water where their terrifying patient had been and that they, finally happy at feeling rescued from the devil, as if Satan himself had left their bewitched institution, did not calm down until they saw the arrival of an exorcist that they had hastily called (Pichois and Ziegler, 567–70).

Although Baudelaire did receive the last rites of the Catholic Church and had a Catholic burial, this was certainly owing to his mother's efforts for, like Nietzsche, Baudelaire himself was insane and unable to speak during the last months of his life (Pichois and Ziegler, 566, 593–97). By anybody's standards, if Baudelaire was a Catholic, he was an odd one, rather along the lines of the rock star Madonna, who was reported to have said that she considered herself to be profoundly Catholic because she used her rosary to masturbate.

Nietzsche made no secret of his antipathy for the Judeo-Christian tradition. He is often viewed as one of the fathers of the post-Christian era and certainly much of his appeal and popularity has come from those eager to cast off shackles of Christianity. [8] In *Human, All Too Human*, he wrote

---

[8] According to H. L. Mencken's 1908 apology for Nietzsche (a colorful mirror of his times and a reminder that Americans and Europeans were not all pious churchgoing Christians until the late 1960s): "Nietzsche himself rejected utterly the Judaic god and he believed that the great majority of intelligent men of his time were of his mind. That he was not far wrong in this assumption is evident to everyone. At the present time, indeed, it is next to impossible to find a sane man in all the world who believes in the actual existence of the deity described in the old testament. All theology is now an effort to explain away this god. Therefore, argues Nietzsche, it is useless to profess an insincere concurrence in a theistic idea at which our common sense revolts, and ridiculous to maintain the inviolability of an ethical scheme grounded upon this idea" (Mencken, 106). In Mencken's eyes, by Nietzsche's early manhood the battle to show that Christianity was "essentially untrue and unreasonable" had practically been won "so he did not spend much time examining the historical credibility of Christianity. He did not try to prove, like Huxley, that the witnesses to the resurrection were superstitious peasants and hysterical women, nor did he seek to show, like Huxley again, that Christ might have been taken down from the cross before he was dead. . . . Tunneling down, in his characteristic way, into the very foundations of the faith, he endeavored to prove that it was based upon contradictions and absurdities; that its dogmas were illogical and its precepts unworkable; and that its cardinal principles presupposed the acceptance of propositions which, to the normal human mind, were essentially unthinkable" (Mencken, 127–29).

of how Christ had hastened the crippling of human intelligence, sided with those lacking intelligence, and impeded the production of great minds (Nietzsche 1878, I §235). Zarathustra considered Jesus noble enough to have recanted his teaching and predicted that had he lived long enough he would have done so (Nietzsche 1883-85, 185).

According to the Gospel according to Friedrich, from the trunk of the tree of vengeance and Jewish hatred, the deepest, most sublime, ideal-producing, value-recreating kind of hatred, grew a new love, of the deepest, most sublime kind. That love did not spring up as any genuine negation of the Jewish thirst for vengeance, did not spring up as the antithesis of that hatred, but rather the opposite happened. It grew out of it and pursued the same goals of conquest, plundering, temptation with the same craving that sank the roots of that hatred ever more thoroughly and greedily down into everything deep and evil. For, according to Nietzsche, as the gospel of love incarnate, Jesus, that "redeemer" bringing bliss and victory to poor, sick, sinful people was precisely temptation in its most sinister and irresistible form, the enticement and roundabout way to precisely those Jewish values and changes of ideal (Nietzsche 1887, I §8).

So it was that even as the Marxists were busy vociferously condemning Christianity for never having helped the poor, defenseless, weak, disadvantaged, Nietzsche was pouncing on Christianity for engaging in the destructive practice of fostering such people. In *The Antichrist* §62, for example, Nietzsche condemned Christianity as "the one great curse, the one great innermost corruption," which had turned "every value into an un-value, every truth into a lie, every integrity into a vileness of the soul." It had "invented 'the equality of souls before God,' this falsehood, this pretext for cover for the rancor of all the base-minded, this explosive concept which eventually became revolution, modern idea, and the principle of decline of the whole order of society—is Christian dynamite" (Nietzsche 1888, 655–56).

In *The Antichrist* §5, Nietzsche trounced Christianity for having sided "with all that is weak and base, with all failures." He portrayed Christianity as having waged a deadly war against his higher men and their instincts, as having "made an ideal of whatever contradicts the instinct of the strong life to preserve itself," as having "corrupted the reason even of those strongest in spirit by teaching men to consider the supreme values of the spirit as something sinful, as something that leads into error—as temptations." Out of these instincts Christianity had "distilled evil and the Evil One: the strong man as the typically reprehensible man, the 'reprobate'" (Nietzsche 1888, 571–72). The fact is, Nietzsche stressed, that with its vengeance and reversal of all values, the values of Israel triumphed over all other ideals, over any nobler ideals. The people, the slaves, the rabble, the herd won.

Everything has become visibly Judaized, Christianized, or rabbled (Nietzsche 1887, I §§8–9).

Just like any other species of animal, the human species produces an excess of failed, sick, degenerate, infirm, necessarily suffering creatures, Nietzsche stressed, as he decried the way in which Christianity and Buddhism had tried to preserve human failures and help them cling to life. These religions had sided with those people because they were religions for suffering people, he argued. By preserving too many people who should have perished, they had contributed in a major way to maintaining humanity at a low level. They offered solace to the suffering, the oppressed, the despondent, were the mainstay of the weak, coaxed mental wrecks and those gone wild into cloisters or mental prisons, and by so preserving everything that was sick and suffering, they had actually worked for the deterioration of the European race (Nietzsche 1886, §62).

He went on to castigate the Church for having made it her business to turn all valuations of values upside down, to shatter the strong, stunt great hopes, cast suspicion on happiness in beauty, twist everything domineering, manly, conquering, tyrannical, all instincts characteristic of the highest and most well-behaved type of human being into uncertainty, pangs of conscience, self-destruction. She had turned all love of what is earthly and of sovereignty over the earth into hatred for the earth and everything of the earth. He complained that people not noble enough to see immense differences in ranks have controlled the fate of Europe with their ideas of equality before God until finally a debilitated, almost laughable species, a gregarious animal, an obliging, sickly, mediocre creature has resulted (Nietzsche 1886, §62).

The Nazi regime was also fundamentally in conflict with Judeo-Christian principles[9] and made no secret of its unhappiness with Christianity on any number of scores. For instance, an official Nazi press release of March 22, 1933 called "Why the *Führer* Does Not Take Part in Catholic Services," read: "The Catholic Bishops of Germany have in the recent past in a series of declarations... designated leaders and members of the Nazi Party as apostates of the Church, who should not come and partake in the sacraments" (Becker, 162–63).[10]

---

[9] Interesting books on Nazi religious beliefs are: Goodrick-Clarke 1985, *The Occult Roots of Nazism, Secret Aryan Cults and their Influence on Nazi Ideology*; Goodrick-Clarke 1998, *Hitler's Priestess. Savitri Devi, the Hindu-Aryan Myth, and Neo-Nazism,*; Rhodes 1980, *The Hitler Movement: A Modern Millenarian Revolution* ; Pois 1986, *National Socialism and the Religion of Nature*; Bernadac 1978, *Le Mystère Otto Rahn, Du Catharisme au Nazisme*. Biographies of such men as Himmler, Goebbels, Bormann, Göring, and other leading Nazis are also of interest.

[10] In countries not subject to Nazi censorship, Vatican opposition to the Nazis was far more apparent to people at the time, who are the ones who count, than decades later. For instance:

A number of diatribes on the subject attributed to Hitler were found recorded in Martin Bormann's *Table Talk 1941-44*. For example, there is his statement of July 1941 that in the long run National Socialism and religion would no longer be able to coexist. The coming of Christianity, Hitler was to have said, was the hardest blow to have struck humanity. Bolshevism was an illegitimate child of Christianity and both were inventions of the Jews.

Of the transvaluation of the Judeo-Christian principle "Thou shalt not kill" under the Nazi regime, Hannah Arendt reflected that:

> just as the law in civilized countries assumes that the voice of conscience tells everybody 'Thou shalt not kill,' even though man's natural desires and inclinations may at times be murderous, so that law of Hitler's land demanded that the voice of conscience tell everybody: 'Thou shalt kill,' although the organizers of the massacres knew full well that murder is against the normal desires and inclinations of most people. Evil in the Third Reich had lost the quality by which most people recognize it —the quality of temptation. Many Germans and many Nazis, probably an overwhelming majority of them, must have been tempted not to murder, not to rob, not to let their neighbors go off to their doom . . . and not to become accomplices in all these crimes by benefiting from them. (Arendt, 150)

In November 1939, Rabbi Jacob Kaplan, a Great Rabbi of France during World War II, lashed out at *Mein Kampf*'s "call to hatred and to violence." "What kind of retrograde doctrine is it," he protested, "that glorifies crushing the weak, subjugating souls, torturing defenseless prisoners, massacring civilian populations, women, children, old people, without

---

Albert Einstein's statement in *Time Magazine* of Dec. 23, 1940, "Only the Church stood squarely across the path of Hitler's campaign for suppressing truth. . . . the Church alone has had the courage and persistence to stand for intellectual truth and moral freedom"; the *New York Times* editorial of Dec. 25, 1941 reported that the Pope's Christmas message was clear. The Gestapo interpreted the Pope's words as one long attack on Nazism: "Here he is clearly speaking on behalf of the Jews." The *New York Times* editorial of Dec. 25, 1942 praised Pius XII as "a lonely voice crying out of the silence of a continent. . . . The Pope expresses as passionately as any leader on our side the war aims of the struggle for freedom." SS leader Heydrich said: "The Pope has repudiated the National Socialist New European Order. . . . He is virtually accusing the German people of injustice toward the Jews and makes himself the mouthpiece of the Jewish war criminals." *New York Times* front page articles of Aug. 6, 1942 reported: "Pope Pius has protested through his Nuncio against mass deportation of Jews from occupied France" and "The Papal Nuncio protested . . . against the inhuman arrests and deportations of Jews from the French occupied zone to Silesia and occupied parts of Russia." In October 1942, the *Times* of London praised Pius XII: "A study of the words which Pope Pius XII has addressed . . . to the Catholics of various nations leaves no room for doubt. He condemns the worship of force and its concrete manifestation in the suppression of national liberties and in the persecution of the Jewish race."

the slightest felling of pity and humanity?" Stressing "the inanity of the racial pretext put forward by Hitlerism to massacre the Jews," Great Rabbi Kaplan maintained that it was for a completely different reason that it baited them. He argued that since racism could not actually become established without previously destroying the great biblical affirmations of which it is the opposite, and consequently, the Jews who, were religious depositaries of those affirmations, and precisely because of this doctrinal incompatibility, Hitlerism was led to attack Christians, liberals, all people who recognize, as he and his fellow Jews do, the principles of fraternity, universal kinship, equality, justice, and Messianic teaching and who, for this reason, were deemed guilty of claiming kinship with Jewish conceptions (Kaplan 1952, 11–12, 80, 211–13).

According to *Mein Kampf,* "God's will gave men their form, their essence and their abilities. Anyone who destroys His work is declaring war on the Lord's creation, the divine will." However, Hitler complained, neither the Lutheran nor the Catholic Church understood how racial disintegration "was dragging down and often destroying the last Aryan values." According to him, the Christian churches were not fighting against that "destroyer of the Aryan man," the Jew who was contaminating Aryan blood. They merely looked on indifferently as "black parasites" systematically "defile inexperienced young blond girls and thereby destroy something which can no longer be replaced in this world." They did nothing to stop the "desecration and destruction of a noble and unique living creature, given to the earth by God's grace . . ." (Hitler, 562). Hitler complained that the churches

> make foolish faces and are full of amazement at the small effect of the Christian faith in their own country, at the terrible 'godlessness,' at this physically botched and hence spiritually degenerate rabble, and try with the Church's Blessing, to make up for it by success with the Hottentots and Zulu Kaffirs. While European peoples are falling into a condition of physical and moral leprosy, pious missionaries wander off to Central Africa where they annoy Negroes with missions until there, too, our 'higher culture' turns healthy, though primitive and inferior, human beings into a rotten brood of bastards. (Hitler, 403)

Be that as it may, the bottom line for Hitler when it came to his dealings with Christianity was surely his conviction that it belonged to the genius of a great leader to concentrate the people's attention upon a single foe. In weak and uncertain characters, he stressed, the knowledge of having different enemies only too readily raises questions about how right they themselves are. Once the vacillating masses see themselves as struggling against too many enemies, objectivity enters to sow doubt as to whether only their own people, or their own movement are in the right and everyone else really wrong. In Hitler's estimation, all truly great national leaders of all times had known how to fit adversaries of even a very different ilk into the same category (Hitler, 118). To Hitler this meant that those who tried to draw the National Socialist movement into religious quarrels were acting damnably because they were consciously, or unconsciously, fighting on the side of the Jews in the mighty struggle against Aryan humanity (Hitler, 654).

Nietzsche's Theories about Sick People

Nietzsche's theories about the deleterious effect that sick people have on society and about the way sick people see things afford interesting insight into why he and the equally syphilitic Baudelaire might have said some of the things that they did about evil and weak, sick people. For example, in a section of *Daybreak* called "Raising oneself above one's own piteousness," Nietzsche writes of proud fellows who in order to establish a sense of their dignity and importance always need other people to hector and do violence to. They need people whose powerlessness and cowardliness allows them to act with impunity in a superior, irate manner in front of them. They need those around them to be wretched in order to raise themselves for an instant above their own wretchedness (Nietzsche 1881, §369).

According to Nietzsche, those who suffer are one and all appallingly ready and inventive when it comes to excuses for painful emotional states. They even relish their suspicions, brooding over depravity and apparent prejudices. They root through the bowels of their past and present for dark, questionable tales where they are free to wallow in torturous suspicions and intoxicate themselves with their own evil poison. They rip open their oldest wounds and from long-healed scars bleed themselves to death. They make friends, women, children, and those around them into miscreants (Nietzsche 1887, III §15).

People who suffer want to find someone to blame for their suffering, Nietzsche emphasized (Nietzsche 1887, III §15). Guilt is always sought wherever there is failure, for along with it comes ill feeling, the instinctively applied cure lying in a new excitation of the feeling of power found in condemning the guilty party. This guilty person is not a scapegoat for the guilt of others, but a sacrifice of the weak, humiliated, depressed who want to prove that they still possess strength (Nietzsche 1881, §140).

In another section of *Daybreak* called "For whom truth is there," Nietzsche suggested that truth, as something whole and coherent was only there for souls who were at once powerful and harmless, joyful, and peaceful, and that it would no doubt be only such souls that would be in a position to seek it, for the others did not seek truth, but only cures for themselves, which was why they took so little real pleasure in science, and criticized it as being cold, dry, and inhuman. It was a matter of sick people judging the games of the healthy (Nietzsche 1881, §424).

In the "On the knowledge of those who are suffering" section of *Daybreak*, Nietzsche complements those reflections by writing of insights acquired by sick people who suffer terribly over long periods of time and whose minds, nonetheless, remain lucid. Those who suffer intensely, he explains, cast a horrifyingly cold eye on things. The supreme sobering up that pain effects pulls them out of any dangerous fantasy world in which they had been living before they fell ill and is perhaps the only means of doing so. All the small, deceptive, magical touches that healthy people commonly see swirling about in things vanish. Sick people themselves even stand plucked and colorless before themselves. With dreadful clearsightedness as to the nature of their being, they challenge themselves to be their own accuser and executioner, to take their suffering as the punishment inflicted by themselves upon themselves, enjoy their superiority as judges, enjoy their willful pleasure, their tyrannical arbitrariness, raise themselves above their lives as above their suffering, look down into the deep and the unfathomable depths (Nietzsche 1881, §114).

The enormous intellectual strain involved in the desire to fight pain, Nietzsche believed, sheds new light upon everything upon which suffering people look, and the unspeakable stimulus that any new light lends is often sufficiently powerful to defy all temptation to suicide and make continuing to live seem most desirable to sufferers. They harbor contemptuous thoughts about the warm, pleasant, nebulous world in which the healthy wander without giving it a second thought. They harbor contemptuous thoughts about the noblest, dearest illusions that they themselves once toyed with. They enjoy conjuring up this contempt as though out of the deepest Hell and causing their souls the bitterest pain. This is how they compensate for physical pain; they feel that this is precisely the compensation needed under the circumstances (Nietzsche 1881, §114).

Himself a very sick man as he theorized about evil, the philosopher of the *Übermensch* possessed keen, personal insight into the minds of sick people and some very specific ideas about people not physically fit to qualify as *Übermenschen*. So it is that midway through the text "On the knowledge of those who are suffering," he tellingly shifts from the third person into the first person plural. In times of great suffering, he explains, our pride rises up as never before to induce us to plead life's cause before the tyranny of pain and all its insinuations that we testify against life. In this state, one bitterly resists all pessimism so that it does not appear to be a consequence of our condition and humiliate us in defeat. But we do not want to be made to feel guilty, but want to show that we can be free of any guilt. We find ourselves in veritable fits of haughtiness, but when the first faint glimmering of relief, of recovery comes, almost we immediately resist the superior force of this haughtiness. We call ourselves silly and vain, as if we had experienced something unique. Ungrateful, we humiliate the almighty pride which was precisely what helped us bear up under the pain; we furiously long for an antidote for the pride which we now see as an ailment and as having been a fit. After pain has too forcibly made us personal for too long, we seek distance from ourselves and depersonalization. We then look upon people and nature with more longing. Smiling sorrowfully, we remember that we know some new and different things about them, that a veil has been lifted, but we find it so refreshing to see life in a subdued light again and to emerge from the awful, sober clearness in which we saw things and saw through things when we were suffering (Nietzsche 1881, §114).

"Was it not always so with Nietzsche," the editor of his correspondence with August Strindberg once commented, "that his philosophy stemmed from most violent struggles against what was most deeply rooted in his self?" (Gilman, 218). Did not Zarathustra advise followers to: "Listen, rather . . . to the voice of the healthy body: that is a more honest and purer voice. More honestly and purely speaks the healthy body that is perfect and perpendicular: and it speaks of the meaning of the earth" (Nietzsche 1883-85, 145).

On Fostering the Strongest and the Healthiest

Nietzsche was adamant in his conviction that sick people were the greatest danger for people in good health. It was not the strong who were the misfortune of the strong, he insisted in *On the Genealogy of Morals*, but the weak. It was they, and not the evil people, not the beasts of prey, who were the greatest danger for humanity. To him, unfortunate, defeated, broken people were those who, more than any others, undermined life, poisoned people, and constituted the most dangerous challenge to people's confidence in life, human beings, and themselves.

According to Nietzsche, superior people should not stoop to being the tools of their inferiors. Their right to exist was a thousand times greater than that of inferior people. They alone were the guarantors of the future. What they could and were obliged to do, the sick could never be able or obliged to do. The upside-down world in which the sick and weak tyrannize the healthy and the strong had to be brought to an end, he insisted (Nietzsche 1887, III §14). He counseled the healthy to stay away from hospitals and madhouses of the civilization, away from the noxious fumes of inner decay and the underhanded maggot-infested sick (Nietzsche

1887, III §14). Taking care of the sick, he said, could not in any way be the work of healthy people (Nietzsche 1887, III §15).

As for Hitler, he did not leave readers of *Mein Kampf* in doubt as to what he himself hoped to achieve when given a chance. As he saw it, human beings "can defy the eternal laws of the will to conservation for a certain time, but sooner or later vengeance comes. A stronger race will drive out the weak, for the vital urge in its ultimate form will, time and again, burst all the absurd fetters of the so-called humanity of individuals, in order to replace it by the humanity of Nature which destroys the weak to give his place to the strong" (Hitler, 132). He further expressed his conviction that the world was not for cowardly peoples. If "a people is defeated in its struggle for human rights, this merely means that it has been found too light in the scale of destiny for the happiness of survival on this earth. For when a people is not willing or able to fight for its existence—Providence in its eternal justice has decreed that people's end" (Hitler, 96).

According to Hitler's world view, in making procreation free, but making it hard to survive, from among an excess number of individuals, nature chooses the best as worthy of living. She thus preserves them alone, and in them she preserves their species. In contrast to this, human beings limit procreation, but are hysterically concerned that a person's life should be preserved at any price. They see this correction of the divine will as both wise and human and delight in having gotten the best of nature and even in having demonstrated her inadequacy. Hitler acknowledged that that was an effective way of reducing the population, but deemed that it diminished the value of the individual, something which, in his words, "the dear little ape of the Almighty does not want to see or hear about." The natural struggle for existence that left only the strongest and healthiest alive, has obviously been "replaced by the obvious desire to 'save' even the weakest and most sickly at any price, and this plants the seed of a future generation which must inevitably grow more and more deplorable the longer this mockery of Nature and her will continues" (Hitler, 132). "*If the power to fight for one's own health is no longer present, the right to live in this world of struggle ends.* This world belongs only to the forceful 'whole' man and not to the weak 'half' man," Hitler was convinced (Hitler, 257).

Hitler saw the struggle against syphilis as being one of the most gigantic tasks of humanity because in this case the sickening of the body was only the consequence of a sickening of the moral, social, and racial instincts. In the struggle against this disease society faced, not the solution of a single question, but the elimination of a large number of evils that bring about this plague as a resultant manifestation. Hitler considered that "the gravest and most ruthless decisions" would have to be made in the medical struggle against syphilis and that no half-measures were admissible. For him, allowing incurably sick people steadily to contaminate the remaining healthy ones in the name of a humanitarianism which, to avoid hurting one individual, let a hundred others perish was one such half-measure. He considered it clearly reasonable to demand that defective people be prevented from propagating equally defective offspring and believed that systematically realized this would represent the most humane act of mankind. In his estimation, it would spare millions of unfortunate people unmerited sufferings, and thus lead to a rising improvement of health overall. He believed that if necessary those who are incurably sick should be pitilessly segregated from the others, "a barbaric measure for the unfortunate who is struck by it, but a blessing for his fellow men and posterity. The passing pain of a century can and will redeem millenniums from sufferings" (Hitler, 255–56).

Hitler's Theories about Idealism in *Mein Kampf*

Given the way in which Hitler and his movement have been (rightly) diabolized, it may at first sight seem perverse, suspicious, or downright disgusting to talk about idealism in connection with Nazism. But, Hitler portrayed himself as an idealist and made no secret of his ideas about the power that ideals exercise over people. That is the very stuff of *Mein Kampf*, a textbook on the subject of manipulating people that is chock-full of talk of ideals. Furthermore, the success that Hitler enjoyed in carrying out his iniquitous plans shows that he must in some sense have been right in his understanding of how to infect people with "idealism" and how to use the power gained to realize his goals.

Upon closer inspection, there is actually ample reason to believe that this is where some important clues to unlocking the "mystery" of the evil of Nazism are to be found, for in trying to understand how people can be led to perform actions that are subsequently almost universally condemned as having been utterly evil, it is essential to take into account how people can be manipulated through an appeal to ideals.

Moreover, it is not at all hard to find instances of people manipulated by Hitler's appeal to ideals. In *Magic Lantern*, Ingmar Bergman tells of how as an exchange student in Nazi Germany "unvaccinated and unprepared," he "fell headlong into an atmosphere glowing with idealism and hero worship" and "was also suddenly exposed to an aggressiveness which to a great extent was in harmony" with his own. "The surface lustre blinded me," he confessed, "and I did not see the darkness" (Bergman, 124). Lincoln Rockwell, founder of the American Nazi Party and a president of the World Union of National Socialists, wondered "at the utter, indescribable genius" of *Mein Kampf* claiming to have discovered in it "abundant 'mental sunshine,' which bathed all the gray world suddenly in the clear light of reason and understanding," a work in which "sentence after sentence stabbed into the darkness like thunderclaps and lightning-bolts of revelation, tearing and ripping away the cobwebs of more than thirty years of darkness, brilliantly illuminating the mysteries of the heretofore impenetrable murk in a world gone mad" (Goodrick-Clarke 1998, 197–98).

Adolf Eichmann, who played a significant role in helping Hitler realize his "ideals," said that the reason that he became fascinated by the Jewish question was his own idealism. He saw Zionists as idealists like himself. As Hannah Arendt explained it:

> An 'idealist,' according to Eichmann's notions, was not merely a man who believed in an 'idea' or someone who did not steal or accept bribes, though these qualifications were indispensable. An 'idealist' was a man who *lived* for his idea—hence he could not be a businessman—and who was prepared to sacrifice for his idea everything and, especially, everybody. When he said in the police examination that he would have sent his own father to his death if that had been required, he... meant to show what an 'idealist' he had always been. The perfect 'idealist,' like everybody else, had of course his personal feelings and emotions, but he would never permit them to interfere with his actions if they came into conflict with his 'idea'. (Arendt, 41–42)

Be that as it may, Hitler was very specific about what he meant by idealism and when it comes to studying his theories about manipulating people through idealism there is really no substitute for his own explanations in *Mein Kampf* (a book, according to its Preface, addressed to those of Hitler's followers "whose intelligence is eager for a more penetrating enlightenment") as to how to "draw from the realm of the eternally true and ideal that which is humanly possible for small mortals, and make it take form" (Hitler, 381).

In *Mein Kampf*, Hitler argued that "in general we must clearly acknowledge the fact that the highest ideals always correspond to a deep vital necessity" (Hitler, 379) and the "purest idealism is unconsciously equivalent to the deepest knowledge" (Hitler, 299). He emphasized that "true idealism" had little "to do with playful flights of the imagination" and how necessary it was "to keep realizing that idealism does not represent a superfluous expression of emotion, but that in truth it has been, is, and will be, the premise for what we designate as human culture. It alone created the concept of 'human being'" (Hitler, 298–99).

By idealism Hitler said he meant "the individual's capacity to make sacrifices for the community and for his fellow men" (Hitler, 298). He defined "true idealism" as being "nothing but the subordination of the interests and life of the individual to the community," and this in turn as being the prerequisite for creating of organizational forms of all kinds, for it corresponded "in its innermost depths to the ultimate will of Nature. It alone leads men to voluntary recognition of the privilege of force and strength, and thus makes them into a dust particle of that order which shares and forms the whole universe" (Hitler, 299).

Hitler professed to believe that "not only do human beings live in order to serve higher ideals, but conversely, these higher ideals also provide the premise for their existence" (Hitler, 379–80). While he preached that one must take care not to underestimate the force of an idea (Hitler, 437), he remained most conscious that "an eternal ideal, serving as the guiding star of mankind must unfortunately resign itself to taking the weaknesses of this mankind into consideration if it wants to avoid shipwreck at the very outset on the shoals of general human inadequacy" (Hitler, 381).

Hitler recognized the need for a new philosophy. He believed that anyone wanting "to cure this era, which is inwardly sick and rotten, must first of all summon up the courage to make clear the causes of this disease . . . to gather and to organize from the ranks of our nation those forces capable of becoming the vanguard fighters for a new philosophy of life" (Hitler, 435). He considered it to be a fundamental principle that after a certain point in their development conceptions, ideas, and movements with a definite spiritual foundation, be they true or false, could only be broken by technical instruments of power if those physical weapons were at the same time used to bolster a new kindling thought, idea, or philosophy (Hitler, 170); he was convinced that any attempt to fight a philosophy by violence was destined to failure unless the struggle took the form of an attack for a new spiritual attitude. "Only in the struggle between two philosophies," he stressed, "can the weapon of brutal force, persistently and ruthlessly applied, lead to a decision for the side it supports" (Hitler, 172). He taught that the

> application of force alone, without the impetus of a basic spiritual idea as a starting point, can never lead to the destruction of an idea and its dissemination, except in the form of a complete extermination of even the very last exponent of the idea and the destruction of the last tradition. . . . the complete annihilation of the new doctrine can be carried out only through a process of extermination so great and constantly increasing that in the end all the truly valuable blood is drawn out of the people or state in question. (Hitler, 170–71)

Hitler was moreover convinced that "if a spiritual conception of a general nature is to serve as a foundation for a future development, the first presupposition is to obtain unconditional clarity with regard to the nature, essence, and scope of this conception, since only on such a basis can a movement be formed which by the inner homogeneity of its convictions can develop the necessary force for struggle" (Hitler, 380–81). He considered such conceptual clarity to be "not only ideal, but in the last analysis also eminently practical." It was "the indispensably necessary means which alone makes possible the achievement of the end" (Hitler, 379).

To make this point, Hitler compared the ideals of his movement to religion. "Without a clearly delimited faith," he maintained, "religiosity with its unclarity and multiplicity of form would not only be worthless for human life, but would probably contribute to general disintegration" (Hitler, 380). As he explained, "since the great masses consist neither of philosophers nor of saints, such a very general religious idea will as a rule mean to individuals only the liberation of their thought and action, without, however, leading to that efficacy which arises from religious inner longing in the moment when, from the purely metaphysical infinite world of ideas, a clearly delimited faith forms" (Hitler, 379). "By helping to raise human beings above the level of bestial vegetation, faith contributes in reality to the securing and safeguarding of their existence. Take away from present-day mankind its education-based, religious-dogmatic principles—or, practically speaking ethical-moral principles—by abolishing this religious education, but without replacing it by an equivalent, and the result will be a grave shock to the foundations of their existence" (Hitler, 379).

The "Idealization" of Humanity

In *Mein Kampf*, Hitler further explained that his movement believed "in the necessity of an idealization of humanity, in which alone it sees the premise for the existence of humanity" (Hitler, 383). The fact of the matter is that by "ideals," Hitler meant racial "ideals," and by the "idealization of humanity," he meant the Aryanization of humanity. It was the Aryans, he taught, who had recognized the need to keep realizing that idealism was not just an excess of emotion, but the premise for human culture that alone had created the concept of human being (Hitler, 298–99). It was precisely to that inner attitude, Hitler wrote,

> that the Aryan owes his position in this world, and to it the world owes human beings; for it alone formed from pure spirit the creative force which, by a unique pairing of the brutal fist and the intellectual genius, created the monuments of human culture. Without this idealistic attitude all, even the most dazzling faculties of the intellect, would remain mere intellect as such—outward appearance without inner value, and never creative force. (Hitler, 298–99)

Hitler saw human culture and civilization in Europe as being inseparably bound up with the presence of Aryans. He believed that if they were to die out or decline, "the dark veils of an age without culture" would again descend upon the earth (Hitler, 383). He also considered the "undermining of the existence of human culture by the destruction of its bearer . . .

the most execrable crime. Anyone who dares to lay hands on the highest image of the Lord commits sacrilege against the benevolent creator of this miracle and contributes to the expulsion from paradise" (Hitler, 383). According to Hitler, the Aryan

> is not greatest in his mental qualities as such, but in the extent of his willingness to put all his abilities in the service of the community. In him the instinct of self-preservation has reached the noblest form, since he willingly subordinates his own ego to the life of the community and, if the hour demands even sacrifices it. . . . This state of mind, which subordinates the interests of the ego to the conservation of the community, is really the first premise for every truly human culture. From it alone can arise all the great works of mankind. (Hitler, 297)

For Hitler, the presence of a certain feeling of cohesion based on similarity of nature and species, and a willingness to stake everything on it with all possible means was the most sensible prerequisite for the formation and preservation of a state and he believed that this was something that would create heroic virtues in peoples having their own soil, but would create lying, hypocrisy, and malignant cruelty in parasites. For him, the State resulted and always would result solely from the action of those qualities that were in line with the will to preserve the species and race. He considered these always to be heroic virtues because the instinct of the existence of a species presupposed a spirit of sacrifice in the individual. He believed that the formation of states originally occurred through the exercise of those qualities and that in the subsequent struggle for self-preservation, those nations possessing the smallest share of heroic virtues, or those not equal to the lies and trickery of the hostile parasite, would be defeated, fall prey to subjugation, and eventually die out (Hitler, 151).

Hitler provided the following explanation of Germany's defeat in World War I in terms of his theories about idealism. What "made people die then was not concern for their daily bread, but love of the fatherland, faith in its greatness, a general feeling for the honor of the nation. . . . when the German people moved away from these ideals to follow the material premises of the revolution, and exchanged their arms for knapsacks, . . . they arrived, not at the earthly paradise, but at the purgatory of general contempt and, no less, of general misery" (Hitler, 437). "In 1914, as long as the German people thought they were fighting for ideals, they stood firm; but as soon as they were told to fight for their daily bread, they preferred to give up the game" (Hitler, 153).

Nothing, Hitler considered, showed the English people's superior psychological understanding of the soul of the people better than the motivation that they gave for fighting. While Germany claimed to be fighting for bread, the English said they were fighting for freedom of small nations.

Germany's laughing at that, or being enraged by it, only demonstrated to Hitler how "empty-headed and stupid the so-called statesmen of Germany had become. . . . We no longer had the slightest idea concerning the essence of the force which can lead men to their death of their own free will and decision" (Hitler, 152–53).

It never became clear to German statesmen, Hitler thought, "that from the moment people begin to fight for economic interests they avoid death as much as possible since death would forever deprive them of their reward for fighting. Anxiety for the rescue of her own child makes a heroine of even the feeblest mother, and only the struggle for the preservation of the species and the hearth or the state that protects it, has at all times driven people against the spears of their enemies" (Hitler, 153). Economic conditions always began to improve when there was an upsurge of political power in Germany, but always whenever economics stifled ideal virtues, the state collapsed and quickly drew down economic life with it (Hitler, 152). People, he insisted, do "not die for business, but only for ideals" (Hitler, 152). He therefore considered it really necessary to confront the "master book-keepers" of the material Weimar Republic with "faith in an *ideal* Reich" (Hitler, 437). "It may be that today gold has become the exclusive ruler of life," he predicted, "but the time will come when people will bow down again before a higher god" (Hitler, 436).

Such considerations led Hitler to advance this "theorem" as an "eternally valid truth": "Never yet has a state been founded by peaceful economic means, but always and exclusively by the instincts of preservation of the species regardless whether these are found in the province of heroic virtue or of cunning craftiness. The one results in Aryan states based on work and culture, the other in Jewish colonies of parasites" (Hitler, 153). The Jew, according to Hitler's theories, lacked "completely the most essential requirement for a cultured people, the idealistic attitude. In the Jewish people the will to self-sacrifice does not go beyond the individual's naked instinct of self-preservation" (Hitler, 301).

Torpor and Turpitude

Ennui, which the *Random House College Dictionary* defines as "a feeling of weariness and discontent resulting from satiety or lack of interest; boredom," is another section of the mosaic we are piecing together. There is the ennui of people who feel buried deep in the dreary routine of existence. There is the ennui of those who have too much, are deadened, numbed by comfort, sated by materialistic, superficial societies, are dying to feel alive and real. There is the ennui of those having nothing to do, the unemployed, the marginalized, of those who, having nothing but time, wallow in the anguish of idleness. . . . There is the ennui that makes people ripe for drugs, drink, or any action to fill the vacuum, that leads them out in pursuit of powerful sensations, of passions, of artificial stimulants to lend existence a meaning that intoxicates them. There is the ennui that causes people to cry out against the stagnation by terrifying and being terrified, by engaging in senseless acts of destruction, kidnapping, killing, martyrdom. There is the ennui that awakens the search for extreme experiences, however ghastly or disastrous, that can shake people free of torpor. There is the ennui of the twelve-year-old fighter in a civil war on the African continent who was quoted as having said: "The first time I killed I did not worry about it. In fact, I felt happy because I had been alone and feeling bored."

The fictional character Sherlock Holmes once offered an explanation of the ennui to which he was prone and of his efforts, in Baudelaire's words, to "cheer up the ennui of our prisons" (Baudelaire 1857, CXXVI, III) by injecting cocaine. When warned by Doctor Watson that rousing and exciting his brain by injections of cocaine was surely "hardly worth the candle" because it was "a pathological and morbid process which involves increased tissue-change and may at least leave a permanent weakness," that it brought about "a black reaction," and that Holmes risked losing the great powers with which he had been endowed for a mere passing pleasure, Holmes explained that he was given to fighting ennui with injections of cocaine because he found the drug "transcendently stimulating and clarifying to the mind" (Doyle 1890, ch. 1). Asked by Watson whether he had any professional inquiry on foot, Holmes responded:

> None. Hence the cocaine. I cannot live without brainwork. What else is there to live for? Stand at the window here. Was [there] ever such a dreary, dismal, unprofitable world? See how the yellow fog swirls down the street and drifts across the dun-coloured houses. What could be more hopelessly prosaic and material? What is the use of having powers, Doctor, when one has no field upon which to exert them? Crime is commonplace, existence is commonplace, and no qualities save those which are commonplace have any function upon earth. (Doyle 1890, ch. 1)

"My mind," Holmes had explained to Watson, "rebels at stagnation. Give me problems, give me work, give me the most abstruse cryptogram, or the most intricate analysis, and I am in my own proper atmosphere. I can dispense then with artificial stimulants. But I abhor the dull routine of existence. I crave for mental exaltation . . ." (Doyle 1890, ch. 1).

Baudelaire, who once wrote in a suicide note: "I am killing myself because I can no longer live, because the fatigue of going to sleep and the fatigue of waking are unbearable for me, and because I am useless to others . . ." (Pichois and Ziegler, 211), was a most eloquent spokesman of the moaning soul prey to long spells of ennui (Baudelaire 1857, LXXVIII). In his "On Tasso in Prison by Eugène Delacroix," he depicted the sixteenth-century Italian poet who went half-mad, as a "genius locked up in an unhealthy hovel," as a "dreamer that the horror of his dwelling awakens" who is emblematic of those "souls with dark dreams that the Real stifles within its four walls!" He is someone who "with a look inflamed with terror sizes up the vertiginous flight of stairs into which his soul is sinking. The intoxicating laughter filling the prison invites his reason to the strange and absurd." He is beset by doubt, and fear, ridiculous, hideous, multiform, circulates about him (Baudelaire 1857).

The poem that serves as the preface to the *Flowers of Evil* closes with thoughts on ennui: "that ugliest and most wicked of monsters, the foulest in the vile menagerie of our vices that, neither making great gestures, nor great cries, would swallow the world in a yawn." The poem ends with the affirmation that among:

> the jackals, the panthers, the hound bitches, the monkeys, the scorpions, the vultures, the snakes, the yelping, howling, grunting, creepy-crawly monsters in the foul menagerie of our vices, there is one that is uglier, more evil, more filthy! Though it neither makes great movements, nor utters great cries, it would willingly make the earth into a wasteland; this is Ennui!—the eye filled with an involuntary tear, it dreams of scaffolds while smoking its hookah. You know it, reader, this delicate monster,—hypocritical reader,—my kindred spirit,—my brother. (Baudelaire 1857, "Au Lecteur")

In his poem "The Voyage," Baudelaire wrote of how the "world, monotonous and small, today, yesterday, tomorrow, ever, makes us see our own image: An oasis of horror in a desert of ennui. Must one leave? Remain? . . . One runs, and another cowers to cheat the watchful, deadly enemy, Time! There are, alas! those who run without respite, like the wandering Jew, and like the apostles, for whom nothing suffices, neither wagon, nor ship, to flee this infamous world of nets . . ." (Baudelaire 1857, CXXVI, VII)

Baudelaire understood well that dormant fantasies, both evil ones and good, come alive in people numbed by ennui. In his poem "The Voyage," he wrote of courting damnation for the sake of a moment's respite from ennui and saw well how ennui is often the scene of the movement from thought to action. There, he wrote: "O Death, old captain, it is time! Let us raise the anchor! This country bores us, O Death! . . . Pour us your poison so that it may comfort us! We wish, this fire is burning our brains so, to plunge into the bottom of the pit, Hell or Heaven, what does it matter? To the depths of the Unknown to find something *new*!" (Baudelaire 1857, CXXVI, VIII). And he alluded to certain, "the least foolish, daring lovers of Madness, fleeing the great herd penned up by Destiny and taking refuge in the immense opium!" (Baudelaire 1857, CXXVI, VI).

In his prose poem "The Bad Windowpane Maker" (Baudelaire 1869, IX), Baudelaire discoursed at length on "a kind of energy that springs from ennui and reverie" that manifests itself in a particularly unexpected way in the most indolent of dreamers. He tells of people who, of a purely contemplative nature and unfit for action, nonetheless, act upon a mysterious, unknown impulse with a rapidity of which they would never have believed themselves capable. Moralists and doctors, who aspire to know everything, the poet says, are at a loss to explain where such mad energy so suddenly comes from to these lazy people, and how voluptuous souls unable to do the simplest, most necessary things come to perform the most absurd and often even the most dangerous deeds.

The poet then describes how one of his friends, the most harmless of dreamers who had ever existed, once set fire to a forest in order to see whether it would catch fire as easily people generally say. His experiment failed ten times in a row, but the eleventh time it succeeded all too well. Another friend lit a cigar next to a powder keg *"to see, to know, to tempt fate,* to force himself to display some energy, to take a gamble, to feel the pleasures of anxiety, for no reason, out of capriciousness, out of a lack of anything to do." Another friend particularly lacking in will and easy to intimidate, too shy to look a person in the eye, would abruptly grab an old person and begin enthusiastically kissing him, probably without ever knowing why.

The poet confesses to having himself more than once been "a victim of these crises and outbursts, which justify us in believing that mischievous Demons slip into us and, without our knowing it, make us carry out their most absurd whims." He begs the reader to note the significant role played in this by the spirit of mystification which, in some people, is not the product of some effort or scheme, but of some chance inspiration, be it only through the ardor of the desire, the product of that mood, called hysterical by doctors, satanic by those who think rather better than the doctors, that pushes us unresisting in the direction of a host of dangerous or unseemly deeds.

One morning, the poet confides, he woke up feeling glum, sad, tired of laziness and pushed, it seemed to him, to do something big, flashy. He opened the window and the first person he saw in the street was a windowpane maker whose piercing, grating cry rose to him through the heavy, dirty Parisian sky. Inexplicably overcome by sudden, despotic hatred for that poor man, the poet beckoned him to come up to his seventh floor room, thinking with some pleasure of how hard it would be for the man to climb the narrow staircase with his windows.

The windowpane maker showed his windows to the poet, who complained that they were not of colored glass, not magical windowpanes, not windowpanes of paradise. So giving the windowpane maker a hardy shove in the direction of the staircase, where he tottered while muttering, the poet chastised him for walking about in poor neighborhoods without even having windowpanes that show life as beautiful.

The poet then went to the balcony and, when the windowpane maker walked out of the building, dropped a flower pot on him, which knocked him over and broke his entire fortune he was carrying with him. With that, intoxicated with his madness, the infuriated poet cried out to the window-pane maker "Life as beautiful! Life as beautiful." The poet acknowledged that such hysterical jokes were not without their risks and that one could often pay dearly for them. But, he asked, "what importance does eternal damnation have for someone who has discovered the infinity of intense pleasure in a single second?"

Insights into links between torpor and turpitude are strewn all throughout Baudelaire's poetry. In his poem entitled "Destruction," it is none other than the Demon himself who, using specious pretexts of doldrums, leads the poet, out of breath and broken with fatigue, far from the sight of God and into the midst of the deep, deserted plains of Ennui, who casts soiled garments, open wounds, and the bloody machinery of Destruction before the poet's confusion-filled eyes (Baudelaire 1857, CIX). In "The Prayer of a Pagan," the poet cries out: "Ah, slow not your flames; rekindle my torpid heart, Voluptuous pleasure, torture of souls! . . . Answer the prayer of a soul bored with waiting who devotes a brazen song to you. Voluptuous pleasure, be ever my queen! Take the mask of a siren . . . or pour me your deep sleep in amorphous, mystical wine, Voluptuous pleasure, elastic phantom!" (Baudelaire 1857). Another of the poems of *The Flowers of Evil* reads:

> You would put the whole universe in your alcove, impure woman! Ennui makes your soul cruel. To use your teeth in this unique game, you must leave your heart in the rack each day. Your eyes, lit like shops and blazing taper-hearses in public celebrations, unabashedly use borrowed power, without ever understanding the law of their beauty. Blind, deaf machine abounding in cruelty! Salutary instrument, drinker of the blood of the world, how is it that you are not ashamed and how is it that you have not seen your charms fade in all the mirrors? Has not the greatness of this evil about which you believe yourself knowledgeable ever made you draw back in horror, when nature, great in its hidden designs, uses you, o woman, o queen of sin,—you vile animal,—to mold a genius, O miry greatness! Sublime ignominy." (Baudelaire 1857, XXV)

Baudelaire's keen awareness of ennui was surely sharpened by the "extraordinary," "astonishing lassitude" and "melancholy" brought on by the incurable malady he had and the deadening effects of the drugs that he used to combat it (Pichois and Ziegler, 180–81). Nietzsche suffered from the same the incurable malady and from the effects of the drugs that he used to combat it. In *On the Genealogy of Morals*, he wrote of how, provided that they burst forth suddenly, basically all the great emotional states, anger, fear, lust, vengeance, hope, victory, despair, and cruelty were fully capable of unhinging the human soul, of submerging it in terror, chills, passion, and rapture of such a kind that, as if by a flash of lightning, it was set free from all the pettiness and paltriness of listlessness, of numbness, of ill humor (Nietzsche 1887, III §20).

As a young man, Adolf Hitler confessed in *Mein Kampf*, he had already been prone to bouts of ennui and harbored angry thoughts concerning his time on earth. Even as a child, he recalled, he had been no pacifist, and all attempts to educate him in that direction had come to naught. He viewed the period of law and order that he feared loomed ahead of him to be a mean, unmerited trick that Fate had played on him (Hitler, 158). The waves of historic events seemed to him to have grown so smooth that the future seemed to belong only to the peaceful contest of nations, a cozy mutual swindling match excluding violent methods of defense. The various nations had begun to be more and more like private citizens cutting the ground out from under each other's feet, stealing each other's customers and orders, trying in every way to get ahead of one another and staging this whole act amid a hue and cry as loud as it was harmless. Nothing, he said, had grieved him more as a child than having been born in days in which shopkeepers and government officials were honored and the whole world seemed to be being remodeled into one big department store in whose vestibules the busts of the shrewdest profiteers and the most lamb-like administrative officials would be garnered for all eternity (Hitler, 157).

In *Explaining Hitler, the Search for the Origins of his Evil*, Ron Rosenbaum speculates that the "despondent and disillusioned" three years that Hitler spent in the men's shelter in Vienna were a crucial time in his development, "one that saw the destruction and loss of his romantic artistic illusions." He notes that some believe that that "was the interlude when other, more sinister illusions took their place" and many have "argued that it was in some encounter there . . . or in some moment of embittered introspection, some vision there, that triggered Hitler's metamorphosis from struggling artist and harmless bohemian to the grim hater he became" (Rosenbaum, 204).

According to Hannah Arendt's understanding of the personality of Hitler's minion Adolf Eichmann in *Eichmann in Jerusalem: A Report on the Banality of Evil*, he was a dweller on the plains of Ennui into whose hands the machinery of destruction had been cast. For her, it was boredom with the dreary routine of existence, not any ill feeling toward his victims, that seemed to have played the more significant role in the decisions that Eichmann made that led to his playing a leading role in the extermination

European Jewry. Hannah Arendt describes him as a once ambitious man who had grown fed up with his job as traveling salesman, "a leaf in the whirlwind of time," who by 1933 had lost all joy in his work and found himself "blown . . . into the marching columns of the Thousand-Year Reich" (Arendt, 30–33). His work for the Nazi regime finally gave him the sense of "elation" that he so craved (Arendt, 53–54). She writes of how:

> From a humdrum life without significance and consequence the wind had blown him into History, as he understood it, namely, into a Movement that always kept moving and in which somebody like him—already a failure in the eyes of his social class, of his family, and hence in his own eyes as well—could start from scratch and still make a career . . . and if he did not always like what he had to do (for example dispatching people to their death by the trainload instead of forcing them to emigrate), if he guessed, rather early, that the whole business would come to a bad end . . . , he never forgot what the alternative would have been. . . . He might have still preferred . . . to be hanged rather than living out his life quietly and normally as a traveling salesman. . . . (Arendt, 33)

Of his time spent in the military, Eichmann said that the humdrum of military service was more than he could stand, "day after day always the same, over and over again the same." Thus "bored to distraction," he found that Himmler's *Sicherheitsdient* had job openings and applied immediately. His job there was also "very, very boring, and he was greatly relieved when . . . he was put into the brand-new department concerned with Jews" that meant the real beginning of his career (Arendt, 30–37). His work to have Jews emigrate being "dead" in 1941, he sought to be named to the *Einsatzgruppen*, the mobile killing units in Eastern Europe (Arendt, 49–51), whose work is described in Part Two of this book.

According to Arendt, what eventually led to Eichmann's capture was his propensity to brag. In the closing days of World War II, he was supposed to have said that he would jump into his grave laughing because the fact that he had the death of five million enemies of the Reich on his conscience gave him extraordinary satisfaction. As she tells it, in exile, "he had nothing to do that he could consider worth doing" and was "fed up with being an anonymous wanderer between the worlds." She reports that he kept bragging "*ad nauseam* to anyone who would listen" about having killed five million enemies of Hitler's Third Reich because it gave him an extraordinary sense of elation (Arendt 1963, 46–47).

The Intoxication of Beauty and Art

Baudelaire, Nietzsche, and Hitler all had a keen sense of the power of beauty and art to release people from the tedium of the real and the rational, to release them from the dreary routine of ordinary existence, from banal realities and constraints, to awaken passions so exhilarating as to lend a sense of meaning to otherwise boring existences. In particular, they were conscious of the intoxicating power of beauty and art, a theme that Baudelaire directly addressed over and over in his writings.

To the question: "Whence comes to you, you were saying, this strange sadness, rising like the sea on a black, naked rock?" The poet of Baudelaire's "Semper Eadem" answers:

> When our hearts have once reaped their harvest, living is an evil. This is a secret known by all, a very simple ache, and not mysterious, and like your joy, blatant to everyone. Cease searching then, oh beautiful curious one, and though your voice be soft, keep quiet, ignorant one! soul ever enraptured, mouth with a infantile laugh. Even more than Life, Death often holds us by subtle ties. Let, let my heart become intoxicated with a *lie*, plunge into your beautiful eyes as into a beautiful reverie, and sleep for a long time in the shadow of your eyelashes. (Baudelaire 1857, XL)

In Baudelaire's poem "Beauty," Beauty says: "I am beautiful, oh mortals! . . . And my breast, where one by one each one has been bruised, is made to inspire an eternal, speechless love in the poet . . ." (Baudelaire 1857, XVII). In his "Hymn to Beauty," the poet tells Beauty: "Whether you come, from heaven or from hell, what does it matter, if your eye, your smile, your foot, open for me the door to an infinite that I love and I never knew? From Satan or from God, what does it matter? Angel or Siren, what does it matter, if you make . . . the universe less hideous and moments less tedious?" After comparing beauty to wine, the poet had said:

> You contain in your eye the sunset and the dawn; you spread fragrances like a stormy evening; your kisses are a philter and your mouth an amphora that make the hero cowardly and the child courageous. Charmed, Destiny follows your skirts like a dog. You sow joy and disaster at random, and you rule everything and are held accountable for nothing. . . . Bedazzled ephemera fly to you candle, crackle, blaze and say: Let us bless this torch! The panting lover leaning over the beautiful woman he loves has the air of a dying man caressing his tomb. (Baudelaire 1857, XXI)

Baudelaire considered it one of the extraordinary prerogatives of art that "set to rhythm and cadenced, *pain* fills the mind with a calm *joy*" (Baudelaire 1859, 504). "When everything ravishes me," Baudelaire has the poet of "Entirely" confess, "I am not aware if something is seducing me . . . and the harmony is too exquisite . . . for a powerless analysis to note its many chords" (Baudelaire 1857, XLI). The poem entitled "Beacons" pays homage to the works of painters. Its poet concludes that, echoing through a thousand labyrinths, the curses, blasphemies, complaints, ecstasies, cries, tears, *Te Deum* of the paintings of Rubens, da Vinci, Rembrandt, Michelangelo, Watteau, Goya, Delacroix are "a divine opium for mortal hearts (Baudelaire 1857, VI).

The "intoxication of Art is more apt than any other to veil the terrors of the pit," Baudelaire wrote in "A Heroic Death." Geniuses, the poet explains there, can play their roles on the edge of the tomb with a joy that keeps them from seeing the tomb, lost as they are in a paradise that precludes any idea of a tomb and destruction. And, no longer dreaming of death, mourning, or punishment, abandoning themselves to manifold pleasurable sensations that the viewing of an artistic masterpiece provides, spectators, no matter how blasé or frivolous they may otherwise be, unworried, rapidly succumb to the almighty dominion of the artist (Baudelaire 1869, XXVII).

In a letter of February 17, 1860 to Richard Wagner, Baudelaire endeavored to describe how he had been immediately "conquered" by Wagner's work:

> The characteristic that principally struck me was the grandeur. That represents what is great, and pushes one toward what is great. . . . Right away, one feels transported and subjugated. One of the strangest bits and one which brought me the new musical sensation was that which was designed to depict religious ecstasy. . . . I felt all the majesty of a life greater than ours. . . . I often had the sentiment of a rather bizarre nature. It was the pride and enjoyment of understanding, of letting myself be penetrated, invaded, truly sensual delight, resembling that of being lifted into the air or travelling upon the seas. . . . Generally those profound harmonies seemed to me to resemble those stimulants that quicken the pulse of the imagination. . . . Everywhere there was something done *con brio* and transporting, something aspiring to go higher, something excessive and superlative. For example, to use comparisons borrowed from painting, I imagined a vast expanse of dark red before my eyes. If this red represented passion, I saw it come gradually, through all the transitions from red and pink, to the incandescence of the furnace. It would seem difficult, even impossible, to me to arrive at something more ardent; and yet a final flare comes to trace a whiter streak of light on the white that serves as a background. This would be, if you wish, the supreme cry of the soul reaching its paroxysm. (Baudelaire 1980, 921–22; Pichois and Ziegler, 407)

In "Evil people and music," Nietzsche asked whether the full bliss of love that lies in unconditional trust could ever be the lot of people who were not deeply mistrustful, evil, and embittered. For they are the ones, he explains, who "enjoy in it the tremendous, unbelieved and unbelievable *exception* in the state of their soul," who one day feel that boundless, dreamlike sensation come over them which, like a precious enigma and miracle, suffused with a golden glory, and quite beyond description, stands out in contrast to the whole of their lives, both secret and visible. Souls oppressed by happiness, he thought, experience a kind of suffering and oppression in the "happy dumbness" of unconditional trust, which usually makes them more grateful to music than other, better people are, for through music, "as though through a coloured mist, they see and hear their love . . . grown *more distant*, more moving and less oppressive; music is the only means they have of *observing* their extraordinary condition and for the first time taking a view of it that is informed with a kind of alienation and relief" (Nietzsche 1881, §216).

In *The Birth of Tragedy*, Nietzsche characterized the highest and truly serious task of art as being to save the eye from gazing into the horrors of night and to redeem individuals from the paroxysms of the stirrings of the will with the healing salve of appearance (Nietzsche 1872, §19). He describes the effect of the third act of Wagner's *Tristan und Isolde* on listeners in terms of "expiring in a frenzied spreading of all the wings of the soul" and asks whether those who have thus pressed their ears right against chambers of the heart of the world's will, who feel the furious desire for existence flow from it as thunderous stream or gently dispersed brook into all the veins of the world would not all of a sudden break to pieces. Are they to suffer this, Nietzsche asks, in the wretched, vitreous frames of human individuals, to hearken to countless cries of pleasure and pain ringing out again from the vast space of cosmic night without impetuously seeking refuge in their primordial home upon experiencing this pastoral roundelay of metaphysics? (Nietzsche 1872, §21).

The Apollonian illusion saves people from the orgiastic self-annihilation (*orgiastischen Selbstvernichtung*) of Dionysian art, which Nietzsche considered, would convince us of the eternal pleasure of existence to be looked for behind appearances. We are compelled to look into the horrors of individual existence and yet not be petrified. Metaphysical consolation instantaneously delivers from the bustle of the world of change. We are really in a quick instant Primordial Being itself, feeling its raging desire for existence and pleasure in existence; the struggle, the pain, the annihilation (*Vernichtung*) of appearances, now appear necessary to us in view of the surplus of countless forms of existence forcing and pushing one another into life, in view of the exuberant fertility of the universal will. We are pricked by the fierce thorns of these torments just as we have become one with the infinite primordial pleasure in existence and enjoy an inkling of the indestructibility and eternity of this pleasure in Dionysian rapture. Despite fear and pity, we are happy living beings, not as individuals, but as the one living being with whose creative joy we are united (Nietzsche 1872, §§17, 21, 24).

In *The Birth of Tragedy*, Nietzsche writes of how art, and through art, life saves those whose gaze has pierced into the very heart of the terrible destructive activities (*Vernichtungstreiben*) of universal history and the cruelty of nature, those who have had conscious insight into the terrible truths about the true nature of everyday reality and perceive it as nauseating and repulsive, who are in danger of longing for a Buddhist negation of the will because knowledge has destroyed any illusion they may have cherished of being able to change the eternal essence of things. It is, then, Nietzsche says, when the will is in the greatest danger, that art draws near as a redeeming and healing sorceress who alone has the power to prevail over nauseating thoughts about the horror and absurdity of existence by artistically subduing horror and providing an artistic release from the nausea of the absurd (Nietzsche 1872, §7).

The Devil

What study of the roots and flowers of evil could be complete without a section on the arch seducer, the notorious spirit of evil, the devil? The scion of a protestant minister's family, Nietzsche likened his own efforts to those of the Antichrist and devil and strew his writings with allusions to the devil of traditional Christianity, to the tempter in the garden of Eden especially. "The devil," he wrote, in *Beyond Good and Evil*, "has the furthest reaching prospects for God. That is why he keeps so far away from him—the devil, namely as the oldest friend of knowledge" (Nietzsche 1886, §129). "Where stands the tree of knowledge is always paradise: thus speak the oldest and youngest snakes," reads another passage of the book (Nietzsche 1886, §152). Zarathustra said that the devil told him once that "'God too has his hell: that is his love of man.' And most recently . . . : 'God is dead; God died of his pity for man'" (Nietzsche 1883-85, 202).

However, although allusions to the devil are not lacking in Nietzsche's writings, the message that Nietzsche ultimately wanted to convey was probably accurately voiced by Zarathustra when he said: "there is no devil and no hell. Your soul will be dead even before your body" (Nietzsche 1883-85, 132). "Verily, you who are good and just, there is much about you that is laughable, and especially your fear of that which has hitherto been called devil. . . . I guess that you would call my *Übermensch* the devil" (Nietzsche 1883-85, 256).

Of the three cognoscenti whose ideas about evil are under study here, only Baudelaire accorded the devil a full, conspicuous role in his writings. In some, the devil appears as a poetic device, but other writings exhibit a very keen sense of the devil's real presence. He is no longer just a fictional entity, or the product of superstition, but is more graphically present, *in propria persona*, not just as some red cartoon character brandishing a pitchfork, not just as an abstraction, but as a real being, a real presence who is sensed, seen, heard, listened to, someone one can address familiarly as *tu*, as a close friend or member of the family, someone in whose company one can live as one lives with someone one loves, admires, adores. So, by following the devil about in his appearances in Baudelaire's different writings, we can chart some of the topography of the realm of evil as Baudelaire chose to depict it.

In a draft to a preface for the *Flowers of Evil*, Baudelaire noted that it was harder for the people of his century "to believe in the Devil than to love him. Everyone serves him and no one believes in him. Sublime craftiness of the Devil" (Baudelaire 1975-76, I 181–83; Baudelaire 1857, 242).[11] *The Flowers of Evil* itself depicts the poet's encounters with the devil with particular earnestness. The book is replete with first person accounts of encounters between him and the narrators of its poems. In "The Possessed One," noting that the sun has covered itself with the crape of mourning, the poet tells Beelzebub, the Moon of his life, to muffle up in shadows, to sleep or smoke as he wishes, be silent, be somber, and plunge entirely into the pit of Ennui. I love you thus, the poet says. "Yet if, like an eclipsed star emerging from the penumbra, you wish today to strut about in the places congested with Madness, that is good! Charming dagger, fly from your sheathe! Light the pupil of your eyes with the flame of the chandeliers! Light desire in the gaze of the uncouth. Everything about you, morbid or irrepressible, is pleasurable to me. Be what you want, black night, red dawn. There is not a fiber in my whole trembling body that does not cry: *O my dear Beelzebub, I adore you!*" (Baudelaire 1857, XXXVII).

In the opening poem of *The Flowers of Evil*, the devil holds the strings that move us. On the pillow of evil is Satan Trismegistus, that learned chemist who for long hours cradles our enchanted spirit, and completely vaporizes the rich metal of our will. "We discover the charms of repugnant objects. Each day we take a step down towards Hell, without horror through stinking darkness. Just as a poor reprobate who kisses and eats the martyred breast of an antique whore, in passing we steal a clandestine pleasure that we squeeze energetically like an old orange. Packed in, teeming like a swarm of parasitic worms, in our brains a flock of demons are on a drinking spree and when we breathe, Death, invisible river, descends into our lungs with muted groans" ("To the Reader," lns. 9–24).

"The Cask of Hatred" portrays the devil piercing secret holes "from which a thousand years of sweat and effort would leak" into the abysses of

---

[11] In quoting Baudelaire as having written that everyone "serves" the Devil, I am citing the more authoritative Pléiade edition, which prints the word '*sert*' (Baudelaire 1975-76, I 181). Interestingly, in its place the less erudite Garnier-Flammarion edition puts '*sent*,' which would be senses, not serves.

a desperate Vengeance hurling "in vain great pails full of the blood and tears of the dead" into her empty darkness (Baudelaire 1857, LXXIII). In "The Irreparable," the devil has forever extinguished, killed the Hope shining in the panes of an inn. The poet "full of anguish and like a dying person that the wounded crush" plies a beautiful, adorable witch with questions about remorse, asks whether she loves the damned, knows what is unpardonable, knows the embittered features of Remorse that uses our hearts as a target, knows whether we can stifle old, long drawn out, implacable Remorse that lives, wriggles, squirms in us, and feeds on us as worms the dead. In what potion, what wine, what decoction, the poet asks shall we drown that old, destructive, greedy, patient enemy? Can one brighten up a muddy, blackened sky, rend darkness denser than pitch, without morning, without evening, without stars, without gloomy flashes of lightning? The poet's queries receive this reply: "I have sometimes seen at the far end of an ordinary theater set ablaze by a resonant orchestra, a fairy kindle a miraculous dawn in an infernal sky. . . . a being that was but light, gold, and gauze crush the enormous Satan, but my heart, which ecstasy never visits, is a theater where one is still awaiting, still in vain, the Being with gauze wings" (Baudelaire 1857, LIV).

In "Destruction," the Demon stirs ceaselessly at the poet's side and, like impalpable air, swims about the poet who inhales it and the meaning that burns the poet's lung and fills it with an eternal, guilty desire. Knowing the poet's great love of Art, the Demon occasionally takes on the form of the most seductive of women and using specious pretexts of doldrums accustoms the poet's lip to foul love potions. Thus, casting before the poet's eyes soiled garments, open wounds, and the bloody machinery of destruction, the Demon leads the poet far from the sight of God and into the deep, deserted plains of Ennui (Baudelaire 1857, CIX, 1–4).

For those who would chant Baudelaire's "Litanies of Satan," Satan is the most knowledgeable and most beautiful of the angels to have reigned in highest heaven, a god betrayed by fate, who has been wronged, but who, vanquished, always rises again in a stronger position. Satan is addressed as one who knows all, as the great king of underground things, the familiar healer of human anguish, who out of love teaches even lepers and pariahs the taste for paradise, who knows in what corners of envious lands the jealous God hid precious stones, whose broad hand hides the precipices from the sleepwalker wandering on the edges of edifices, as the adopted father of those whom, in dark anger, God the Father cast out of the earthly paradise. . . . "O, Satan, take pity on my long misery," is the refrain.

This recitation of Satan's attributes ends with the "prayer:" "Glory and praise to you, Satan, in high heaven, where you reigned, and in the depths of Hell, where, vanquished, you dream in silence! Have my soul rest near you, one day, beneath the Tree of Knowledge, at the time its branches spread out like a new Temple on your forehead!" (Baudelaire 1857, CXX).

In "The Monster or the Paranymph of a Macabre Nymph," the poet laments being unable to accompany "an old monster" whose favors he enjoys to a witches Sabbath. He says, "Fool, you are going straight to the Devil! I would willingly go with you, if this appalling speed didn't agitate me a bit. Go, therefore, all alone, to the Devil! My loin, my lung, my knee, no longer allow me to pay homage to this Lord as one should. . . . Oh! Very sincerely I suffer from not going to Sabbaths, to see, when he farts sulfur, how you kiss his ass. Oh! Very sincerely I suffer!" The poet goes on to say that he is "devilishly afflicted not to be your torchère and to ask to take leave of you . . . Since I have long loved you, being perfectly logical! Indeed, wishing Evil searching for the cream, and loving only a perfect monster, truly yes! old monster, I love you" (Baudelaire 1857).

Complementing the experiences of the devil portrayed in *The Flowers of Evil*, are two, more tongue in cheek, stories of devils in *The Spleen of Paris*. In "The Temptations, or Eros, Pluto, and Glory" (Baudelaire 1869, XXI), two "superb Satans and a no less extraordinary lady Devil" climb the mysterious staircase that Hell uses to assault the sleeping in their weakness and communicate secretly with them. Proud and domineering, with a sulfurous splendor emanating from them that sets them off in contrast to the backdrop of the night, the three stand gloriously before the poet who initially takes them for true gods.

Looking at the poet with "inconsolably anguished eyes, out of which flows an insidious intoxication," the first Satan proposed to make the poet the lord of souls and the master of living matter. He promised that he would experience the "endlessly renewed pleasure" of coming out of himself to forget himself in others, and of attracting other souls to the point of confusing them with his own. Less beautiful and sly, the second, eyeless, Satan offered the poet "what obtains everything, what is worth everything, what replaces everything!" The third visitor, the lady Devil, conveyed her power to the poet by placing a gigantic trumpet in her mouth decorated with all the newspapers of the universe that blared his name "through space with the sound of a hundred thousand claps of thunder and echoed back to him from the furthest planet." The poet refused all their offers, but upon waking, regretted having been so scrupulous and wished his visitors would come back. He even called out to them, imploring them to forgive him, and offering to disgrace himself as often as needed to merit their favors. But they never came back.

In "The Generous Gambler" (Baudelaire 1869, XXIX), the poet is brushed in the street by a mysterious being whom, without seeing him, the poet immediately recognizes. Having always wanted to get to know this mysterious being, the poet follows him attentively. They go down into a dazzling, luxurious underground dwelling where an exquisite, though heady, atmosphere reigns that instantly makes one practically forget all the tiresome horrors of life and where one inhales a somber beatitude. Strange faces marked with fatal beauty inspire fraternal sympathy in the poet, who had never seen eyes that shone so fiercely with the horror of ennui and the immortal desire to feel alive.

Having already become old and perfect friends, the mysterious being and the poet sat down, ate, and drank to excess. The poet gambled and ended up losing his soul "in part in connection with heroic carelessness and frivolity." "The soul," the poet explains, "is something so impalpable, so often useless, and sometimes so cumbersome that in losing it he had only felt a bit less emotion than if he had lost his calling card while on a walk."

The two companions then smoked cigars and chatted about the universe, its creation and its future destruction, about the great nineteenth-century idea of the progress and perfectibility of mankind, about all the forms of human infatuation, a subject about which his interlocutor expressed himself with suaveness of diction and droll tranquility. The mysterious companion discoursed about the absurdity of the different philosophies that had taken possession of the human brain, conveyed some principles whose benefits and ownership it would not be appropriate to share with anyone whatsoever. He did not complain about his bad reputation, stated that he himself was the one most interested in the destruction of superstition, and confessed that he was only afraid for his own power one day when a churchman proclaimed from the pulpit that, when hearing people boast of the progress brought about by the Enlightenment, one should not forget that the devil's cleverest ruse consists of persuading us that he does not exist. The mysterious being also declared that he had many times inspired the pen, the works and the minds of pedagogues and had been in attendance "almost always in person, though invisibly so, at all the sessions of the academy."

Encouraged by his companion's display of goodness, the poet asked for news of God and whether his interlocutor had seen him recently. With an insouciance tinged with sadness, the mysterious being replied that when their paths crossed they greeted one another when like old gentlemen for whom a certain inherent politeness could not entirely extinguish former hard feelings.

Finally, "the quivering dawn brightening the windowpanes," "this celebrated personality, sung by so many poets and served by so many philosophers who work for his glory without knowing it," tried to prove that he was sometimes a "good devil" by compensating the poet for the irremediable loss of his soul by giving him what was at stake had he won, had fate been on his side. He would have had the opportunity to relieve and vanquish throughout his entire life that bizarre feeling of ennui that was the source of all his ailments and of all pitiable progress. He would never have a desire that his mysterious companion would not help him realize. He would reign over his common peers, be the object of flattery, and even adoration. Money, gold, diamonds, fairy castles would run after him and beseech him to accept them without his having made any effort to merit them. He would travel as he liked, enjoy a surfeit of revelry, without growing weary in countries where it is always hot and the women smell as good as the flowers, etc. etc. At the end, the poet confesses that, but for fear of degrading himself, he would have fallen at the feet of the generous gambler to thank him for his incredible munificence. Yet, little by little, no longer daring to believe in such a prodigious happiness, he found himself praying to God that the devil would keep his word to him.

The Magical Powers of Words

Of the *Flowers of Evil*, the literary critic Sainte-Beuve wrote to Baudelaire "You wanted to snatch the secrets of the demons of the night from them. By doing that with subtlety, with refinement, with curious talent, and a quasi *affected* abandon of expression, and by *perfecting* the details, by *Petrarchisizing* about what is horrible, you give the impression of having played around. Yet, you have suffered. You have tortured yourself parading your worries, your nightmares, your inner torment" (Pichois and Ziegler, 377).

Baudelaire was keenly aware of the power of language and how to wield it. Words, he knew, are not neutral marks upon paper. Whether meaningful or meaningless, whether what they mean is real, or imagined, or nothing at all, words have the power to please, charm, arouse, romanticize, inspire, exhilarate, fascinate, tempt, inveigle, shock, distract, deceive, confuse, excite, entice, seduce . . .

"Poetry," Baudelaire realized, "comes close to music through a prosody whose roots plunge deeper into the human soul than any classical theory indicates" (Baudelaire 1975-76, I 183). He saw that, like music or mathematics, poetical language can imitate "the horizontal line, the straight ascending line, the descending straight line; that it can go straight up to heaven, without running out of breath, or go perpendicularly down to hell with the swiftness of any gravitational force.... can spiral, trace a parabola, or zigzag representing a series of superimposed angles . . ." (Baudelaire 1975-76, I 183). "There is in words, in the *logos*," he saw, "something *sacred* that prohibits us from making them into a game of chance. . . . color speaks like a deep, vibrant voice . . . monuments rise and jut out against deep space . . . animals and plants, representatives of what is ugly and bad, articulate their unambiguous grimaces . . . scents induce the corresponding thoughts and memories . . . passion murmurs or howls its eternally unchanged language" (Baudelaire 1859, 501). He understood how poetry was "connected with the art of painting, of cooking and of cosmetics through the ability to express any sensation of gentleness, bitterness, of beatitude or horror through the pairing of one noun or another with one adjective or another, analogous or opposite" (Baudelaire 1975-76, I 183).

Language also has the power to repel, disgust, estrange, bore . . . In one of the truly inimitable passages of *Mein Kampf*, Hitler tells of how, "inwardly repelled" he was by the "new-fangled pettifogging phraseology" of the official party literature of Social Democracy and the style in which it was written. "With an enormous expenditure of words, unclear in content or incomprehensible as to meaning," he complained, "they stammer an endless hodgepodge of phrases purportedly as witty as in reality they are meaningless." He felt that only "decadent metropolitan bohemians" could "feel at home in this maze of reasoning and cull an 'inner experience' from this dung-heap of literary dadaism, supported by the proverbial modesty of a section of our people who always detect profound wisdom in what is most incomprehensible to them personally" (Hitler, 50).

And, words whose actual meaning may actually be shocking, offensive, stupid, or horrible, or which may have no meaning at all, can be artfully manipulated to provoke a reaction quite alien to the reality of what is being expressed. By capitalizing on form divorced from content, by pursuing pleasing formal perfection, radiant words, images, resonant, sonorous syllables, bewitching lyricism, appealing rhythms and rhymes, sensual pleasure, delight, enjoyment at the expense of content, language can effectively belie what it ordinarily means or efface the reality of what is being said.

Baudelaire was a master at divorcing content and the language in which he clothed it. Was not his mother (who was not actually the thoroughly conventional, straight-laced bourgeois Catholic lady that French literature teachers used to say she was) prepared to admit that, though certain of Baudelaire's poems were not very Christian, his "Litanies of Satan" (Baudelaire 1857, CXX) displayed an extraordinary display of talent and the form of its verses was so harmoniously, musically cadenced as to make her believe she was singing when reading them? (Pichois and Ziegler, 606–7).

Baudelaire, Nietzsche, and Hitler knew how to sculpt words to make them speak to the real or imaginary feelings, fears, fantasies, desires that really lurk in people, and a large part of the appeal and success that all three had surely lies precisely in the promises of flight from what is real, routine, rational, moral, conventional, mundane that they were able to make through language. "Wielding words knowledgeably is practicing a kind of evocative sorcery," Baudelaire once wrote (Baudelaire 1859, 501). Even words whose meaning may not be well determined, he was keen to point out, can have a magical influence (Baudelaire 1980, 465).

Like Nietzsche, Baudelaire and Hitler were most conscious that the "real world is much smaller than the fanciful one" (Nietzsche 1881, I §10). They saw how words can appeal to a longing for a world built on the imagination in which one could find and invent meaning, how words can build such a world and impose its charm; they saw how to use words to draw people into an unreal world and to impose the vision created by its logic. "We shall embark on the sea of Darkness with the joyous heart of a young passenger," invites the poet of "The Voyage." "Do you hear these voices, charming and gloomy that sing: 'Over here! You who wish to eat the fragrant Lotus! It is here that the miraculous fruits your heart hungers for are harvested. Come and intoxicate yourself with the strange sweetness of this endless afternoon?" (Baudelaire 1857, CXXVI, VII).

Once unhinged from reality, words can go a long way to liberate evil from the repulsive images usually associated with it. Framed in the right language, even the destructive character of an idea can become decisive for the success of a poet, philosopher, or politician whose virtuosity or showmanship it is what one especially applauds. Words can so distract from the real content of what is said, so overshadow what is actually depicted or implied behind or beneath them as to make it dwindle in importance and even seem to vanish. Words can romanticize the deeds of, say, a troop of triumphant brutes without painting the real gore, horror, cruelty, anguish, and torment that necessarily accompanies their deeds and makes the real experience intolerable. They can make evil look easy, attractive, exhilarating, and free of tangible consequences. None of that is present in the moment. Dressed up, terrible evils can conjure up sensually pleasant images in the reader, can come to appear actually quite preferable to something good clothed in more ordinary language.

Confusing what is meaningful and what is meaningless, what is real and what is imaginary, objectivity and subjectivity, truth and falsehood, good and evil in this way can drive people off course and set them on a journey beyond morality, can crush to death, pulverize their remnants of morality. Nietzsche showed that he was privy to this intelligence when he reflected in *On the Genealogy of Morals* that one may admit the possibility that taking delight in cruelty had not actually died out, but would only need to undergo a certain refinement. In particular, he theorized, it would have to be presented soulfully and imaginatively and translated into language so reassuring that it did not awaken any suspicion even among the most sensitive of hypocrites (Nietzsche 1887, II §7).

Of course, what has been said about the magical powers that words have independently of what they really mean, of whether they have a clear meaning, or of whether they have any meaning at all also applies to the *spoken* word. Speaking can itself make flights of lyricism seem expressive. It can make words sparkle independently of content. It too can mold ambiguous or nonsensical language to make it appear meaningful. So it proves to be a particularly effective and insidious way of ungluing words from reality, people from reality.

Baudelaire, Nietzsche, and Hitler all impressed people by their power to wield the spoken word. After hearing Baudelaire read his poems, one of his contemporaries confessed:

> The crudest language, marvelously enshrined, the boldest descriptions come one after the other and we listened, completely dumbfounded, blushing, folding our seraphic poems and feeling the startled wings of our guardian angels, frightened away by the scandal, beating against our foreheads. It was besides, superbly alluring, but that was so foreign to our literary principles that we felt timorous admiration for this excellent and depraved poet. (Pichois and Ziegler, 176)

One of Nietzsche's students recalled how "the strongly agreeable trait" of Nietzsche's teaching "was immediately communicated to the hearer, the irresistible power" that led "toward ideas which, merely read, would have aroused me to the most vehement contradiction. Even today, the enchantment of this voice continues to affect me! It lays a mitigating, transfiguring veil over the most heterogeneous of his pronouncements. Whoever has not experienced the interpretive melody of his spoken word only half knows Nietzsche" (Gilman, 66–67).

Politicians surely fall into one of the categories of people having the keenest sense of the particular impact of speech. And, while Baudelaire and Nietzsche were literary virtuosos adept at unhinging the words from reality, Hitler was the one who took advantage of the mind-altering power of spoken words to link ideas to action, to form bridges to flesh-and-blood realities. It was he who did most of the actual talking, and did it to thundering applause.

Hitler saw his specialty as being oration and cast his lot with what he termed the "magic power" of the spoken word. In *Mein Kampf*, he told of how he had seen how to use the spoken word to inflame and excite people. When he first began to have the idea of going into politics, he said that that was what caused him to decide to become a speaker (Hitler, 107, 175). He believed that

> the power which has always started the greatest religious and political avalanches in history rolling has been from time immemorial the magic power of the spoken word. . . . the broad masses of the people can be moved only by the power of speech. And all great movements are popular movements, volcanic eruptions of human passions and emotional sentiments, stirred either by the cruel Goddess of Distress or by the firebrand of the word hurled among the

masses. . . . Only a storm of hot passion can turn the destinies of peoples, and only those can arouse passion who bear it within themselves. It alone gives its chosen one the words which like hammer blows can open the gates to the heart of a people. (Hitler, 106–7)

"Let no one believe," Hitler emphasized, "that the French Revolution would ever have come about through philosophical ideas if it had not found an army of agitators led by demagogues in the grand style, who whipped up the passions of the people tormented to begin with, until at last there occurred that terrible volcanic eruption which held all Europe rigid with fear" (Hitler, 475). In Hitler's estimation the Russian revolution was not "brought about by Lenin's writings, but by the hate-fomenting oratorical activity of countless of the greatest and the smallest apostles of agitation. The illiterate common people were not . . . fired with enthusiasm for the Communist Revolution by the theoretical reading of Karl Marx, but solely by the glittering heaven which thousands of agitators themselves . . . all in the service of an idea, talked into the people" (Hitler, 475). What had won millions of workers to the Marxist cause, he stressed, was "less the literary style of the Marxist church fathers" than the work of orators standing upon tables and hammering away at the masses during hundreds of thousands of meetings in smoky taverns and the gigantic "parades of hundreds of thousands of men, which burned into the small, wretched individual the proud conviction that, paltry worm as he was, he was nevertheless a part of a great dragon, beneath whose burning breath the hated bourgeois world would some day go up in fire and flame . . ." (Hitler, 472–73).

In *Explaining Hitler: The Search for the Origins of His Evil*, Ron Rosenbaum studied the ideas of George Steiner,[12] described by Rosenbaum as someone with the "fascination and distrust of speech, the love and hate for the power and terror of language" at the heart of his career. For Rosenbaum, in *Language and Silence* Steiner came close "an almost black-magic view of the dark power of words: that they have a spell-like power to bring into being that which had been inconceivable before they were uttered." In *The Portage to San Cristóbal of A. H.*, to quote Rosenbaum, Steiner "raised the question of the potential diabolism within language itself and implicitly addressed the relationship between Hitler and language." His "Hitler is a kind of medium for the evil genius of the German language itself" (Rosenbaum, 303–5).

---

[12] George Steiner is the author of: *Language and Silence: Essays on Language, Literature and the Inhuman*, 1967; *After Babel, Aspects of Language and Translation*, 1975; *The Portage to San Cristóbal of A.H.*, 1999.

What Rosenbaum calls Steiner's "lifelong horrified fascination with Hitler" began when, as a boy of five Steiner listened to the master's voice on the radio. In *The Portage to San Cristóbal of A. H.*, Steiner says he tried to show Hitler as one of the "greatest masters" of German who "drew on a kind of rhetorical power which . . . allies highly abstract concepts with political, physical violence in a most unusual way. . . ." Steiner characterized Hitler as being "easily a genius at that, absolutely no doubt about it." For Steiner, the essence of Hitler's genius was in the embodied voice. "It's a hard thing to describe, but the voice itself was mesmeric. . . . It was specifically the physicality rather than the metaphysicality that mesmerized . . . " (Rosenbaum, 300–303).

Stripping Truth of Its Authority and Power

Baudelaire, Nietzsche, and Hitler made no secret of their conviction that truth was one of the first victims of artful work to manipulate media of expression. Regarding the "Revolt" poems of the *Flowers of Evil*, Baudelaire wrote of how he, as a perfect actor, had had "to fashion his mind to all the forms of sophistry as well as to all forms of corruption" (cited Pichois and Ziegler, 346). In passages of "Théophile Gautier" and "Notes nouvelles sur Edgar Poe" that are identical but for a single word, Baudelaire twice affirms that poetry "does not have Truth as her goal. . . . Truth has nothing to do with songs. Everything that constitutes the charm, the grace, the irresistibility of a song would strip Truth of her authority and her power" (Baudelaire 1859, 498; Baudelaire 1855-57, 598). "Rhythm," he pointed out, "is necessary to the development of the idea of beauty, which is the greatest and most noble goal of poems. However, the artifices involved in rhythm are an insurmountable obstacle to that meticulous development of thoughts and expressions whose goal is the *truth*" (Baudelaire 1855-57, 596). "Poetry," he wrote in "Since Realism There Is," "is what is most real. It is what is only completely true in another world" (Baudelaire 1980, 466).

As for Nietzsche, *Beyond Good and Evil* opens with an expression of his wish to question the very idea of pursuing objective truth. He inquires into the value of the will to truth and asks why one might not want untruth instead (Nietzsche 1886, §1). What may be strangest about his new way of speaking, he admitted, is that for him the falseness of a judgment is no objection to a judgment. The question for him is whether the judgment, true or false, promotes life, sustains life, sustains the species, even improves it, perhaps even cultivates it. He says that he is fundamentally inclined to declare that false judgments are most indispensable to us and that the abandonment of false judgments would be an abandonment of life, a denial of life.

Nietzsche saw recognizing untruth as the condition of life as putting up dangerous resistance to conventional values and believed that any philosophy venturing this already was positioning itself beyond good and evil (Nietzsche 1886, §4). In the 1886 forward to *Human, All Too Human*, he affirmed that life "*wants* deception, it *lives* on deception," that he himself needed falsity to realize the luxury of his truthfulness (Nietzsche 1878, Foreword §1). Two sections later, he has his free spirits ask whether "everything is perhaps ultimately false . . . and if we have been deceived, are not we also by this very fact deceivers. . . . *Must* we not also be deceivers?" (Nietzsche 1878, Foreword §3).

In a manner fully appropriate to a philosopher preaching the transvaluation of values, Nietzsche asked in *Beyond Good and Evil* how something could originate in its opposite, how, for example, truth could originate in error, the will to truth in the will to deceive, selfless deeds in self-interest, or the pure, sunny gaze of the sage in covetousness. Whatever value it is that one may accord truth, truthfulness and selflessness, he proposed, it could be that pretense, the will to deceive, to self-interest and the appetites should be ascribed a higher and more fundamental value for life. It is quite possible, he conjectured, that what constitutes the value of these good and venerable things lies precisely in the fact that they are kindred, mix, and become insidiously confused with things that are bad and apparently opposed to them, in the fact that they are perhaps of the same nature. To find anyone concerned about such maybes, he believed one would have to await the arrival of a new variety of philosophers, philosophers whose tastes and inclinations are the reverse of those who have preceded them, philosophers of the dangerous maybe, in every sense (Nietzsche 1886, §2).

In Nietzsche's opinion no one, except for some charming idealists, who gush over the good, the true, and the beautiful and allow all kinds of muddled clumsy and cheery desiderata to swim about confusedly in their ponds, would easily accept that a theory was true merely because it made people happy or virtuous.[13] Even circumspect minds, though, in Nietzsche's opinion, gladly forget that making people unhappy and making people evil are just as little of an objection. Something, he considered, should be true independently of whether it is pernicious and dangerous in the extreme. As he saw it, it could even be a fundamental fact of existence that full knowledge of it may mean a person's ruination, so that strength of mind might be measured by how much truth it could bear, at what

---

[13] In "For Whom Truth Is There" Nietzsche wrote of how his contemporaries had come to expect consolation from known truths and had been waiting for that for some time. But what, he asked, if truths are precisely incapable of that? What, he wanted to know, do have they in common with the inner states of suffering, stunted, sick human beings that would necessarily make them of any use to them? (Nietzsche 1881, §424).

point diluting, cloaking, sweetening, muffling, falsifying might be called for. He did consider it certain, however, that evil and unhappy people were in a better position to discover certain parts of truth and much more likely to have success in so doing (Nietzsche 1886, §39).

In *On the Genealogy of Morals*, Nietzsche continued to gnaw away at the idea of pursuing objective truth. He called for a critique, a justification of the will to truth. For once, he said, the value of truth had to be tentatively put into question (Nietzsche 1887, III §24). He expressed his heartfelt desire that those investigating the human soul "might fundamentally be brave, magnanimous, and proud animals who know how to keep both their hearts and their pain in check and have been educated to sacrifice all desirability of truth, of *every* truth, even homely, bitter, ugly, unpleasant, unchristian, unmoral truth . . ." (Nietzsche 1887, I §1). If anywhere he was to be a solver of puzzles, he wrote, he wanted to be so by affirming that those who still believe in the truth are far from being free spirits. According to him, the Crusaders received a hint of the creed that "Nothing is true, everything is permitted" when they came up against the invincible order of Assassins in the Middle East, "that order of free spirits *par excellence.*" That conviction, Nietzsche considered, was an expression of freedom of spirit. With it belief in truth itself was revoked (Nietzsche 1887, III §24).

Hitler made no secret of his desire to unhinge people from the notion that there were objective truths and to loose them from the real and rational into the subjective attitudes conducive to Nazi-like endeavors. *Mein Kampf* is strewn with suggestions as to how to cure Germans from the "mania of objectivity" from which he saw them suffering. "Let not Germans be contaminated with the curse of 'objectivity,' even in matters regarding the preservation of their own ego," he counseled. Hitler taught that the task of propaganda was "not to make an objective study of the truth," but to serve one's "own right, always and unflinchingly" (Hitler, 113–14, 182–83).

The art of propaganda, Hitler had found, is to be found in understanding the emotional ideas of the broad masses of people and in discovering the psychologically correct manner of capturing their attention and hence their heart. He studied how to "upset emotional prejudices, moods, sentiments, etc., and to replace them by others." It was his avowed purpose to convince the masses, who in his estimation "in their overwhelming majority are so feminine by nature and attitude that sober reasoning determines their thoughts and actions far less than emotion and feeling. . . ." He viewed them as governed by sentiment that "is not complicated, but very simple and all of a piece. It does not have multiple shadings; it has a positive and a negative; love or hate, right or wrong, truth or lie, never half this way and half that way, never partially, or that kind of thing" (Hitler, 107, 180, 183, 473).

"Anyone who wants to win the broad masses," he plainly said, "must know the key that opens the door to their heart. Its name is not objectivity (read weakness), but will and power. . . . What they desire is the victory of the stronger and the destruction of the weak or his unconditional subjection." The "impetus to the mightiest upheavals on this earth has at all times consisted less in a scientific knowledge dominating the masses than in a fanaticism which inspired them and sometimes in a hysteria which drove them forward." "The more modest its intellectual ballast, the more exclusively it takes into consideration the emotions of the masses, the more effective it will be." Following his prescriptions, he maintained, one would see "what tremendous results such perseverance leads to—to results that are almost beyond our understanding" (Hitler, 180–85; 337–38).

In *Albert Speer: His Battle with the Truth*, Gitta Sereny remarks that "one of the great psychological mysteries about the Third Reich has always been Hitler's ability to convince a nation of culturally sophisticated men and women that wrong was right" (Sereny 1995, 546). Speer once explained to her that "the whole point is that eighty million people were *not* persuaded to follow Hitler because they knew he was going to murder people in lime ditches and gas chambers; they did not follow him because he seemed evil, but because he seemed extraordinarily good. . . . whatever was known or not known, it was our society that had produced these horrors or, better said, had given monsters a licence for horrors . . . as a consequence of our moral disintegration" (Sereny 1995, 595). Maria von Below, the wife of Hitler's longtime adjutant Colonel von Below, explained to Sereny: "I have never understood how diminishing the gifts that Hitler so clearly did have made it any easier for people to live with having become bewitched by him. After all, he didn't gain the loyalty of decent and intelligent men by telling them his plan was murder and allowing them to see that he was a moral monster. He persuaded them because he was fascinating. I don't know why people want to deny that extraordinary . . . spark in him" (Sereny 1995, 113).

Vice, Crime, Beauty

In the hands of its best beauticians, vice undergoes a sea-change. Baudelaire was one of their number. He was keenly aware that, approached from the right angle, anything, including what is most execrable, could be made attractive. Discovering terrible beauty in what is most abhorrent, establishing relations between beauty and vice, and exhibiting his findings in his poetry were, in fact, among his principal occupations. "Your *flowers of evil*," Victor Hugo once wrote to him, "shine and sparkle like stars" (cited Pichois and Ziegler, 377).

Baudelaire deemed it one of the "wondrous prerogatives of Art that, artistically expressed, what is horrible becomes beauty" (Baudelaire 1859, 504). In his "Verses for the Portrait of M. Honoré Daumier," he expressed his conviction that "the energy with which he [Daumier] paints Evil and its aftermath proves the beauty of his heart" (Baudelaire 1857). In "Au lecteur," the opening poem of *The Flowers of Evil*, Baudelaire had concluded that if rape, poison, the dagger, fire, burning had not yet embroidered their pleasing designs on the banal fabric of our pitiful destinies, it was because, unfortunately, our souls were not hardy enough (lns. 25–28). In his "Hymn to Beauty," the poet asks Beauty:

> Do you come from deep heaven or do you come from out of the abyss, O beauty! your gaze, infernal and divine, spills out good deeds and crime in obscure ways. . . . Do you come from out of the black pit or down from the stars? . . . You trample the dead, Beauty, whom you mock; among your jewels, Horror is not the least charming, and Murder, among your most cherished charms, dances amorously on your proud belly, Beauty. (Baudelaire 1857, XXI)

"Vice is seductive," Baudelaire affirmed (Baudelaire 1980, 457). "What above all exasperates people of taste in the spectacle of vice," he confided, "is that it is misshapen, out of proportion. Vice detracts from what is right and true, is revolting to the mind and conscience. . . . as an insult to harmony, as a discordant note, it would particularly wound certain poetic minds," but he did not himself believe it "scandalizing to consider all moral infractions an infraction of moral beauty, a sort of transgression against universal rhythm and prosody" (Baudelaire 1859, 498). And he defied people to find him "a single work of the imagination that combines all the conditions of beauty and is not a pernicious work" (Baudelaire 1980, 457).

Cognizant that vice actually did, in any case, often take on the most unappealing and repulsive forms, Baudelaire took up the challenge of presenting evils in appealing ways. In notes for a preface to the *Flowers of Evil*, a book that he characterized as being "of sinister, cold beauty" (cited Pichois and Ziegler, 349), he wrote: "It seemed pleasant to me, and all the more agreeable because the task was more difficult, to extract beauty from evil. This book, essentially useless, and absolutely innocent, was not made with any other goal than to entertain me and practice my impassioned taste for obstacles" (Baudelaire 1975-76, I 181; Baudelaire 1857, 243).

In a draft for a preface of *Flowers of Evil*, he wrote: "Some people have told me that this poetry could be harmful. I did not rejoice over it. Others, good souls, that it could do good, and that did not distress me." That draft begins: "It is not for my women, my daughters, or my sisters that this book was written, no more than for the women, the daughters, or the sisters of my neighbor. I leave this function to those who have a stake in confusing good actions with beautiful language. I know that passionate lovers of beautiful style leave themselves open to the hatred of the crowd. But no human respect, no false modesty, no universal suffrage is going to constrain me to speak the incomparable *patois* of this century, or to confuse ink and virtue" (Baudelaire 1975-76, I 181; Baudelaire 1857, 242–43).

Along the same lines, he wrote to his mother: "You know that I have only ever considered literature and the arts as pursuing a goal foreign to morality, and that the beauty of conception and of style is enough for me" (Pichois & Ziegler, 353). In the first version of the dedication of the *Flowers of Evil* to Théophile Gautier, Baudelaire wrote: "I know that Evil, no more than Good, is not in the ethereal regions of genuine Poetry, and that this miserable dictionary of melancholy and crime can legitimate the moral reactions as the blasphemer confirms religion" (Baudelaire 1975-76, I 187).

Nietzsche made no secret of his eagerness to find ways to free evil from the reputation for dirtiness and ugliness in which he felt moralizers, Christians, women, and Jews had enveloped it, and the kind of expert plastic surgery that Baudelaire was so adept at performing on vices was one step in the direction of venturing eyes open into that realm of dangerous, morality crushing knowledge that Nietzsche enthused about when writing of theories that derive "all good instincts from bad ones" and "affirmations of the mutual interdependency of 'good' and 'bad'" in *Beyond Good and Evil* (Nietzsche 1886, §23).

Nietzsche too wrote of making evil alluring and he did his share to make it so in a way in step with Baudelaire's propensity for scavenging about in search of unsuspected treasures and exalting what is commonly deemed most execrable in human existence. Just as Baudelaire once wrote of Paris in an epilogue for the 1861 edition of his *Flowers of Evil*:

> My heart content, I climbed the mountain, from which one can contemplate the city in its fullness, hospital, brothel, purgatory, hell, prison, where all enormity flowers as a flower. You know well, O Satan, patron of my distress, that I did not go there to shed a vain tear; but, like a dirty old man with an old mistress, I wanted to inebriate myself with the enormous whore whose infernal charm endlessly rejuvenates me. Whether you are still asleep in morning's sheets, heavy, obscure, sick with a cold, or whether you strut about in the veils of evening, trimmed in fine gold, I love you O infamous capital! Courtesans, and bandits, to such you often offer your favors, which the common and ungodly do not understand. (Baudelaire 1975-76, I 191)

. . . so Nietzsche suggested in "The Realm of Beauty is Bigger" section of *Daybreak* that, just as

> artfully and glad, we go about in nature in order to discover the beauty characteristic of every thing and, as it were, to catch it unawares, as now in the sun-

shine, now under stormy skies, now in the dimmest twilight, we make an attempt to see how that piece of coastline with its rocks, coves, olive trees and pines attains its perfection and mastery, so we ought also to go about among people as discoverers and watchers of them, showing them their good and evil, so that the beauty characteristic of them, which displays itself radiantly in one, stormily in another, and in a third only when it is half dark and under rainy skies, may reveal itself. (Nietzsche 1881, V §468)

Nietzsche then goes on to ask whether it is forbidden to enjoy evil people as wild scenery with their own bold lines and lighting if, while presenting themselves as good and law abiding, they appear to our eyes as a distortion and caricature and cause us pain as a blemish in nature. To which question the product of a parsonage responded: "Yes it is forbidden: up until now one has only been allowed to look for beauty in what is morally good—reason enough that one has found so little of it and has had to look around for imaginary, spineless forms of beauty!—As certain as it is that there are a hundred kinds of happiness for the wicked about which the virtuous have no inkling, so too there are a hundred kinds of beauty for them and many have not yet been discovered" (Nietzsche 1881, V §468).

Nietzsche too was keenly aware how, approached from the right angle, what is execrated could be made attractive, and how making vice attractive stirs up fantasies, produces fascination, makes evil alluring, enhances its ability to seduce. Asking whether anything was beautiful in itself, Nietzsche wrote in *Daybreak* of how those who are used to delighting only in abandoning reality, in plunging into the depths of appearance, consider reality ugly and think neither about the fact that perceiving even the ugliest reality is beautiful, nor that those who perceive a lot and often are ultimately very far from finding ugly the vast amount of that reality whose discovery always gave them happiness (Nietzsche 1881, §550).

Nietzsche was also keen about showing crime and vice in a better light. For example, he wrote in *Beyond Good and Evil*, "Quite often criminals are not up to their act: they diminish it and denigrate it" (Nietzsche 1886, §109). "The lawyers for criminals," he followed up in the next section, "are rarely artists enough to turn the beautiful horror of the perpetrator's acts to their best advantage" (Nietzsche 1886, §110).

In *The Birth of Tragedy*, Nietzsche studied the story of Prometheus, which he calls "an original possession of the entire Aryan ethnic community." What especially characterizes the Aryan conception, in Nietzsche's opinion, is the magnificent view of active sin as the genuinely Promethean virtue, as the justification of human evil, of human guilt, as well as of the suffering incurred thereby. According to his interpretation of the myth of Prometheus, the best and highest that people can partake in can only be attained by them through a crime for which they are obliged to face the consequences—a whole flood of sufferings and sorrows visited upon the nobly striving human race by the offended divinities. Nietzsche sees this as an unpleasant thought which, by the dignity that it confers on crime sets this myth in strange contrast to the Semitic myth of Adam and Eve, in which a series of chiefly womanly sentiments like curiosity, false pretenses, susceptibility to temptation, lasciviousness are regarded as the origin of evil.[14] He suggests that it is not entirely improbable that the myth of Prometheus had the same characteristic significance for the Aryan genius that the myth of the Garden of Eden had for the Semitic, and that they are in this way related as "brother to sister." Just as crime is understood by the Aryans to be a man and sin by the Semites as a woman, Nietzsche says, so the original crime was committed by the man and the original sin by the woman (Nietzsche 1872, §9).

Patterns observed by specialists trying to understand what it is that attracts serial killers to repeat their horrible crimes tie in with Baudelaire's and Nietzsche's reflections on vice, crime, and beauty. According to observers of criminal behavior, serial killers have poorly structured personalities, and constantly totter on the edge of an emotional abyss. The first murder inevitably happens in an unexpected way, during robbery or sexual aggression, and surprises the killers themselves. Then the murder suddenly begins shaping the killer's personality. Captivated by the experience, the murderer feels a kind of intense jubilation at being able to annihilate another person, a feeling of omnipotence, indestructibility, perhaps accompanied by sexual excitement, to the point of what specialists have referred to as a genuine narcissistic orgy. The thrill experienced during the first murder awakens an irresistible fascination, and then is pursued, either compulsively, or as a reaction to destabilizing situations. Whence the repetition. The cruelty and the sadism intensifies as if the murderer was seeking to have the pleasure last. Observers of criminal behavior hypothesize that serial killers sometimes keep body parts, or objects belonging to their victims in order to prolong their feelings of intense pleasure. To understand the extreme horror of these crimes, they say, one has to understand that the murderer feels neither compassion, nor animosity, just abysmal indifference. The victim was made into a thing, a tool. England's "Doctor Death," Dr. Harold Shipman, who killed hundreds of his patients in the late twentieth century, was depicted as someone who, in addition to being addicted to the drug pethidine, was "addicted to killing."

In this connection, it is interesting to note that the words *euphoria* and *elation*, used by the media to describe the reaction of Americans to the bombing of Baghdad in 1991, recur in descriptions of the emotional reac-

---

[14] *The Birth of Tragedy* is dedicated to Richard Wagner, under whose influence it seems Nietzsche actually was anti-Semitic in his youth. See the essays in Golomb 1997.

tions that mass murderers and serial killers are found to have to their crimes. For instance, Hannah Arendt reported that Adolf Eichmann, a serial killer if there ever was one, who made known his extraordinary satisfaction about having "the death of five million enemies" on his conscience, outraged and disconcerted his judges because "whenever, during the cross-examination, the judges tried to appeal to his conscience, they were met with 'elation,'" (Arendt, 46–47, 53, 244–48, 252). The outrage provoked in France by the publication of the memoirs of the serial torturer and killer General Aussaresses (discussed in the torture section of Part Two) was surely caused by the sense of enjoyment in torturing and killing and the unrepentant attitude about it conveyed in the work.

Jung on the Sight of Evil

In "After the Catastrophe" published in the wake of World War II, Carl Jung (who once asked Sigmund Freud: "[M]ust we not love evil if we are to break away from the obsession with virtue that makes us sick and forbids us the joys of life?" [Jung 1910, 25]) discoursed about how evil exercises its power on the human psyche. Jung said that he considered it to be an undeniable fact that "the wickedness of others becomes our wickedness because it enkindles something evil in our own hearts," that the "sight of evil kindles evil in the soul." "Was not Plato aware," Jung asks, "that the sight of ugliness produces something ugly in the soul?" (Jung 1945, 184–85).

Evil, Jung explained, disrupts our whole circle of psychic protection. "When evil breaks at any point into the order of things," he wrote, something "of the abysmal darkness of the world has broken in on us, poisoning the very air we breathe and befouling the pure water with the stale, nauseating taste of blood." He believed that since "no man lives within his own psychic sphere like a snail in its shell, separated from everybody else, but is connected with his fellow-men by his unconscious humanity, no crime can ever be what it appears to our consciousness to be: an isolated psychic happening" (Jung 1945, 185).

The "great fire of evil" that flares in a crime sets something aflame, Jung maintained. He considered that "we are all so much a part of the human community that every crime calls forth a secret satisfaction in some corner of the fickle human heart." "Everybody," Jung claimed, "harbours his 'statistical criminal' in himself, just as he has his own private madman or saint. Owing to this basic peculiarity in our human make-up, a corresponding suggestibility, or susceptibility to infection, exists everywhere." He acknowledged that "in persons with a strong moral disposition, this reaction may arouse contrary feelings in a neighbouring compartment of the mind. But a strong moral disposition is a comparative rarity, so that when the crimes mount up, indignation may easily get pitched too high, and evil then becomes the order of the day" (Jung 1945, 184).

In reality, Jung maintained, a crime "always happens over a wide radius." "The sensation aroused by a crime," he points out, "the passionate interest in tracking down the criminal, the eagerness with which the court proceedings are followed, and so on, all go to prove the exciting effect which the crime has on everybody who is not abnormally dull or apathetic." "Everybody joins in, feels the crime in his own being, tries to understand and explain it" (Jung 1945, 184). "True, we are innocent, we are the victims, robbed, betrayed, outraged; and yet for that, or precisely because of it, the flame of evil glowers in our moral indignation." "Indignation leaps up, angry cries of 'Justice!' pursue the murderer, and they are louder, more impassioned, and more charged with hate the more fiercely burns the fire of evil that has been lit in our souls." "The victim is not the only sufferer; everybody in the vicinity of the crime, including the murderer suffers with him." "The murder has been suffered by everyone, and everyone has committed it; lured by the irresistible fascination of evil, we have all made this collective psychic murder possible; and the closer we were to it and the better we could see, the greater our guilt. In this way we are unavoidably drawn to the uncleanness of evil, no matter what our conscious attitude may be. No one can escape this . . ." (Jung 1945, 184–85).

"Action inevitably calls up reaction, and in the matter of destructiveness, this turns out to be just as bad as the crime, and possibly even worse, because the evil must be exterminated root and branch. In order to escape the contaminating touch of evil we need a proper *rite de sortie*, a solemn admission of guilt by judge, hangman, and public, followed by an act of expiation." "It must be so, for it is necessary that someone should feel indignant, that someone should let himself be the sword of judgment wielded by fate. Evil calls for expiation, otherwise the wicked will destroy the world utterly, or the good suffocate in their rage which they cannot vent, and in either case no good will come of it" (Jung 1945, 185).

Guilty of Realism?

One question to be raised upon drawing to the end of this first part about evil and theory and preparing to enter into Part Two about evil and reality is whether Baudelaire, Nietzsche, and Hitler were realists as concerns evil. Both defenders and detractors have applied this term to each of them. And each in his own way claimed the title for himself. Moreover, a measure of their success surely lies in the fact that their claims to realism strike a certain chord in society.

Baudelaire was tried for offending public morality in the sixth correctional chamber of the Palace of Justice that tried swindlers, pimps, and prostitutes. The main reason for his conviction was that the poems being condemned necessarily led "to the excitation of senses through a coarse realism offensive to people's sense of decency." The prosecutor had called upon the judges to react "against that unwholesome passion that brings one to portray everything, to say everything as if crimes against public morality had been rescinded and as if this morality were nonexistent" (Pichois and Ziegler, 360–63).

Those were days when realism and immorality were often linked in the public's mind, when there was talk of the "rubbish of the Bohemian and realist press." The Count of Montalembert had just denounced society, and the youth in particular, for lacking all "passion for higher things," for being corrupted by "the gross slackness of invasive empiricism that teaches people . . . to abandon taste and morality, reason and honor, conscience and faith. By the name of *realism*," he said, "this moral influence is already infecting literature, art, and even philosophy" (Pichois and Ziegler, 363–67).

Baudelaire displayed a keen sense of the alluring, enticing, seductive aspects of vices that he said he was painting and describing as they were. "Vice is seductive. It must be painted as seductive, but it brings along with it singular psychological pains and illnesses. They must be described .... Indeed, vices must be painted as they are, or not see them," he averred (Baudelaire 1980, 457). In his defense, his lawyer claimed that, while depicting vice, Baudelaire was showing it to be odious in order to make people detest it (Pichois and Ziegler, 361). Of Baudelaire, a contemporary wrote: "The poet does not delight in the spectacle of evil. He looks vice in the face, but as an enemy he knows well and confronts." Baudelaire himself wrote to a minister of the imperial government that he was "proud to have produced a book that only exudes the terror and horror of Evil" (cited Pichois and Ziegler, 353, 354).

At the time he was afflicted with the paralysis that marked the onset of his final illness, Baudelaire was characterized in the press as an "unbridled realist" (Pichois and Ziegler, 572). At his graveside, Théodore de Banville contrasted Baudelaire's and Victor Hugo's work saying that while "Hugo always transfigured man and nature in the image of a certain desired ideal. In contrast, Baudelaire . . . accepted all of modern man, with his failings, unwholesome (*maladive*) grace, futile aspirations, triumphs mingled with so much discouragement and so many tears!" (cited Pichois and Ziegler, 595–97)

Be that as it may, while Baudelaire can be said to have been a realist about evil in the sense of looking it in the face, he cannot be said to have been a realist in the sense of painting and describing it as it is. He intentionally beautified evil and beautifying evil cannot be said to be merely depicting the evil that really exists as it really exists. He said that it was mud that he had been given and out of which he had made gold, that the task had seemed pleasant to him and all the more agreeable because it was so difficult to extract beauty from evil, that in his writing he was indulging his impassioned taste for obstacles (Baudelaire 1957, 214, 243). Isn't this a clear case of varnished, not unvarnished, evil here? If evil is really beautiful, it would not need the beautification that he labored to effect.

The realism in question cannot therefore be one of a faithful depiction of the way evil really is, of some thoroughgoing portrayal of objective realities. But, it can be one of being realistic about manipulating people's perceptions. The kind of realism common to Baudelaire, Nietzsche, and Hitler is a realism about the way human beings are behind appearances and any masks they wear. The kind of conscious plastic surgery they performed belies a realistic sense on their part of the raw material upon which they worked, a realistic sense of human nature, of the human mind. And that is indeed being realistic about the true nature of evil.

Nietzsche was openly at odds with conventional notions about reality and ardent in his desire to transform them. In *The Birth of Tragedy*, he wrote of how the

> sphere of poetry does not lie outside the world, like some fantastic figment of a poet's brain; it seeks to be the very opposite, the unembellished expression of truth, and for this very reason it must reject the deceitful finery of that supposed reality of civilized people. The contrast between this genuine truth of nature and the lie of civilization that poses as the only reality, is similar to that existing between the eternal core of things, the thing in itself, and the entire world of appearance. (Nietzsche 1872, §8)

In *Beyond Good and Evil*, he remarked that one could never cease to wonder at the strange simplification and falsification in which people dwell, how we make everything around us bright, free, easy, and simple, how we have understood from the beginning to maintain our ignorance in order to enjoy scarcely conceivable freedom and an uncritical, carefree, dauntless, serene attitude toward life. "The will to know," he observed, "is built on the foundations of a much more powerful will, of the will not to know, to uncertainty, and to falseness" (Nietzsche 1886, §24).

While Nietzsche surely felt that there was much to learn from Baudelaire about portraying the beautiful horror of crimes to their best advantage, Hitler was in a position to use such knowledge to his advantage and to do so on a large scale. *Mein Kampf*, is replete with practical ideas about just how to impose a Hitlerian logic on the masses and have them dwell in a world simplified and suitably falsified to Hitler's tastes. Although on the closing page of the book, Hitler presented himself as the disseminator of ideas that were so accurate that the National Socialist Workers'

Party would "with almost mathematical certainty some day emerge victorious from its struggle," it is safe to say that the conscious, intentional falsification of reality was one of Hitler's specialties. He made no secret of his desire to manipulate minds. His advice about the "correct application of propaganda" is revealing in this regard.

The purpose of propaganda, he declared in *Mein Kampf*, was to convince. As he saw it, the whole art of propaganda consisted in calling the attention of the masses to certain facts, processes, necessities, whose significance is placed within their field of vision for the first time and done so in such a skillful manner that they will be convinced that those facts are real, those processes necessary, those necessities justified. Propaganda, he maintained, must target the emotions and aim at the "so-called intellect" only to a very limited extent. The intellectual level must be adjusted to the most limited intelligence among those to which it is being addressed. In most cases, Hitler believed, "even the most beautiful idea of a sublime theory" can only be promulgated "through the small and smallest minds." The important thing was not what the creator of the idea had in mind, but in what form, and with what success it was transmitted it to the broad masses of people. He judged the receptivity of the masses of people to be very limited, their level of intelligence low, and their power to forget immense. He believed that they would only finally remember the simplest ideas after they had been repeated thousands of times (Hitler, 107, 176, 179, 180, 183, 342, 473).

In the "Art of Evil" part of *Explaining Hitler*, Rosenbaum studied the theories of Berel Lang[15] about "artistic consciousness in the design and enactment of evil." Rosenbaum cites Lang's reflections on the "similarities between the thinking process of the artist and that of the conscious evildoer," in which attention is drawn to:

> an element of deliberation and pride. We think of style in artwork as presupposing the choice among alternatives, a systematic series of choices which excludes some and includes other alternatives and then build on each other. And where moral issues are at stake, then one . . . could speak of moral style using the moral as an aesthetic; there has to be at least the consciousness of evil which plays its role: consciousness of the road *not* taken, awareness that the road taken is one that's believed to be evil. And the presence of inventiveness, imagination. (Rosenbaum, 216)

Inventiveness seems to Lang "in some ways really to come to the heart of the matter; even though it's subtler than the brutality. . . . There seems

---

[15] Berel Lang is author of *Act and Idealism in the Nazi Genocide*, 1990; *Holocaust Representation: Art within the Limits of History and Ethics*, 2000; "Misinterpretation as the Author's Responsibility (Nietzsche's fascism, for instance)," in Golomb and Wistrich, 47–65.

to be this imaginative protraction, elaboration that one finds best exemplified in art forms and which in art we unusually take to be indicative of a consciousness, an artistic consciousness, of an overall design" (Rosenbaum, 215). The dehumanization process that the Nazis engaged in, Lang points out, was "an elaborately staged one, requiring not just a highly conscious awareness of what is being done but an intention to provide false covering, false color for the subsequent killing—killing that might have looked wrong before dehumanization but 'right' afterward" (Rosenbaum, 214).

In the "Art of Evil" part of his book Rosenbaum presents Hitler as an artist, as an alienated figure on the margins of the German Reich "who fashioned a vision, an art, out of despair and dispossession." He considers that "looking at Hitler's evil through the lens of the artistic consciousness it exhibited," there is at "the very least" "a conscious *relish* in the horrific transgressiveness of the dehumanization process—a kind of artistic process in reverse, a *decreation*, in which humans are reconfigured, resculpted into subhumans—a relish in the process that cannot be defended as a self-sacrificing descent into ruthless methods for an idealistic cause. The methods were the essence," Rosenbaum maintains, "the methods were the madness" (Rosenbaum, 218–19).

Behind the Masks

Claiming to be acting in the name of realism can itself be a form of "artful" dissembling. Does not, as a corollary to Lang's ideas about the thinking process of artists and of conscious evildoers, the very effort to beautify, glorify, romanticize evil itself imply that one really knows that evil is not really beautiful, glorious, romantic? There are obviously unbeautiful ways of presenting the horror of, for example, criminal acts that cannot fail to sicken. The horror of any horror, if real horror it is, can surely be presented in ways that horrify.

Baudelaire, Nietzsche, and Hitler were realistic about the need to perform plastic surgery on what naturally inspires repugnance. In them evil found talented make-up artists. With them we are really talking about playing on a particular kind of seductiveness really inherent in evil in step with a Nietzschean campaign to burnish evil's tarnished reputation by dissociating it from the ugliness in which moralizers envelop it. With them we are talking about beautifying, adulterating, doctoring, camouflaging what is naturally offensive, repulsive, horrible, dangerous to make presentable, palatable, digestible, appealing, tempting in order to entice people into the realm of a new logic that seems to promise release from well-trodden, all too familiar, realities and rationales, from well-trodden, all too familiar notions about good and evil.

The kind of realism involved in manipulating people's perceptions plays on the existence of realities cloaked behind appearances of one kind or another. And pulling away the veils masking certain realities while veiling others (say those of Part Two of this book) can be an effective way of enticing people into an alternative vision of reality. But baring certain realities (no matter how buried, suppressed, masked, anathematized, censured, weird, scandalous, shocking, forbidding, or forbidden they may normally be) to obscure others, still plays on a love of, or a need for, lies that it is not realism. It is not a matter of portraying everything, saying everything, but is rather a form of intentional blinding that is quite the opposite of realism.

In *The Birth of Tragedy*, Nietzsche writes of Greek tragedy's attempt to show the god Dionysus as a radiant visionary figure real, present, and visible to all. It was the chorus's job, according to Nietzsche's book, to stimulate the audience's feelings to such a degree that when the tragic hero appeared on the stage, he was not seen as an ungainly masked man, but as a visionary figure born out of the spectators' own rapture, a god with whose sufferings they had already come to feel identified. Instinctively they would transfer the whole image of the god magically quivering before their souls over to that masked figure and dissolve its reality into the spectral unreality of a dream state in which the world of daytime was veiled and a new, clearer, more comprehensible, more captivating, yet more shadowy, perpetually changing world was freshly born before their eyes (Nietzsche 1872, §8).

Nietzsche invites readers to take our minds off the character of the hero that surfaces and comes into sight and who actually amounts to no more than luminous images cast on a dark wall, just appearance through and through. Entering into the myth being projected in these bright reflections, Nietzsche reflects, we suddenly experience a phenomenon that is the reverse of the familiar one we have when we fix our eyes on the sun, turn away blinded, and have dark spots appear to help our eyes heal. Here, the opposite happens. Here the tragic hero's appearances in the form of a luminous image, the dream character of the mask, are the necessary product of a glimpse into the inner core and horror of nature, shining spots for healing sight wounded by the horrible night (Nietzsche 1872, §9).

By viewing reality from one or a few chosen perspectives, we narrow experience, not broaden it. We view realities from a limited perspective, not in all their dimensions. That was the method that Hitler explicitly prescribed for altering states of mind through propaganda. According to him, the first axiom of all propagandist activity, was the fundamentally subjective, one-sided attitude that it had to take toward every question it dealt with. He taught that all effective propaganda had to be limited to a very few points that had to be harped on over and over and that it was a grave error to be many-sided. The moment propaganda recognized so much as a glimmer of right on the other side, the foundation for doubt in one's own right had been laid, he warned. He underscored the importance of taking a one-sided approach because he believed that an objective study of the truth would confuse the masses of people, whose intelligence he considered limited (Hitler, 180–85).

But this kind of one-sided approach is obviously a form of double-thinking and double dealing. It is two-faced and ultimately two-edged. By giving into the temptation to allow one's vision to be blinded by one facet of reality to the exclusion of others, one risks finding oneself in the situation described in Baudelaire's poem "The Mask." Initially charmed by a one-sided experience of a statue of a woman, the poet is drawn to her "delicate face, completely framed by a thin veil, whose each feature tells us with a triumphant air: 'Sensuous Pleasure calls me and Love crowns me!'" and to the "exciting charm kindness gives this being endowed with so much majesty." But upon drawing closer to turn around her beauty, the poet cries out:

O blasphemy of art! O fatal surprise! The woman with a divine body, promising happiness, finishes on top as a two headed monster! But no! it is only a mask, a seductive façade, this face brightened with an exquisite grimace, and, look there is, atrociously contorted, the true head, and the sincere face reversed, in the shelter of the face that lies. Poor great beauty! The magnificent river of your tears ends in my anxious heart; your lie intoxicates me, and my soul drinks deep of the tide that Pain causes to spring from your eyes! (Baudelaire 1857, XX)

Once Hitler's spell was broken and the masks stripped from the leading characters of the tragedy of the Third Reich before the eyes of a shocked world plunged into the depths of pain, Carl Jung depicted the unmasked Hitler as a man suggesting "a psychic scarecrow (with a broomstick for an outstretched arm) rather than a human being," delivering "ranting speeches . . . in shrill, grating, womanish tones," whose "theatrical, obviously hysterical gestures struck all foreigners (with a few amazing exceptions) as purely ridiculous." Jung saw a "sorry lack of education, conceit that bordered on madness, a very mediocre intelligence combined with the hysteric's cunning and the power fantasies of an adolescent" written all over Hitler's face. "His gesticulations were all put on, devised by an hysterical mind intent only on making an impression. He behaved in public like . . . the sombre daemonic 'man of iron' of popular fiction, the ideal of an infantile public whose knowledge of the world is derived from the deified heroes of trashy films." Jung called him a "theatrical hysteric and transparent imposter," who was "exalted to the skies" as a "nation of eighty millions crowded into the circus to witness its own destruction" (Jung 1945, 188–89).

Jung characterized the unmasked Göring as "the good fellow and *bon vivant* type of cheat, who takes in the simple-minded with his jovial air of respectability." As Jung saw it, he "was popular on account of his weaknesses; few people would believe his crimes." For Jung, Goebbels was "a no-less-sinister and dangerous character . . . the typical *Kaffeehausliterat* and card-sharper, handicapped and at the same time branded by nature." Jung thought that Goebbels had been tolerated "because many think that lying is inseparable from success, and that success justifies everything" (Jung 1945, 189).

Jung's Reflections on Hitler, Nazism, and Realism

In "After the Catastrophe" (Jung 1945) and "The Fight with the Shadow" (Jung 1946), Jung searched for answers to what he termed a "gigantic tangle of questions" about the meaning of the whole tragedy of World War II, which had left most of Europe in ruins and had seen, as he put it, the Germans fall on their fellow Europeans like beasts of prey and torture and murder them (Jung 1945, 181, 183). He addressed the issue of realism, Hitler, and his followers.

Jung diagnosed the history of Third Reich as "the case-chart of an hysterical patient" from whom the truth should not be withheld because hysteria is never cured by hushing up the truth. According to Jung's diagnosis, the kind of lack of reality evident in Goethe's Faust produces a corresponding lack of realism in Germans, who boast of an "ice-cold" realism, but whose realism is really nothing more than "a pose, a stage-realism." Jung interpreted Faust as "split," as someone who "never attains the character of reality . . . is not a real human being and cannot become one," who "sets up 'evil' outside of himself," and neither has real insight, nor suffers real remorse. According to Jung, if "Faust strikes a chord in every German soul, this chord has certainly gone on ringing. We hear it echoing in Nietzsche's Superman, the amoral worshipper of instinct, whose God is dead, and who presumes to be God himself, or rather a demon 'six thousand feet beyond good and evil.'" If it seems intelligent to ask how people let themselves be seduced by Hitler, Jung seems to imply, then how did so many people let themselves be seduced by Nietzsche? (Jung 1945, 191–97)

In Jung's opinion, Germans merely act the part of someone who has the sense of reality. They explain away their failures by means of lies that are immediately invented and believed. "Believing one's own lies when the wish is father to the lie is a well-known hysterical symptom," Jung points out. He considers that the "bloodbath of the First World War . . . glory, conquest, and bloodthirstiness acted like a smoke-screen on the German mind, so that reality, only dimly perceived at best, was completely blotted out. . . ." "When a whole nation finds itself in this condition," he says, "it will follow a mediumistic Führer over the house-tops with a sleep-walker's assurance, only to land in the street with a broken back" (Jung 1945, 191–93).

According to Jung's analysis, an "accurate diagnosis of Hitler's condition would be *pseudologia phantastica*, that form of hysteria which is characterized by a peculiar talent for believing one's own lies"(Jung 1945, 188). "Nothing," Jung points out, "has such a convincing effect as a lie one invents and believes oneself, or an evil deed or intention whose righteousness one regards as self-evident. At any rate, they carry far more conviction than the good man and the good deed, or even than the wicked man and his purely wicked deed" (Jung 1945, 188). Jung says that "it is part and parcel of the pathological liar's make-up to be plausible. Therefore it is no easy matter, even for experienced people, to form an opinion, particularly while the plan is still apparently in the idealist state. It is then quite impossible to foresee how things are likely to develop . . ." (Jung 1945, 190). "For a short spell," Jung warns, "such people usually meet with astounding success, and for that reason are socially dangerous (Jung 1945, 188). "A whole nation," according to Jung's analysis,

> as well as countless millions belonging to other nations, were swept into the blood-drenched madness of a war of extermination. No one knew what was happening to him, least of all the Germans, who allowed themselves to be driven to the slaughterhouse by their leading psychopaths like hypnotized sheep. Maybe the Germans were predestined to this fate. . . . But their peculiar gifts might also have enabled them to be the very people to draw helpful conclusions from the prophetic example of Nietzsche. . . . Thus they were led to imitate their prophets and to take their words literally, but not to understand. And so it was that the Germans allowed themselves to be deluded by these disastrous fantasies and succumbed to the age-old temptations of Satan, instead of turning to their abundant spiritual potentialities, which because of the greater tension between the inner opposites would have stood them in good stead. But, their Christianity forgotten, they sold their souls to technology, exchanged morality for cynicism, and dedicated their highest aspirations to the forces of destruction. (Jung 1945, 195)

In "After the Catastrophe," Jung even entertained the possibility that whites might be possessed. The reasons that a New Mexican Pueblo chieftain gave Jung for believing that the white men he knew were crazy led Jung to reflect how:

> For the first time since the dawn of history we have succeeded in swallowing the whole of primitive animism into ourselves and with it the spirit that ani-

mated nature. Not only were the gods dragged down from their planetary spheres and transformed into chthonic demons, but, under the influence of scientific enlightenment, even this band of demons, which at the time of Paracelsus still frolicked happily in mountains and woods, in rivers and human dwelling-places, was reduced to a miserable remnant and finally vanished altogether. (Jung 1945, 194)

The times, the first half of the twentieth century in particular, had prepared the way for crime, Jung maintains:

> For the first time, we are living in a lifeless nature bereft of gods. No one will deny the important role which the powers of the human psyche, personified as 'gods,' played in the past. The mere act of enlightenment may have destroyed the spirits of nature, but not the psychic factors that correspond to them, such as suggestibility, lack of criticism, fearfulness, propensity to superstition and prejudice—in short, all those qualities that make possession possible. Even though nature is depsychized, the psychic conditions which breed demons are as actively at work as ever. The demons have not really disappeared. . . . Just when people were congratulating themselves on having abolished all spooks, it turned out that instead of haunting the attic or old ruins the spooks were flitting about in the heads of apparently normal Europeans. Tyrannical obsessive, intoxicating ideas and delusions were abroad everywhere, and people began to believe the most absurd things, just as the possessed . . . (Jung 1945, 194)

Jung asks where now was "sanction for goodness and justice, which was once anchored in metaphysics" and if it was "really only brute force that decides everything?" This was a state of affairs that was a matter of concern to many thinking people in the final years of the nineteenth century and the early years of the twentieth. [16] In a course that he gave in 1898/99, the German philosopher Edmund Husserl studied how the hard questions about the objectivity of knowledge raised in the wake of work of the German philosopher Immanuel Kant could determine one's entire conception of being in the world. He saw the metaphysical needs of his time going unmet and a concomitant rise in spiritism, occultism, and supersti-

---

[16] As Jung notes, the Western world was not a passel of pious church going Christians until the 1960s. The state of Western civilization at the turn of the twentieth century much resembled the state it was in at turn of the twenty-first century. Deschristianization was widespread, as was a concomitant rise in occult practices and neo-paganism. A number of very interesting scholarly works treat different facets of the phenomenon addressed here by Jung and Husserl. Among those that went into the making of this book are: Goodrick-Clarke 1985, *The Occult Roots of Nazism: Secret Aryan Cults and their Influence on Nazi Ideology*; Goodrick-Clarke 1998, *Hitler's Priestess: Savitri Devi, the Hindu-Aryan Myth, and Neo-Nazism*; Harrington 1996, *Reenchanted Science: Holism in German Culture from Wilhelm II to Hitler*; Rhodes 1980, *The Hitler Movement: A Modern Millenarian Revolution*.

tions of every kind. He called for a science of metaphysics to study problems lying beyond empirical investigation and provide ultimate and deepest knowledge of reality (Husserl 1898/99, 223–55).

In "After the Catastrophe," Jung suggested an answer that announces the theme of Part Three of this book: "But as the 'thousand-year Reich' of violence and infamy lasted only a few years before it collapsed in ruins, we might be disposed to learn the lesson that there are other equally powerful forces at work which in the end destroy all that is violent and unjust, and that consequently it does not pay to build on false principles" (Jung 1945, 197).

PART TWO

. . . To Reality

The pen, I stressed in Part One, has the power to create myths and illusions, fake facts and history, dupe people, divorce them from reality, beautify what is horrible . . . Artfully and masterfully manipulated, expressed in exquisite, compelling language, ideas and theories can be undeservedly appealing, seductive, even intoxicating. They can even so unglue, unhinge people from reality as to bring them to justify, temporarily, or even permanently, the worst atrocities. Moreover, the price in terms of the real, raw human suffering that is the fruit of evils that words, theories, dreams, and ideas can glorify, rarely makes itself felt in theories. As Nietzsche rightly observed in *Daybreak*, "People who act freely are at a disadvantage compared with freethinkers because people suffer more obviously from the consequences of deeds than from those of thoughts" (Nietzsche 1881, §20).

So, any study of the roots and flowers of evil inevitably needs to make the transition from theory to reality. No matter how much some may wish, or plead in words, that there is no objective reality, that truth and facts are illusions, flourishes of pen cannot blot out the real cruelty, slaughter, massacres, torture, terrorism, purges that really have occurred and really do occur with all their millions of victims and cadavers, blood, suffering, loss, destruction that make up much of this second part of this study of the roots and flowers of evil. Those who in armchairs, offices, libraries, classrooms, or lulled by drugs delight in pleasingly expressed ideas or sentiments divorced from reality really leave themselves open to charges of hypocrisy, or worse. And if a Baudelaire, a Nietzsche, or a disciple of one or the other, is to be excused because they just wrote about those things and did not act on them, then should those who fell under Hitler's spell not be readily forgiven for not having taken his words in earnest? So, the theories of Part One need to be confronted with the realities of what they glorify and the causes that they champion. In other words: *Let's get real!*

Making Action the Sister of One's Dreams

Baudelaire, Nietzsche, and Hitler, each in his own inimitable manner, addressed the matter of the difference between thinking about evil and actually engaging in it. In Baudelaire's "The Denial of Saint Peter," the poet boldly proclaims: "—Of course, as for myself, satisfied, I shall leave a world where action is not the sister of dreams; may I use the sword and perish by the sword!" (Baudelaire 1857, CXVII). The poet of Baudelaire's "To the Reader" expresses his conviction that "if rape, poison, the dagger, fire, have not yet embroidered their pleasant designs on the banal story of our pitiable destinies, it is that our soul, alas, is not hardy enough" (Baudelaire 1857). What the poet of Baudelaire's poem "The Ideal" needs to satisfy his "heart deep as an abyss" is a "soul powerful in crime" (Baudelaire 1857, XVIII).

Baudelaire actually saw action during the 1848 rebellion in Paris. In *Souvenirs d'un septugénaire*, Charles Toubin recalled the heady atmosphere of those days and its effect on Baudelaire who experienced it alongside him. The emotional climate that Toubin described was one of hatred to the point of rage existing between the people and the Paris military police, whom the people detested and insulted whenever the occasion offered itself and who, according to Toubin, were no longer men, but had become veritable ferocious beasts stabbing harmless people with their bayonets (Pichois and Ziegler, 257–58).

In his whole life, Toubin wrote, he had never seen such an "outburst of enthusiasm, nor anything comparable to that intoxicating display, magnificent spell of good weather born of a storm that was to end that very evening in a dreadful unleashing of the elements." He had never seen Baudelaire so gay, so agile, so untiring. He seemed to him to be "enchanted" by the events; his eyes sparkled. Baudelaire, Toubin thought, loved "revolution as he did everything that was violent and abnormal" (Pichois and Ziegler, 258, 263).

Jules Buisson remembered how, sporting a beautiful, shiny, unused double-barreled shotgun and a superb yellow leather ammunition pouch just as immaculate, Baudelaire threw himself into the revolution. Another witness remembered Baudelaire as "nervous, excited, feverish, agitated," told of how he held forth, ranted, bragged, jumped about in order to race to martyrdom (Pichois and Ziegler, 261–62, 270).

Of the "intoxication" that he had felt in 1848, Baudelaire himself confessed in *Mon cœur mis à nu*, that it was a matter of a "taste for vengeance," of the "natural pleasure of demolition." Of the violence in May of that year, Baudelaire exclaimed: "Ever a taste for destruction, a legitimate taste if everything that is natural is legitimate." Of what he once called the "horrors" of June 1848, he wrote: "Madness of the people and madness of the bourgeoisie. Natural love of crime" (Baudelaire 1949, V).

Of the Pen and the Sword

For all their bravado and big words, however, there is little to indicate that, even if they were not sick, weak, and had not ultimately lost their minds to syphilis, Baudelaire and Nietzsche would have ever have actually made action the sister of their dreams. Both used the pen, not the sword, and both perished in a most pathetic fashion.

In Baudelaire's case, in *Mon cœur mis à nu*, he commented that the revolution of 1848 was "only fun because each one fabricated utopias then, like castles in Spain." He follows that statement with a statement of his conviction that Maximilien de Robespierre, the architect of the Reign of Terror during the French Revolution, "was only worthy of esteem because he constructed some beautiful sentences" (Baudelaire 1949, VI).

As for Nietzsche, Paul Deussen, a friend of his during their university years, once recalled the "amusing" way in which Nietzsche behaved himself when challenged to a duel:

> With some foreboding I saw the day approaching when our friend, who was somewhat corpulent, not like Hamlet through a printer's error ("fat" for "hot") but in reality, and moreover very myopic, would have to undergo an adventure for which his qualifications were so ill-suited. The blades were tied and the sharp rapiers flashed around their bare heads. After barely three minutes the opponent applied a cut diagonally across the bridge of Nietzsche's nose right where too hard a pinch leaves a red mark. The blood was dripping to the ground, and the experts determined it to be sufficient atonement for all past injury. I loaded my well-bandaged friend into a carriage and took him home to bed, cooled the wound diligently, denied him visitors and alcohol, and in two or three days our hero had recuperated. . . . (Gilman, 22–23)

According to Nietzsche admirer H. L. Mencken, Nietzsche tried in vain to escape his term of compulsory military service on the grounds that he was near-sighted and the only son of a widow. Confides Mencken, "soldiering was scarcely his forte, and he cut a sorry figure on a horse. After a few months of unwilling service, in fact, he had a riding accident and came near dying. . . . As it was he wrenched his breast muscles so badly that he was condemned by a medical survey and discharged from the army" (Mencken, 17).

With the advent of the Franco-Prussian War in 1870, Nietzsche who was, in Mencken's eyes, "at bottom a good citizen and perfectly willing to suffer and bleed for his country" went to the front, but having taken Swiss nationality, was obliged to go, not as a warrior, but as a member of the medical corps. Even so, Mencken recounts, Nietzsche still nearly lost his life. Not strong physically, a victim of severe headaches, and weakened by his own hard work, he fell ill on the battlefields of France and when he finally reached home again he was a neurasthenic wreck. Ever thereafter his life was one long struggle against disease. "Diphtheria and what seems to have been cholera morbus attacked him. . . . He suffered from migraine, that most terrible disease of the nerves, and chronic catarrh of the stomach made him a dyspeptic. Unable to eat or sleep, he resorted to narcotics. . . . Nietzsche, indeed, was a slave to drugs, and more than once in after life, long before insanity finally ended his career, he gave evidence of it" (Mencken, 23).

An acquaintance of Nietzsche in Basel in the Summer of 1878 found that the "horrible experiences in the battlefields of the Franco-Prussian

War had shaken him so much psychologically that his delicate nervous system was permanently damaged. Insomnia, which was not improved by repeated overwork, by chloral and potassium bromide, but made worse, excruciating headaches, and other neuralgic ailments tormented his life" (Gilman, 100).

In 1914, Louis Bertrand hypothesized that Nietzsche's entire literary output was in reality conditioned by his experiences during that war and is explainable from beginning to end by the nervous shock that the direct experience of war had upon his sickly sensibility. His short period of time on the battlefield as an ambulance worker in the midst of the victorious armies of his country, that short-lived contact with brute force, was enough to have an inebriating effect upon him. Bertrand considered that:

> Until he breathed his last breath, he was intoxicated with this bad intoxication. The man of the pen . . . became enamoured of the man of the sword. The civilized man became the mad admirer of the brute beast. The chronically ill man extolled the exuberantly healthy, joyous, vigorous man who smashes everything around him. But since he was also a professor . . . his pedantry had to turn his warlike enthusiasms to his account. The scholarly barbarity he was singing had to seem to him . . . as "borrowed from the Greeks." The destructive intoxication of the German armies became for him the Dionysian drunkenness, the orgiastic madness of the dithyramb (Bertrand, 292).

Imagining Adolf Eichmann

In a book of reflections on Adolf Eichmann's 1961 trial, Harry Mullisch addressed the matter of the pen and the sword in an essay on horror and its representation. To underscore the fundamental difference between the written word and actual deeds, Mullisch asked to what extent the representation of atrocities could be said to be the cause of atrocities. He says that he himself once wrote that he was one of those people "who delighted in tossing infants into the air and catching them at sword point," but he stresses that his statement about catching infants at sword point did not make him into a Nazi, that he remained a writer, and that it was essential to understand the difference between those who depict a world destroyed and those who destroy worlds (Mullisch, 144–45).

In the essay in question, Mullisch also theorizes that Nazism was incontestably born from certain images rather than certain ideas, that innumerable images *preceded* Nazism, images in which its universe was already perceptible in works of art that cast shadows heralding future events (Mullisch, 138–39). Figuring on Mullisch's list of literary harbingers of brutal force and unleashed passions are Goethe, who in *Faust* revealed a new world, the world of darkness, and the Marquis de Sade, who saw in crime the revelation of the most profound reality. Then there was the person whom Mullisch just calls Jean Paul, who had written of a revolution greater and more spiritual than a political revolution, and just as murderous, that was beating in the heart of the world. Among the early, still blurry images prefiguring the universe of Hitler in the nineteenth century, Mullisch cites E. T. A. Hoffmann's odious, ugly phantom who, wherever he went, brought affliction, misery, and perdition in this world and in the other, and the hero of Lautréamont's *Les Chants de Maldoror* who has a little girl torn to pieces by his bulldog on the sacrificial altar (Mullisch, 142).

Mullisch suggests (without providing the references) that three quarters of a century later, Heinrich Himmler would almost be repeating the words of Nietzsche when he wrote of the need to attain that monstrous energy of grandeur in order to be able to form the people of the future by education and the annihilation of millions of human failures and not die of the pain that one *creates*, pain of which there has never been an equivalent. For a long time ago, Mullisch remarks, Baudelaire had already noted that it was only on the strongest that the attractiveness of horror had an intoxicating effect (Mullisch, 143).

With time, the picture came more clearly into focus, Mullisch contends. He cites: Heinrich Mann's clear depiction of the coming decadence of German intellectuals; the medium's killing under hypnosis in *Doctor Caligari*; Doctor Mabuse's gang of killers and counterfeiters; the German expressionist Arnolt Bronnen's declaration that it was "better to scream a lot than to be very intelligent;" the father of surrealism André Breton's admission that if he obeyed his strongest and most frequent drives, there would be nothing left for him to do but to take a revolver, go out in to the street, and see quite well what happened (Mullisch, 143).

Mullisch takes care to point out that Hitler, who did in reality what the above artists did with forms, recognized the artists that he considered degenerate to be his worst enemies. So it was that, before it ever took on a concrete form, Hitler's world was especially portrayed by his "opponents," whose talent, Mullisch concludes, saved them. "Less privileged people, like Hitler, were only able to get rid of their nostalgia by real destruction" (Mullisch, 144–45).

In chronicling all this, Mullisch stresses that not even the greatest geniuses had been able to imagine Eichmann: "The staid, conscientious bureaucrat who holds out the little girl to Maldoror's bulldog. The staid, conscientious bureaucrat who brings the surrealist a passerby at which to shoot. The staid, conscientious bureaucrat who offers the medium's blade to the student. The staid, conscientious bureaucrat who leads the Jews of Europe to Rudolf Hoess' gas chambers." And this, to Mullisch's mind, illustrates all the difference between the artist and the assassin. While he has said that works of art are shadows portending events to come, Mullisch is intent on affirming that "Eichmann did not cast any shadow because he was not that *about which* the artists were writing, but *why* they were writing: the new factor that, worried, they were presenting and that out of the paper Caligari made a quite real Hitler—the symbol of 'progress'" (Mullisch, 146–47).

On Setting Aside Aesthetics

Baudelaire and Nietzsche wrote about the "beauty" of cruelty, but our third man, Adolf Hitler, was a man really intent upon making action the sister of his dreams and one most adamant in his belief that people's destinies were not turned by "the lemonade-like outpourings of literary aesthetes and drawing-room heroes." He was not one to risk leaving it to the "designs" of "rape, poison, the dagger, fire" themselves to prove as universally pleasant as Baudelaire and Nietzsche implied in their writings, but had a keen, practical sense of what to do about the power that flows from arms, torture, scaffolds, firing squads. He considered that one should "let the writer remain by his ink-well engaging in theoretical activity, if his intelligence and ability are equal to it; for leadership he is neither born nor chosen." "Hard reality alone," Hitler stressed, "must determine the road to the goal" (Hitler, 106–7).

While, as seen in Part One, Hitler firmly believed that any attempt to combat a philosophy with the sword would fail unless the fight took the form of attack for a new spiritual attitude, he was at the same time intent upon eliminating the criteria of humanitarianism and beauty from the struggle (Hitler, 178). He complained that instead of taking "one of those creatures" who tried to dampen the exuberance during the first World War "by his long ears, tying him to a long pole and pulling him up on a long cord, thus making it impossible for the cheering nation to insult the aesthetic sentiment of this knight of the inkpot, the authorities actually began to issue remonstrances against 'unseemly' rejoicing over victories. It did not occur to them in the least that enthusiasm once scotched cannot be reawakened at need. It is an intoxication and must be preserved in this state" (Hitler, 167).

Hitler maintained that in terms of the principles valid for the struggle for the existence of the German people, "the most cruel weapons were humane if they brought about a quicker victory; and only those methods were beautiful which helped the nation to safeguard the dignity of its freedom" (Hitler, 178–79). He maintained that "the nobility of the most exalted beauty lies in the last analysis only in what is logically most expedient" (Hitler, 379). As he explained:

When the nations on this planet fight for existence—when the question of destiny, 'to be or not to be,' cries out for a solution—then all considerations of humanitarianism or aesthetics crumble into nothingness; for all these concepts do not float about in the ether, they arise from man's imagination and are bound up with man. When he departs from this world, these concepts are again dissolved into nothingness, for nature does not know them. . . . Humanitarianism and aesthetics. . . . become secondary when a nation is fighting for its existence; in fact, they become totally irrelevant to the forms of the struggle as soon as a situation arises where they might paralyze a struggling nation's power of self-preservation. And that has always been their only visible result. As for humanitarianism . . . in war it lies in the brevity of the operation, and that means that the most aggressive fighting technique is the most humane. But when people try to approach these questions with drivel about aesthetics, etc. really only one answer is possible: where the destiny and existence of a people are at stake, all obligation toward beauty ceases. The most unbeautiful thing there can be in human life is and remains the yoke of slavery. (Hitler, 185)

In this second part on the reality of evil, I too shall be setting aside aesthetics. I have no intention to try to show evil acts figuring in it as beautiful. In so doing, I shall surely leave myself open to the charge that I am not displaying the beauty of evil to its best advantage, something which, of course, in my opinion, would in itself be an evil thing to do.

A Soul Powerful in Crime

Adolf Hitler did make action the sister of his dreams, and the success he knew in so doing must have exceeded his wildest dreams. He and his henchmen were souls powerful in crime who lived by the sword and perished by the sword. They so effectively translated his words into action as to leave the lives of millions of real people and much of the real world in shreds.

Mein Kampf is a book replete with very practical advice about precisely how to take the step from its theories to reality. In it Hitler stressed that, while it had always been reserved to the pen to provide theoretical foundations for the greatest revolutions in this world, those revolutions had "never been directed by a goose-quill," that without the mighty force of the mass of a people, no great idea, however lofty and noble it may seem, could be realized (Hitler, 106–7). "To draw from the realm of the eternally true and ideal that which is humanly possible for small mortals and make it take form," he especially preached there, "the search after truth must be coupled with knowledge of people's psyche" (Hitler, 381). Tactics "based on precise calculation of all human weaknesses," he promised, would "lead to success with almost mathematical certainty" (Hitler, 43–44).

Hitler characterized the people whose psyche one needed to understand as consisting neither of professors nor of diplomats, or even of people capable of forming a rational opinion, but of plain mortals having a scanty amount of abstract knowledge . . . wavering and inclined to doubt and uncertainty (Hitler, 183, 337–38). "The psyche of the great masses," he considered,

> is not receptive to anything that is half-hearted and weak. Like the woman, whose psychic state is determined less by grounds of abstract reason than by an indefinable emotional longing for a force which will complement her nature, and who consequently, would rather bow to a strong man than dominate a weakling, likewise the masses love a commander more than a petitioner and feel inwardly more satisfied by a doctrine, tolerating no other beside itself, than by the granting of liberalistic freedom with which, as a rule, they can do little, and are prone to feel that they have been abandoned. (Hitler, 42)

Hitler characterized national bodies as being "divided into three major classes: the best humanity, possessing all virtues, especially distinguished by courage and self-sacrifice; the worst scum, bad in the sense that all selfish urges and vices are present. . . . And the great, broad middle stratum, in which neither brilliant heroism nor the basest criminal mentality is embodied" (Hitler, 519). He felt confident that in case of the victory of one of the extremes, the broad masses in the middle would complaisantly submit to the victor . . . offer no resistance, never fight (Hitler, 520).

Hitler further considered that "the realization of philosophical ideals and of the demands derived from them no more occurs through men's pure feeling or inner will in themselves than the achievement of freedom through the general longing for it. Only when the ideal urge for independence gets a fighting organization in the form of military instruments of power can the pressing desire of a people be transformed into glorious reality" (Hitler, 380). "Every philosophy of life," he taught, "even if it is a thousand times correct and of highest benefit to humanity, will remain without significance for the practical shaping of a people's life, as long as its principles have not become the banner of a fighting movement which for its part in turn will be a party as long as its activity has not found completion in the victory of its ideas and its party dogmas have not become the new state principles of a people's community" (Hitler, 380). As he saw it, "from general ideas a political program must be stamped, from a general philosophy of life a definite political faith. The latter, since its goal must be practically attainable, will not only have to serve the idea in itself, but will also have to take into consideration the means of struggle which are available and must be used for the achievement of this idea." He saw the "transformation of a general, philosophical, ideal conception of the highest truth into a definitely delimited tightly organized political community of faith and struggle, unified in spirit and will" to be "the most significant achievement" since the possibility of a victory of an idea depended on its "happy solution alone" (Hitler, 381).

So it was, according to him, that the "abstractly correct intellectual concept which the theoretician has to proclaim must be coupled with the practical knowledge of the politician" and from "the army of often millions of men . . . one man must step forward who with apodictic force will form granite principles from the wavering idea world of the broad masses and take up the struggle for their sole correctness, until from the shifting waves of a free thought world there will arise a brazen cliff of solid unity in faith and will" (Hitler, 381).

Awakening Latent Tendencies in Society

In *Warrant for Genocide: The Myth of the Jewish World Conspiracy and the Protocols of the Elders of Zion*, Norman Cohn writes of "a subterranean world where pathological fantasies disguised as ideas are churned out by crooks and half-educated fanatics for the benefit of the ignorant and superstitious. There are times," he explains, "when this underworld emerges from the depths and suddenly fascinates, captures, and dominates multitudes of usually sane and responsible people, who thereupon take leave of sanity and responsibility. And it occasionally happens that this underworld becomes a political power and changes the course of history" (Cohn, xiv).

Hitler saw well how the ideas, theories, pathological fantasies of poets, artists, philosophers, politicians, crooks, and half-educated fanatics could be made to emerge from the depths to fascinate, capture, and dominate the masses, and how they would be particularly likely to do so by giving voice and promising to lend meaning to tendencies already latent in society but not yet well articulated and channeled. To a large extent National Socialism came to power because Hitler, just as he predicted he would be, was successful in translating such tendencies into action.

"Every deed in the grand manner on this earth," Hitler held forth in *Mein Kampf*, "will in general be the fulfillment of a desire which had long since been present in millions of people, a longing silently harbored by many" (Hitler, 509). "The common people themselves," he maintained, "harbor indefinite desires and have general convictions, but cannot obtain precise clarity regarding the actual nature of their aim or of their own desire, let alone the possibility of its fulfillment" (Hitler, 510). Making his appeal to "the hundreds of thousands who fundamentally long for the same thing without as individuals finding the words to describe outwardly what they inwardly visualize" (Hitler, 330), Hitler defined his "own task" as "especially in extracting those nuclear ideas from the extensive and unshaped substance of a general world view and remolding them into more or less dogmatic forms which in their clear delimitation are adapted for holding solidly together those men who swear allegiance to them" (Hitler, 385).

Hitler told the German people that the "internal decline of the German nation had long since begun, yet, as often in life, people had not achieved clarity concerning the force that was destroying their existence. Sometimes they tinkered with the disease, but confused the forms of the phenomenon with the virus that had caused it" (Hitler, 156). "The fact that millions bear in their hearts the desire for a basic change in the conditions obtaining today," he affirmed, "proves the deep discontent under which they suffer. It expresses itself in thousandfold manifestations, with one in despair and hopelessness, with another in ill will, anger, and indignation; with this man in indifference, and with that man in furious excesses" (Hitler, 330).

As witnesses to the inner dissatisfaction to which he was referring, Hitler named "those who are weary of elections as well as the many who tend to the most fanatical extreme of the Left." He said that it was particularly to the most fanatical extreme of the Left that his own movement was intended primarily to appeal, that it was not meant "to constitute an organization of the contented and satisfied, but to embrace those tormented by suffering, those without peace, the unhappy and the discontented, and above all it must not swim on the surface of a national body, but strike roots deep within it" (Hitler, 330–31). "Yes," he exclaimed, "it can come about that centuries wish and yearn for the solution of a certain question because they are sighing beneath the intolerable burden of an existing condition and the fulfillment of this general longing does not materialize." Then "Fate some day bestows . . . the man endowed for this purpose, who finally brings the long yearned-for fulfillment" (Hitler, 509–10).

It may be presumed that Hitler saw himself as the leader who could finally make the fulfillment of long present desires and silently harbored longings of millions a reality, who could find the long yearned for "solution of a certain question," who profoundly recognized his people's distress and then, after attaining ultimate clarity regarding the nature of the disease, seriously tried to cure it (Hitler, 513). Reading *Mein Kampf*, one senses that he thought that he himself might be just the man to light the match that would bring the end to what many saw as a decaying "old world," to an antiquated way of life and set of moral values just asking to be destroyed.

Civilization and Its Discontents

In *Human, All Too Human*, Nietzsche warned that: "We live in a time in which civilization is in danger of being ruined by its own means of civilization" (Nietzsche 1878, I §520). This was a theme that Sigmund Freud made one of the major planks of his theorizing about the state in which he found European Christian civilization during the first decades of the twentieth century. Freud's writings are in fact rife with reasons to destroy European civilization as he and his contemporaries knew it.

"Reality," Freud wrote in *Civilization and Its Discontents*, "shows us that civilization is not content with the ties we have so far allowed it" (Freud 1930, 299). He viewed civilization as he knew it as having generally been built up through prohibitions by which it began to detach people from what he called their "primordial animal condition" (Freud 1927, 189). "The psychical modifications that go along with the process of civilization are striking and unambiguous," he maintained. "They consist in a progressive displacement of instinctual aims and a restriction of instinctual impulses. Sensations which were pleasurable to our ancestors have become indifferent or even intolerable to ourselves" (Freud 1933, 361). He professed to have been surprised to have found the privations involved in the suppression of the instinctual wishes of "incest, cannibalism, and lust for killing," which he claimed were "born afresh with every child," to be "still operative and still form the kernel of hostility to civilization" (Freud 1927, 189). He designated war as being in the "the crassest opposition to the psychical attitude imposed on us by the process of civilization" (Freud 1933, 362).

The problem, according to Freud, was "how to get rid of the greatest hindrance to civilization—namely, the constitutional inclination of human beings to be aggressive towards one another" (Freud 1930, 336). Civilization's efforts to solve this problem involved "the use of methods intended to incite people into identifications and aim-inhibited relationships of love, hence the restriction upon sexual life, and hence too the ideal's commandment to love one's neighbor as oneself," a commandment which Freud saw as "really justified by the fact that nothing else runs so strongly counter to the original nature of man" (Freud 1930, 303).

According to Freud's theories about civilization's attempts to tame unruly members, it "obtains mastery over the individual's dangerous desire for aggression by weakening and disarming it and by setting up an agency within him to watch over it, like a garrison in a conquered city" (Freud 1930, 316). "The man who, in consequence of his unyielding constitution, cannot fall in with this suppression of instinct becomes a 'criminal', and an 'outlaw', in the face of society—unless his social position or his exceptional capacities enable him to impose himself upon it as a great man, a 'hero'" (Freud 1908, 39). Civilization, Freud wrote, "hopes to prevent the crudest excesses of brutal violence by itself assuming the right to use violence against criminals, but the law is not able to lay hold of the more cautious and refined manifestations of human aggressiveness." Freud considered that "it would be unfair to reproach civilization with trying to eliminate strife and competition from human activity. These things are undoubtedly indispensable. But opposition is not necessarily enmity; it is merely misused and made an occasion for enmity" (Freud 1930, 303).

Freud expressed pessimism as to whether civilization's efforts to tame the constitutional inclination of human beings to be aggressive towards one another had so far achieved very much (Freud 1930, 303). "If a man, for example, has become over-kind as a result of a violent suppression of a constitutional inclination to harshness and cruelty, he often loses so much energy in doing this that he fails to carry out all that his compensatory impulses require, and he may, after all, do less good on the whole than he would have done without the suppression" (Freud 1908, 55).

Freud was, however, prepared to concede that "if these forces are turned to destruction in the external world, the organism will be relieved and the effect must be beneficial. This would serve as a biological justification for all the ugly and dangerous impulses against which we are struggling. It must be admitted that they stand nearer to Nature than does our resistance to them . . ." (Freud 1933, 358). He deemed it was "always possible to bind together a considerable number of people in love, so long as there are other people left over to receive the manifestations of their aggressiveness" and that this represented "a convenient and relatively harmless satisfaction of the inclination to aggression, by means of which cohesion between the members of the community is made easier." He adds that in this regard "the Jewish people, scattered everywhere, have rendered most useful services to the civilizations of the countries that have been their hosts" (Freud 1930, 305).

He also conceded that civilization's common assets in material and ideal wealth had grown out of individuals surrendering some part of their sense of omnipotence or of the aggressive or vindictive inclinations in their personality. He saw this renunciation as having been progressive and the individual steps in it to have been sanctioned by religion (Freud 1908, 38–39). However, he observed, the "unmistakable situation" in his day was that religion no longer had the same influence on people that it had had in the past and that that was not so because it had come to promise less, but because people find its promises less credible. He gave the reason for this change to be:

the increase of the scientific spirit in the higher strata of human society. Criticism has whittled away the evidential value of religious documents, natural science has shown up the errors in them, and comparative research has been struck by the fatal resemblance between the religious ideas which we revere and the mental products of primitive peoples and times . . . the greater the number of men to whom the treasures of knowledge become accessible, the more widespread is the falling-away from religious belief . . . (Freud 1927, 220–21).

Freud thought that that was all fine so long as "the uneducated and oppressed, who have every reason for being enemies of civilization" do not find out that people no longer believe in God. Freud considered, however, that they were inevitably bound to discover that that was the case and that there was, therefore, a danger that the hostility that those masses felt toward civilization would "throw itself against the weak spot that they have found." He reasoned that if

the sole reason why you must not kill your neighbor is because God has forbidden it and will severely punish you for it in this or the next life—then, when you learn that there is no God and that you need not fear His punishment you will certainly kill your neighbour without hesitation, and you can only be prevented from doing so by mundane force. Thus either these dangerous masses must be held down most severely and kept most carefully away from any chance of intellectual awakening, or else the relationship between civilization and religion must undergo a fundamental revision. (Freud 1927, 221–22)

People themselves, Freud observed, show by their behavior what is the purpose and intention of their lives. What it is that they demand of life and wish to achieve in it can hardly be in doubt, he deemed: "They strive after happiness; they want to become happy and to remain so. . . . what decides the purpose of life is simply the programme of the pleasure principle. This principle dominates the operation of the mental apparatus from the start. There can be no doubt about its efficacy, and yet its programme is at loggerheads with the whole world. . . . There is no possibility at all of its being carried through; all the regulations of the universe run counter to it . . ." (Freud 1930, 263). Freud considered that what "we call happiness in the strictest sense comes from the (preferably sudden) satisfaction of needs which have been dammed up to a high degree" (Freud 1930, 264).

In "Thoughts for the Times on War and Death," Freud found that within each of the nations at war during World War I, "high norms of moral conduct were laid down for the individual, to which his manner of life was bound to conform if he desired to take part in a civilized community. These ordinances, often too stringent, demanded a great deal of him—much self-restraint, much renunciation of instinctual satisfaction. He was above all forbidden to make use of the immense advantages to be gained by the practice of lying and deception in the competition with his fellow-men. The civilized states regarded these moral standards as the basis of their existence . . ." (Freud 1915, 62–63).

Unleashing Pent-up Desires

In his book *Himmler: Reichsführer-SS*, Peter Padfield wrote of Nietzsche and the warlike tendencies latent in German culture that "his writings were inspired revelations from the deepest subconscious levels of his own psyche which mirrored the culture that produced him. Since that culture was about to burst forth on the world stage they were also extraordinary books of prophecy touched with genius. . . . He was expressing in extreme, grotesque form the masculine, martial code . . . and . . . justified intellectually the compulsions of a warrior caste. Had his visions not corresponded to those of his countrymen he would not have spawned so many in his own image" (Padfield, 33).

Born into the discontented civilization described by Freud, Adolf Hitler was himself a product of the culture reflected in Nietzsche's writings. As a boy and a young man, Hitler wrote in *Mein Kampf*, he had "often wanted to prove at least once by deeds" that for him national enthusiasm was "no empty whim." It had often seemed to him "almost a sin to shout hurrah perhaps without having the inner right to do so." For who, he asked, "had the right to use this word without having proved it in the place where all playing is at an end and the inexorable hand of the Goddess of Destiny begins to weigh people and men according to the truth and steadfastness of their convictions?" (Hitler, 163).

Hitler recalled that in his youth he had often indulged in angry thoughts concerning his earthly pilgrimage, which, it seemed to him, had begun too late. He said that he had regarded the period of law and order that seemed to be ahead of him as a mean and undeserved trick of Fate (Hitler, 158). He said that as "a young scamp" in his "wild years," nothing had grieved him so much as having been

> born at a time which obviously erected its Halls of Fame only to shopkeepers and government officials. The waves of historic events seemed to have grown so smooth that the future really seemed to belong only to the 'peaceful contest of nations'; in other words, a cozy mutual swindling match with the exclusion of violent methods of defense. The various nations began to be more and more like private citizens who cut the ground from under one another's feet, stealing each other's customers and orders, trying in every way to get ahead of one another, and staging this whole act amid a hue and cry as loud as it is harmless. This development seemed not only to endure but was expected in time (as was

universally recommended) to remodel the whole world into one big department store in whose vestibules the busts of the shrewdest profiteers and the
most lamblike administrative officials would be garnered for all eternity.
(Hitler, 157)

Why, Hitler lamented, could not he have been born a hundred years
earlier, "when a man, even without a 'business', was really worth something" (Hitler, 157). How, he wondered could the German people "have
succumbed to such a sickening of its political instinct" as to come to
believe "that the world could be peacefully opened up to, let alone conquered for, the German people by a commercial and colonial policy"
(Hitler, 153).

Hitler saw Germany in the years preceding World War I as facing
"forces of decay which in truly terrifying number soon began to flare up
like will-o'-wisps, brushing up and down the body politic, or eating like
poisonous abscesses into the nation, now here and now there." It seemed
to him "as though a continuous stream of poison was being driven into the
outmost blood-vessels of this once heroic body by a mysterious power, and
was inducing progressively greater paralysis of sound reason and the simple instinct of self-preservation" (Hitler, 154).

Looking back as he wrote *Mein Kampf*, Hitler said that what as a boy
had seemed to him to have been "a lingering disease" began to seem to
him to be the

> quiet before the storm. . . . the Balkans were immersed in that livid sultriness
> which customarily announces the hurricane, and from time to time a beam of
> brighter light flared up, only to vanish again in the spectral darkness. The time
> lay . . . on the chests of men like a heavy nightmare, sultry as feverish tropical
> heat, so that due to constant anxiety the sense of approaching catastrophe
> turned at last to longing: let Heaven at last give free rein to the fate that could
> no longer be thwarted. And then the first mighty lightning flash struck the
> earth; the storm was unleashed and with the thunder of heaven there mingled
> the roar of World War batteries. (Hitler, 158)

The civilization that Hitler deplored tore apart along the seams of its
alliances. Austria declared war on Serbia on July 28, 1914 . . . Germany
declared war on Russia on August 1, 1914 . . . Germany declared war on
France on August 3, 1914 . . . France declared war on Germany on
August 3, 1914 . . . Great Britain declared war on Germany on August 3,
1914 . . . Belgium declared war on Germany on August 4, 1914 . . .
Montenegro declared war on Austria on August 8, 1914 . . . Austria
declared war on Montenegro on August 9, 1914 . . . Montenegro
declared war on Germany on August 9, 1914 . . . France declared war on
Austria on August 13, 1914 . . . Great Britain declared war on Austria on

August 13, 1914 . . . Japan declared war on Germany on August 23, 1914 . . . Austria declared war on Japan on August 27, 1914 . . . Austria declared war on Belgium on August 28, 1914 . . . Russia declared war on Turkey on November 3, 1914 . . . France declared war on Turkey on November 5, 1914 . . . Great Britain declared war on Turkey on November 5, 1914 . . . Turkey declared war on the Allies on November 23, 1914 . . . Portugal declared war on Germany on November 23, 1914 . . . Serbia declared war on Turkey on December 2, 1914 . . . Italy declared war on Austria on May 24, 1915 . . . San Marino declared war on Austria on May 24, 1915 . . . Italy declared war on Turkey on August 21, 1915 . . . Bulgaria declared war on Serbia on October 14, 1915 . . . Great Britain declared war on Bulgaria on October 19, 1915 . . . France declared war on Bulgaria on October 16, 1915 . . . Serbia declared war on Bulgaria on October 16, 1915 . . . Italy declared war on Bulgaria on October 19, 1915 . . . Russia declared war on Bulgaria on October 19, 1915 . . . Germany declared war on Portugal on March 9, 1916 . . . Rumania declared war on Austria on August 27, 1916 . . . Italy declared war on Germany on August 28, 1916 . . . Turkey declared war on Rumania on August 29, 1916 . . . Germany declared war on Rumania on September 14, 1916 . . . Greece declared war on Germany on November 28, 1916 . . . Greece declared war on Bulgaria on November 28, 1916 . . . the United States declared war on Germany on Germany on April 6, 1917 . . . Panama declared war on Germany on April 7, 1917 . . . Cuba declared war on Germany on April 7, 1917 . . . Siam declared war on Austria on July 22, 1917 . . . Siam declared war on Germany on July 22, 1917 . . . Liberia declared war on Germany on August 4, 1917 . . . China declared war on Austria on August 14, 1917 . . . Brazil declared war on Germany on October 26, 1917 . . . the United States declared war on Austria and Hungary on December 7, 1917 . . . Panama declared war on Austria on December 10, 1917 . . . Cuba declared war on Austria and Hungary on December 16, 1917 . . . Costa Rica declared war on Germany on May 23, 1918 . . . Nicaragua declared war on Germany on May 24, 1918 . . . Guatemala declared war on Germany on April 22, 1918 . . . Guatemala declared war on Austria and Hungary on April 22, 1918 . . . Haiti declared war on Germany on July 15, 1918 . . . Honduras declared war on Germany on July 19, 1918. . . .

On the Fulfillment of Long Present Desires

In the "War Indispensable" section of *Human, All Too Human*, Nietzsche expressed his conviction that human beings as highly cultivated (*hochkultivierte*), and hence necessarily jaded, as his European contemporaries were needed not only wars, but the biggest and most awful wars—therefore occasional lapses back into barbarity—in order to not to suffer the loss of their civilization (*Kultur*) and its very existence to the means of civilization (*Kultur*). For the time being, he maintained, no means other than a big war was known for communicating to a people growing jaded that raw energy of the bivouacs, that deep impersonal hatred, that cold-bloodedness of one who murders in good conscience, that collective fervor in annihilating (*Vernichtung*) the enemy, that splendid lack of concern about major casualties, about one's own existence as well as that of those befriended, that muffled, earthshaking tremor of the soul. He was confident that, while admittedly having all sorts of stones and rubbish churning in them, and laying to waste fields of tender cultures (*Wiesen zarter Kulturen*), from the brooks and streams bursting forth from this, the wheels of the workshop of the mind would afterward turn with newfound strength amid favorable circumstances. Civilization (*Kultur*), he affirmed, can by no means dispense with passions, burdens, and evils. He points out how, when the Romans were growing rather weary of war, they tried to win new strength by hunts, gladiator fights, and persecuting Christians (Nietzsche 1878, I §477).

In *Daybreak*, Nietzsche reflected that the most powerful tide that drives individuals and a people forward is the need for the feeling of power that from time to time gushes out of ever-flowing wells, not only in the souls of princes and the powerful, but right in the humbler classes of the people. Over and over, the hour comes, he says, when the masses are ready to place their lives, their resources, their consciences, their virtue on the line in order to procure for themselves that highest pleasure, and as a victorious, tyrannical capricious nation rule, or think it is ruling, over other nations. Then extravagant, sacrificing, hopeful, trusting, over-daring fantastic feelings well up in profusion (Nietzsche 1881, §189).

Of his own "view of the destiny which few have the iron nerve and masculine force to bear," the German World War I soldier of Ernst Jünger's *Copse 125* wrote:

> Time works with heavy tools, and in the battle for some slag-heap of horror, over whose wreathed smoke rival conceptions of the world's future are locked in demoniac strife, it is not a question of the few thousand men who may perhaps be rescued from destruction, but of the dozen or two survivors who are there in the nick of time to turn the scales with their machine-guns or their bombs. . . . Though few may emerge from these flaming plains that offer no shelter but the mettle in a man's own heart. . . . a gain will be scored that can never be scored out. . . . And so I see in old Europe a new and commanding breed rising up, fearless and fabulous, unsparing of blood and sparing of pity, inured to suffering the worst and to inflicting it and ready to stake all to attain their ends—a race that builds machines and trusts to machines, to whom machines are not soulless iron, but engines of might which it controls with cold

reason and hot blood. This puts a new face on the world. (Jünger 1930, 20–21)

As for Hitler, he said that he greeted the advent of World War I as the fulfillment of long present desires and silently harbored longings of millions. The coming of the war seemed to him like a release from the painful feelings of his youth. He was not ashamed to say that, "overpowered by stormy enthusiasm," he fell down on his knees and thanked Heaven from an overflowing heart for granting him the good fortune of being permitted to live at that time. As he saw it, a "fight for freedom had begun, mightier than the earth had ever seen; for once Destiny had begun its course . . ." (Hitler, 161).

That war, Hitler swore in *Mein Kampf,* was not forced upon the masses. It was desired by the whole people. In their overwhelming majority, the people "had long been weary of the eternally uncertain state of affairs." What people want is what they hope and believe, Hitler explained. "People wanted at length to put an end to the general uncertainty. Only thus can it be understood that more than two million German men and boys thronged to the colors for this hardest of struggles, prepared to defend the flag with the last drop of their blood." "For the last time in many years the people had a prophetic vision of its own future. Thus, right at the beginning of the gigantic struggle the necessary grave undertone entered into the ecstasy of an overflowing enthusiasm" (Hitler, 161–62).

When World War I broke out, Hitler's heart, he said, like that of a million others, overflowed with proud joy that at last he would be able to redeem himself from that paralyzing feeling that he had not proved at least once by deeds the truth and steadfastness of his convictions. He recalled how it seemed to him almost a belated act of grace to be allowed to stand as a witness in the divine court of the eternal judge and proclaim the sincerity of his convictions. From the first hour he was convinced that in case of war he would at once leave his books (Hitler, 163).

It was with trembling hands, Hitler recalled, that he opened his summons to serve in a Bavarian regiment. His joy and gratitude knew no bounds as he was to begin the greatest and most unforgettable time of his earthly existence. Compared to this gigantic struggle, he said, everything past seemed to him to recede to shallow nothingness. But a single worry tormented him at the time. Like so many others, he was afraid that he would reach the front too late. Time and time again this alone banished his calm. So it was that a slight drop of bitterness was concealed in every opportunity to rejoice over a new heroic victory, for every new victory seemed to increase the danger of arriving too late to take part in the action (Hitler, 163–64).

Ernst Jünger expressed kindred sentiments about the "irresistible attraction" that had led his contemporaries into the war. "When I joined up, the thought of all that lay hidden in the darkness of the future rejoiced me as indeed it did every other young fellow in those days," wrote the soldier of *Copse 125*. "We knew already that an experience awaited us whose imprint on our development would be sharp and deep. . . . We had seen the generation before us grow old in security, and it seemed a wonderful dream to be permitted to fight as soldiers. . . . All of military age, to a man, thronged to the colours, eager to show by deeds that they were ready for the task their times laid upon them and that their country might rely upon them" (Jünger 1930, vii).

In *Storm of Steel*, Jünger writes: "We had all grown up in a material age, and in each one of us there was the yearning for great experience, such as we had never known. The war had entered us like wine. We had set out in a rain of flowers to seek the death of heroes. The war was our dream of greatness, power, and glory. It was a man's work, a duel on fields whose flowers would be stained with blood" (Jünger 1929, 1).

"The horrible," Jünger wrote, "was undoubtedly a part of that irresistible attraction that drew us into the war. A long period of law and order, such as our generation had behind it, produces a real craving for the abnormal, a craving that literature stimulates. Among other questions that occupied us was this: what does it look like when there are dead lying about?" (Jünger 1929, 23)[1]

Wilfred Owen, English poet and soldier who died in the conflict, left poignant descriptions of what it looked like when there dead lying about on the battlefield.

"The Show" by Wilfred Owen (1893–1918)

We have fallen in the dreams the ever-living
Breathe on the tarnished mirror of the world,
And then smooth out with ivory hands and sigh.

W. B. Yeats

My soul looked down from a vague height with Death,
As unremembering how I rose or why,
And saw a sad land, weak with sweats of dearth,
Gray, cratered like the moon with hollow woe,

---

[1] Actually there is no dearth of evidence to corroborate of Hitler's recollections of the general enthusiasm that accompanied the outbreak of World War I. See, for example, Zweig 1964; Russell 1968; Reid 1986; Monk 1990; Monk 1996; Dillard 1947.

And pitted with great pocks and scabs of plagues.
Across its beard, that horror of harsh wire,
There move thin caterpillars, slowly uncoiled.
It seemed they pushed themselves to be as plugs
Of ditches, where they writhed and shrivelled, killed.
By them had slimy paths been trailed and scraped
Round myriad warts that might be little hills.
From gloom's last dregs these long-strung creatures crept,
And vanished out of dawn down hidden holes.
(And smell came up from those foul openings
As out of mouths, or deep wounds deepening.)
On dithering feet upgathered, more and more,
Brown strings, towards strings of gray, with bristling spines,
All migrants from green fields, intent on mire.
Those that were gray, of more abundant spawns,
Ramped on the rest and ate them and were eaten.
I saw their bitten backs curve, loop, and straighten,
I watched those agonies curl, lift, and flatten.
Whereat, in terror what that sight might mean,
I reeled and shivered earthward like a feather.
And Death fell with me, like a deepening moan.
And He, picking a manner of worm, which half had hid
Its bruises in the earth, but crawled no further,
Showed me its feet, the feet of many men,
And the fresh-severed head of it, my head.

Horror Replaces the Romance of Battle

Hitler left for the front. After marching in silence, one damp, cold night in Flanders, daylight began to emerge from the mists and "an iron greeting" suddenly came whizzing at them over their heads. With a sharp report little pellets went flying through their ranks and "from two hundred throats the first hurrah rose to meet the first messenger of death. Then a crackling and a roaring, a singing and a howling began, and with feverish eyes each one of us was drawn forward, faster and faster, until suddenly past turnip fields and hedges the fight began, the fight of man against man. . . . and . . . Death 'plunged a busy hand' into our ranks" (Hitler, 164–65).

When they came back four days later, Hitler noticed that they had aged and even their gait had changed. Things went on like that year after year, he recalled, but the romance of battle had been replaced by horror. The enthusiasm grad-ually cooled and the exuberant joy was stifled by mortal fear. . . . every man had to struggle between the instinct of self-preservation and the admonitions of duty. . . . Always when Death was on the hunt, a vague something tried to revolt, strove to represent itself to the weak body as reason, yet it was only cow-ardice, which in such disguises tried to ensnare the individual. (Hitler, 165)

While during the first days, he had brimmed over with rejoicing and laugh-ter, he now found himself calm and determined. The entire army issued old and hard from the endless battles, and those who could not stand up under the storm were broken (Hitler, 165).

Jünger too related how "so mysterious, and so impersonal" the war had showed "its claws and torn off its pleasant mask" (Jünger 1929, 3). The soldier of *Storm of Steel* recounts how his "attention was caught by a sickly smell and a bundle hanging on a wire. . . . The putrid flesh, like the flesh of fishes, gleamed greenish-white through the rents in the uniform." Then he "started back in horror" as he saw a "figure cowered beside a tree. . . . Empty eye-sockets and the few wisps of hair on the black and weathered skull" told him that this was "no living man. Another sat with the upper part of the body clapped down over the legs as though broken through the middle. All round lay dozens of corpses putrefied, calcined, mummified, fixed in a ghastly dance of death" (Jünger 1929, 21–22). The soldier con-fessed that he had

> never for a moment dreamt that in this war the dead would be left month after month to the mercy of wind and weather, as once the bodies on the gallows were. And now at our first glance of horror we had a feeling that is difficult to describe. Seeing and recognizing something are matters, really, of habit. In the case of something quite unknown the eye alone can make nothing of it. . . . We looked at all these dead with dislocated limbs, distorted faces, and the hideous colours of decay, as though we walked in a dream through a garden full of strange plants, and we could not realize at first what we had all round us. (Jünger 1929, 23)

"What," he asked, "was a man's life in this wilderness whose vapour was laden with the stench of thousands upon thousands of decaying bodies?" (Jünger 1929, 109).

Though World War I did succeed to a considerable degree in satisfy-ing an urge for the destruction of European civilization, it failed, as is well known, to have the energizing effect that many hoped and expected it would. Adolf Hitler was among those dissatisfied by its outcome. In his estimation, by draining the extreme of the best humanity almost entirely of its blood, four and a half years of bloody warfare had disturbed the inner balance of society. As he saw it, "the year 1914 set up whole armies of so-called volunteers who, thanks to the criminal unscrupulousness of . . . parliamentary good-for-nothings . . . became helpless cannon fodder at the mercy of the enemy." Those who did not fall were either shot to pieces and crippled, or they gradually crumbled away as a result of their small remaining number (Hitler, 520–21). In his estimation, the four hundred thousand soldiers who had fallen or were maimed in Flanders were irreplaceable:

> By their loss the scale, too lightly weighted on the good side, shot upward, and the elements of baseness, treachery, cowardice, in short the mass of the bad extreme, weighed more heavily than before . . . Not only . . . the extreme of the best had been most frightfully thinned on the battlefields in the course of the war, but the bad extreme had meanwhile preserved itself in the most miraculous way. . . . And so the end of the War gives us the following picture: The middle broad stratum of the nation has given its measure of blood sacrifices; the extreme of the best, with exemplary heroism, has sacrificed itself almost completely; the extreme of the bad . . . has unfortunately been preserved almost completely. This well-preserved scum, deserters, pimps, and other rabble of our people then made the revolution and was able to make it only because no longer opposed by the extreme of the best elements who were no longer among the living. (Hitler, 520–22)

The "Hidden Power of Evil" Released

In the wake of World War II, Carl Jung analyzed how it seemed to him that in the early part of the twentieth century a subterranean world of pathological fantasies disguised as ideas could be made to emerge from the depths to become a political power in Europe that changed the course of history.

In "After the Catastrophe," Jung wrote of how there were "symptoms of the mental change taking place in Europe" even before World War I. "The medieval picture of the world," he explained, "was breaking up and the metaphysical authority that ruled it was fast disappearing, only to reappear in man. Did not," Jung asked, "Nietzsche announce that God was dead and that his heir was the Superman, that doomed rope-dancer and fool?" (Jung 1945, 196–97). In "The Fight with the Shadow," Jung told of his conviction that World War I had "released the hidden power of evil, just as the war itself was released by the accumulation of unconscious masses and their blind desires." He saw Kaiser Wilhelm as "one of the first victims," as someone who "not unlike Hitler . . . voiced these lawless, chaotic desires and was thus led into war, and into the inevitable catastrophe." Jung viewed World War II as a "repetition of the same psychic process but on an infinitely greater scale" (Jung 1946, 177).

In the wake of World War I, Jung recalled, he had witnessed peculiar disturbances, an "uprush of darkness" deploying itself in the unconscious of every single one of his German patients. He ascribed this, not to their personal psychology, but to a disturbance of the collective unconscious. The archetypes, or typical modes or forms in which the collective phenomena he was observing "expressed primitivity, violence, and cruelty: in short, all the powers of darkness." Jung told of how he watched as those forces "broke through the individual's moral and intellectual self-control, and as they flooded his conscious world." After encountering a number of such cases, he turned his attention to the peculiar state of mind then prevailing in Germany. He could only see "signs of depression and a great restlessness." At the time, he suggested "that the 'blonde beast' was stirring in an uneasy slumber and that an outburst was not impossible" (Jung 1946, 174–76).

Jung "was fully aware of the immense dangers involved when such people crowd together." "When such symbols occur in a large number of individuals and are not understood," Jung explained, "they begin to draw these individuals together as if by a magnetic force, and thus a mob is formed. Its leader will soon be found in the individual who has the least resistance, the least sense of responsibility and, because of his inferiority, the greatest will to power. He will let loose everything that is ready to burst forth, and the mob will follow with the irresistible force of an avalanche." He saw the Germans as having a marked proneness to mass psychology and that defeat and social disaster had increased the herd instinct in Germany making it vulnerable to becoming a "victim of a mass movement brought about by an upheaval of forces lying dormant in the unconscious, ready to break through all moral barriers" (Jung 1946, 175).

He considered that "the uprush of mass instincts was symptomatic of a compensatory move of the unconscious . . . because the conscious state of the people had become estranged from the natural laws of human existence." Industrialization had uprooted vast segments of the population and herded people together in large centers. Jung considered that this "new form of existence—with its mass psychology and social dependence on the fluctuation of markets and wages—produced an individual who was unstable, insecure, and suggestible." People were aware that their lives were dependent on boards of directors and captains of industry and rightly or wrongly presumed that the latter were chiefly motivated by financial interests. There was a feeling that no matter how conscientiously one worked, one could fall prey to economic changes beyond one's control. And there was nothing else upon which people could rely. In addition to this, "the system of moral and political education prevailing in Germany had already done its utmost to permeate everybody with a spirit of dull obedience, with the belief that every desirable thing must come from above, from those who by divine decree sat on top of the law-abiding citizen, whose feelings of personal responsibility were overruled by a rigid sense of duty" (Jung 1946, 177). People's

> feeling of weakness, indeed of non-existence, was thus compensated by the eruption of hitherto unknown desires for power. It was the revolt of the powerless, the insatiable greed of the 'have-nots.' By such devious means the unconscious compels man to become conscious of himself. Unfortunately, there were no values in the conscious mind of the individual which would have enabled him to understand and integrate the reaction when it reached consciousness. Nothing but materialism was preached by the highest intellectual authorities. The Churches were evidently unable to cope with this new situation; they could do nothing but protest and that did not help very much. Thus the avalanche rolled on in Germany and produced its leader, who was elected as a tool to complete the ruin of the nation. (Jung 1946, 177)

"Long before 1933," Jung recalled in "After the Catastrophe," "there was a smell of burning in the air, and people were passionately interested in discovering the locus of the fire and in tracking down the incendiary. And when denser clouds of smoke were seen to gather over Germany, and the burning of the Reichstag gave the signal then at last there was no mistake where the incendiary, evil in person, dwelt. . . . the esteemed public had not the faintest idea how closely they themselves were living to evil" (Jung 1945, 185).

Expressing Primitivity, Violence, and Cruelty

Nietzsche advocated a transvaluation of values according to which what conventional morality considered to be evil should be viewed as being good. One step in the direction of realizing that reversal of values would be to begin to show vilified evils in a new and appealing light, an undertaking that Nietzsche also advocated and in which he energetically engaged. An example of this is to be found in what he had to say in praise of cruelty, something commonly condemned as being decidedly evil.

Cruelty, Nietzsche announced in *Daybreak*, "is one of mankind's oldest festive joys" (Nietzsche 1881, §18). In *On the Genealogy of Morals*, he went into greater detail about what he meant about the festive nature of cruelty. He lamented the fact that having any robust sense of the extent to which cruelty was an occasion of joyous celebration for people of other times and an ingredient mixed in with all their pleasures, of how naively and innocently their need for cruelty appeared, of how fundamentally they understood this disinterested evil to be a normal human characteristic and thus something to which their consciences heartily gave assent, all went against the grain of the sensibilities, and even more so of the hypocrisy, of the docile domestic animals that modern human beings had become (Nietzsche 1887, II §§6, 7).

Rather than unabashed pleasure in cruelty, Nietzsche perceived antipathy to suffering among his contemporaries. Much to his regret, he saw them even thinking of suffering as presenting the primary argument against existence, as raising the most difficult questions concerning it. He suggested it would do them good to recall the times when people thought the contrary because they did not want to give up making people suffer and found it highly fascinating and a genuine enticement to live (Nietzsche 1887, II §7).

Nietzsche felt that, however distressing affirmations about enjoying cruelty might be to modern pessimists, witness should expressly be borne to the fact that in times when people were not yet ashamed of their cruelty, life on earth was merrier than in his day. The weary, pessimistic look, distrust before the riddle of life, the icy no of the aversion to life, Nietzsche contended, were not characteristic of the most evil periods of the human race, but rather first surfaced when pampering and moralizing taught human beasts to be ashamed of all their instincts (Nietzsche 1887, II §7).

Nietzsche also set about to illustrate his convictions about the pleasure and gratification that comes with seeing and causing suffering. His reading of human history furnished him with a number of specific examples of the enjoyment of cruelty by people of other times. As one example, he named the ancient Greeks who, according to him, knew no more pleasing way to add to the happiness of the gods than to offer them the joys of cruelty. There was no doubt, he said, that the Trojan War and other tragic horrors were ultimately intended as festival performances for the gods. In another passage, he reminisced about the times when princely weddings or great popular celebrations were unthinkable without executions, acts of torture, or burning people at the stake, and when no noble household was without beings upon whom one could unhesitatingly vent one's evil and one's cruel ridicule (Nietzsche 1887, II §§6, 7).

While realizing that it was a harsh statement to make, Nietzsche was prepared to affirm that "seeing suffering does one good and causing suffering even more so" and to defend that pronouncement as the expression of one of the chief, "old, powerful, human all too human" principles. According to his theories, in the most evil times, human beasts were not ashamed of their instincts, were not repulsed by their animal innocence. He even went on to suggest that the apes would have perhaps subscribed to it as well, for it had been said that in devising bizarre forms of cruelty the apes had already amply heralded the coming of human beings and were, so to speak, a prelude to them. No cruelty, no celebration. That is, Nietzsche said, what the oldest, longest history of mankind teaches. There is so much that is *festive* about punishment, he enthused. There is so much that is festive about *punishment*, he repeats a few pages later with a change of emphasis (Nietzsche 1887, II §§6, 7).

In *Daybreak*, Nietzsche asked what the supreme form of enjoyment was for people in a state of war of that small, constantly endangered community where the strictest morality prevails,—thus for powerful, revengeful, hostile, malicious, distrustful souls ready for the most horrible things and hardened by want and morality. His answer was that it was the "enjoyment of *cruelty*," just as it is also reckoned a virtue in a soul to be inventive and insatiable in cruelty under such circumstances. In the act of cruelty the community refreshes itself and casts off the gloominess of constant fear and circumspection, he said (Nietzsche 1881, §18).

Many Nazi SS-men would fit Nietzsche's description of hardened, powerful, revengeful, hostile, malicious, distrustful people ready for the most horrible things and inventive and insatiable in cruelty. In his memoirs, Commandant of Auschwitz Rudolf Hoess recalled in that there were "plenty of SS-men among the troops who regarded the sight of corporal punishment being inflicted as an excellent spectacle, a kind of peasant merry-making" (Hoess, 70). More than enough accounts of such "merry-making" on the part of SS-men and others of their ilk have survived to bear that out.

In *Rue de la Liberté*, the memoirs of his time in Dachau, Edmond Michelet recalled one of the spectacles of cruelty that Hitler's SS-men forced him and fellow captives to witness. Arrested for resistance activities, Michelet was first sent to a camp, which he describes as a sort of quadrilater of lugubrious barracks set up around a basin of water.

Upon arrival at the camp, all the prisoners were invited to line up. After entertaining them with a speech designed to sharpen their awareness of the new existence awaiting them, an SS-man announced that they were then going to see just how one treats the dirty pig Jews responsible for the war in the great Germany of Adolf Hitler. The six or seven Jews of the convoy were then ordered to step forward. For sixteen consecutive hours, from six in the morning until ten at night, they were then forced to engage, without respite, in the humiliating, painful disciplinary exercise called "leap frog," which consisted of jumping forward with their legs bent and their hands crossed behind their necks, the sun beating down mercilessly on their shaved heads.

When one of the leap-froggers could not go on any longer, an SS-man would first hit him with a rubber nightstick to make him stand up again and then send him with a good kick to finish reviving in the basin of water around which the "merry-making" was taking place. Once the patient was back on the road to recovery, in a sugary voice the interpreter would remind the Aryans, obliged to stand still at attention and watch this spectacle, which fatigue and the heat had made hallucinating, that any of them who felt like objecting to the treatment that they were witnessing always had a perfect right to go and join the leap-froggers.

When night finally fell, the prisoners had to carry the inert bodies of the two youngest leap-froggers into the block on improvised stretchers and deposit them on the wooden platforms that served as beds. They had been out of the running for several hours and, sated by the spectacle, the SS-men had abandoned them, inanimate at the edge of the basin. Convinced that their fellow prisoners would never regain consciousness after such an ordeal, their companions were all gripped with rage and dead tired. They gobbled down their potatoes without even having the energy to peel them and went to bed on bare boards provided for the purpose (Michelet, 50–54).

In *Himmler: Reichsführer-S.S.*, Padfield preserved Maurice Lampe's description of the execution of forty-seven British, American, and Dutch pilots at Mauthausen concentration camp. According to Lampe's account, the pilots were first forced to undress and then assemble in front of the camp office shoeless and wearing only a shirt and underpants. The Kommandant then informed them that they had all been sentenced to death. As Lampe recalled:

> at the bottom of the steps they loaded stones on the backs of these poor men and they had to carry them to the top. The first journey was made with stones weighing 25 to 30 kilos and was accompanied by blows. Then they were made to run down. For the second journey the stones were still heavier; and whenever the poor wretches sank under their burden, they were kicked and hit with a bludgeon. Even stones were hurled at them. . . . In the evening . . . the road which led to the camp was a bath of blood . . . I almost stepped on the lower jaw of a man. Twenty-one bodies were strewn along the road. Twenty-one had died on the first day. The twenty-six others died the following morning. (Padfield, 435)

Mullisch's book of essays on the Eichmann trial lists a string of cruel spectacles: children playing in the street, all of a sudden accosted by SS-men and thrown into trucks, piled by thousands into freight trains and sent to gas chambers. . . . sick children thrown from the fourth floor of a hospital. . . . babies torn to pieces like bits of cloth before their mothers' eyes . . . neighborhoods chosen at random, surrounded, starved, and finally set afire . . . inhabitants who jumped out the windows and with crushed limbs crawled along the road to the laughter of soldiers who throw them into the fire to finish them off . . . churches filled with worshippers set afire . . . elderly priests forced to race carrying people on their backs . . . elderly women cleaning a square with toothbrushes . . . orchestras playing lively music while thousands of completely naked families were executed . . . an old lady with hair as white as snow holding a child in her arms and singing songs and tickling it . . . the child laughing with pleasure . . . the couple looking at them with tear-filled eyes . . . the father taking a ten year old boy by the hand, speaking softly to him . . . the child trying not to cry . . . the father pointing to the sky, patting his head and seeming to explain something to him before the order is given . . . dogs rewarded by a bit of sugar for having torn a bit of thigh from a little girl . . . mountains of cadavers, mountains of shoes, mountains of eyeglasses, mountains of artificial limbs, barns filled with women's hair, pails full of gold teeth, fields covered with skulls and bones . . . people sprinkled with water in the middle of winter and left to freeze . . . people killed by injection and cooked in big pots to show their bodies in museums . . . others who ate them . . . people eating long black cadavers . . . a man having to choose whether to have his wife or his mother shot, or else the two would be shot . . . torture and executions in cellars in the heart of towns . . . gas chambers filled with naked people so crushed together that they have to raise the arms in which they are holding children . . . a man forced to sort through a mountain of cadavers who finds the body of his daughter, then that of his father, and finally that of his wife (Mullisch, 139–41).

Evaluating Nietzsche's arguments for the revaluation of cruelty in light of real scenes of cruelty, some will surely be tempted to cry out: "Machine, blind and mute, prolific in cruelty! Instrument of salvation, drinker of the blood of the world, how is it that you are not ashamed and how is it that you have not seen your allurement pale in every mirror? Has not the magnitude of this evil you believe yourself skilled at ever made you draw back in terror when, great in her hidden designs, nature uses you . . . ?" (Baudelaire 1857, XXV).

The Use of Terror

Hitler told of how he achieved an understanding of the method and importance of both psychological and physical terror toward the individual and the masses. It was during his first encounters with Social Democrats when employed as a building worker, he said, that he came to understand the "infamous" psychological terror exerted by this movement and came to the realization that "based on precise calculations of all human weaknesses," it would "lead to success with almost mathematical certainty unless the opposing side learns to combat poison gas with poison gas" (Hitler, 43–44).

Hitler recalled how, while drinking his bottle of milk and eating his piece bread off to one side during lunchtime, he cautiously studied his coworkers, or reflected on his own miserable lot. He remembers how infuriated he felt as he heard everything,—capitalism, the nation, classes, the

fatherland, the bourgeoisie, the authority of law, school, religion, morality—"drawn through the mud of a terrifying depth" and how he engaged
in heated discussions with the Social Democrats, "until one day they made
use of the weapon which most readily conquers reason: terror and violence." They forced him "either to leave the building at once or be thrown
off the scaffolding." Since he "was alone and resistance seemed hopeless,"
he chose the former alternative. However, "Poverty" soon enfolded him
"in her heartless arms" and finally forced him to return to work whether
he liked it or not. He acknowledged that the more familiar, he became
with the methods of physical terror, the more indulgent he grew toward
all the hundreds of thousands who succumb to it (Hitler, 39–44).

After two years of "reflection and cogitation" on the inner nature of
the Social Democratic thought processes and the inner causes of its successes, Hitler said, both the theory and the technical methods of Social
Democracy became clear to him. He observed how, "at a given sign," it
"unleashes a veritable barrage of lies and slanders against whatever adversary seems most dangerous, until the nerves of the attacked persons break
down and, just to have peace again, they sacrifice the hated individual.
However, the fools obtain no peace. The game begins again and is
repeated over and over until fear of the mad dog results in suggestive paralysis" (Hitler, 41–43).

Hitler found that, conscious of the value of force from their own experience, the Social Democrats reserved their most violent attacks for people "in whose nature they detect any of this substance which is so rare."
On the other hand, he found them enthusiastically commending every
weakling "in both mind and force" in the opposition. Hitler found Social
Democrats to be aware of how to create the illusion that this was the only
way to preserve peace, while all the time, "stealthily but steadily" conquering "one position after another, sometimes by silent blackmail, sometimes by actual theft." He said that he came to see that, not being
receptive to anything that is half-hearted and weak, and unaware of the
shameless psychological terrorization being exercised on them, the psyche
of the great masses only sees "the ruthless force and brutality of its calculated manifestations, to which they always submit in the end."
Nonetheless, he felt certain that, though it may require the bitterest
struggle, if opposed by a doctrine of greater truth, but equal brutality of
methods, Social Democracy could be vanquished. He saw it as his "duty
to inform all weaklings that this is a question of to be or not to be"
(Hitler, 41–44).

*"Terror at the place of employment, in the factory, in the meeting hall, and
on the occasion of mass demonstrations will always be successful unless opposed
by equal terror,"* Hitler emphasized. He believed that the impression that
the successful use of terror made on the minds of both supporters and

adversaries could only be measured by those who had come to know the soul of a people from life, and not from books, for while the great masses of supporters judge the success as a victory of the justice of their own cause, in most cases, the defeated opponents despair of the success of any further resistance. Hitler saw this as being another area in which the psychological impact could be precisely calculated (Hitler, 44).

Hitler taught that the very first requirement for struggling with the "weapons of naked force" is, and remains, persistence, that "only the continuous and steady application of the methods for repressing a doctrine, etc., makes it possible for a plan to succeed. . . . Only in the steady and constant application of force lies the very first prerequisite for success." The persistence needed, he further considered, could "always and only arise from a definite spiritual conviction. Any violence which does not spring from a firm, spiritual base, will be wavering and uncertain. It lacks the stability which can only rest in a fanatical outlook. It emanates from the momentary energy and brutal determination of an individual, and is therefore subject to the change of personalities and to their nature and strength" (Hitler, 171).

A Satisfied Torturer

In *Mon Cœur mis à nu* (XII), Baudelaire identified cruelty and sensual pleasure. As an art for discovering the truth, he reflected, torture is barbarous silliness. It is applying a material means to a spiritual goal. Torture, he jotted down, "is born from the foul part of the heart of people, thirst for sensual pleasure. Cruelty and sensual pleasure, identical sensations, like extreme cold and extreme cold" (Baudelaire 1949, 63). However, this was the same poet who at the same time believed in what he called a "satanic side to love" and twice professed to believe that love strongly resembled torture or a surgical operation. "The sole, supreme sensual pleasure of love," he claimed, "lies in the certitude of doing *evil.—*And men and women know from birth that in evil all sensual pleasure is found" (Baudelaire 1949, 10–11; 24–25).

In *Services Spéciaux, Algérie 1955–1957*, France's General Aussaresses successfully conveyed the pleasure torturing can represent for a soul inventive and insatiable in cruelty. The opportunity that he had had to engage in torture during the Algerian war was apparently a quite welcome one for Aussaresses, who obviously relishes relating his experiences. His book offers a unique opportunity to enter the mind of a contented torturer (Aussaresses 2001).

In an interview granted to Florence Beaugé in May 2001, General Aussaresses acknowledged that a life counts very little for him, his own no more than that of others. He was tough with his adversaries, he admitted, but was so first of all with himself. He said that he had to admit that he and his henchmen were a death squad. To the question as to whether that raised problems for his conscience he said that he had to admit that it did not, that he had grown accustomed to all that (Beaugé, 6).

It is not hard to see General Aussaresses as a hardy soul in Baudelaire's sense, one pleased that rape, poison, the dagger, fire had embroidered the most agreeable designs on what might have otherwise been the banal destiny of a family man and classicist. If ever one has been in the secret services, Aussaresses assured readers, everything one does afterward has the flavor of mystery. He said that he knew that in opting for a career in special services he would clandestinely steal, assassinate, vandalize, terrorize, perform actions condemned by ordinary morality, often punishable by the law, and for this reason clothed in secrecy. He was trained to pick locks, to kill without leaving traces, to lie, to be indifferent to his own suffering and that of others, to forget, and have himself be forgotten. Given his chosen profession, he had killed and engaged in nerve-racking activities. He had often thought that he would be tortured one day, but before the Algerian war he had not imagined that he would one day torture people. For him the army and his work in special services was in service of an ideal. He and his henchmen had the quality most important in his eyes, patriotism (Aussaresses 2001, 14–15, 29, 94; Beaugé, 6).

When General Aussaresses arrived in Algeria, many boats had inexplicably sunk. Many people had fallen sick in bizarre ways, or had had sudden urges to commit suicide. The Algerian police confided in him in plain terms the critical nature of the situation and the dangers threatening the city. These men, who Aussaresses describes as "neither monsters, nor brutes, but ordinary men, people devoted to their country, with a profound sense of duty, but put in exceptional circumstances," made no secret of the methods that they were obliged to use given the paltry resources at their disposal. They operated according to the principle that when one "had to interrogate a person who had, even for the sake of an ideal, shed innocent blood, torture became legitimate if there were urgent reasons for it" (Aussaresses 2001, 16, 31).

In no time, Aussaresses was convinced that the circumstances explained and justified the methods they used (Aussaresses 2001, 28, 30). He says that he found one of their arguments particularly convincing. It ran:

> Imagine for a moment that you are in principle opposed to torture and that you arrest someone obviously involved in preparing an attack. The suspect refuses to talk. You don't force the issue. Then the attack occurs and it is particularly deadly. What would you say to the families of the victims, to the parents of a

child, for example, cut to pieces by the bomb, to justify the fact that you had not done everything you could to make the suspect talk? (Aussaresses 2001, 31–32).

If Aussaresses always conducted himself as if he were in that situation, the police advised, he would definitely see whether it was harder to torture a presumed terrorist or to explain to the families that it is better to let dozens of innocents die rather than make a single guilty person suffer. After giving brief thought to this argument, he said, any scruples he had had vanished. He concluded from it that no one would ever have the right to judge their actions and that even if his job led him to engage in some very unpleasant activities, he should never have any regrets. In his book, he speculates that if some of the idealists in France who were opposed to torture ever had to make terrorists talk, they might themselves become the most zealous of inquisitors (Aussaresses 2001, 31–32).

Without qualms, the police showed Aussaresses the techniques used for "thorough" interrogation. First there were the beatings, which often sufficed, then the other means, electrodes applied to the ears or testicles, water torture. The last technique was the most dangerous for the prisoner. It rarely lasted more than an hour and consisted of tying the suspect's hands behind his back and forcing a water hose into his mouth. If the suspect refused to talk, a handkerchief was placed on his face and watered to prevent air from passing. Out of fear of these techniques, or owing to them, prisoners gave him very detailed information and names with which he could proceed with new arrests (Aussaresses 2001, 33–34).

Aussaresses rapidly acquired the names of suspects undeniably involved in the bloodiest of crimes, and when they were arrested, he did not find them to be heroes, but just mere brutes. Once the suspects had talked, he killed them if they had links with terrorist activities. The first man that Aussaresses tortured had split open the head of a French Algerian that he knew well with an ax. Aussaresses tortured him in order to find out whether seven bombs that had exploded that day had been the work of an organization and who the members were. The torture proved useless. The man died without talking. Aussaresses says that he did not think of anything. He was not sorry about the death. He was only sorry that the man had not talked before dying. The man had used violence against a person who was not his enemy (Aussaresses 2001, 33, 34, 44–45, 156).

The experience of an attack on Europeans who worked with Algerians in a mine confirmed Aussaresses's views on torture. He recalls that what had been done to the Europeans was beyond imagining. They found thirty-five bodies. Fifteen people were wounded and two had vanished. Aussaresses says that when he saw the children cut to pieces, throats slit or crushed, women disemboweled or decapitated, he says that he thinks that he forgot what pity was. The most incredible thing for him was that these people had been massacred and mutilated by Moslem neighbors with whom they had often been on good terms. Aussaresses remembered the sight of the priests coming back in tears from the mine. He had to supply them with whisky for them to return to gather the bits of children in the hope of piecing the bodies together on sheets (Aussaresses 2001, 64, 158).

Aussaresses' next assignment was in Algiers where the principal leaders of the organization they were combating had their base of operations in the Casbah. He had been deemed the right man for the job of liquidating the organization. He was to do it quickly and resort to whatever methods were necessary (Aussaresses 2001, 97). Soon, he was made privy to a plot supposedly being hatched by a group of the most influential French Algerians who were growing determined to take the law into their own hands if the legal system continued to prove incapable of handling the situation. These influential people wanted to begin by doing something spectacular. The Casbah was on a hill. At the top was a broad avenue. They were planning to form a convoy of trucks of combustible fuel. The first truck would stop and the convoy would close ranks. Then they would open the sluice gates to the cisterns and once the combustible fuel had flooded the Casbah, they would set it afire. It was estimated that seventy thousand people would die. The French Algerians in question, Aussaresses was assured, were not kidding. He would have to be pitiless, which would meant torture and extra-judicial executions,—not of the influential French Algerians ostensibly seriously plotting to kill tens of thousands of innocent people, but of members of the opposition (Aussaresses 2001, 97–100).

Aussaresses said that the very thought of such a massacre of innocent people in the Casbah vanquished any feeling of reticence that he might have otherwise had and he made up his mind to do his best, no matter what. It was his role to relieve people of the most unpleasant jobs and to cover up their own deeds. He proceeded to draw up lists of suspects, organize arrests, oversee interrogations and executions. People often denounced others to him out of personal spite. Women denounced their husbands in exchange for a guarantee of widowhood (Aussaresses 2001, 100, 115–20, 145, 146).

The torturers quickly found a big, abandoned two-story house with a cellar. It had four rooms on each floor, was surrounded by a garden, and located in an isolated area with no neighbors to disturb them. At sundown, they would dress in camouflage and the cavalcade would begin. The team would go out at eight o'clock and do their best to return before midnight with around a half dozen suspects to proceed with the interrogation. They had enough to keep them busy and the night was over in no time at all. Most of those arrested were interrogated; others were purely and simply liquidated on the spot. Torture was systematically used if the prisoner refused to talk, which was often. It was rare for prisoners interrogated during the night to be still alive in the morning. Whether they talked or not, they were generally neutralized. All those brought to the house were considered sufficiently dangerous that they could not be allowed to survive. Most of the time his men went out and machine-gunned the suspects, then buried them. The executions were often attributed to failed attempts to escape. No one ever asked Aussaresses to kill any one in particular. It was something that was taken for granted (Aussaresses 2001, 144–47, 153, 155).

To his more scrupulous superior who would have preferred to see him resort to "cleaner" methods more in keeping with humanistic traditions, Aussaresses explained that his work obliged him to think not in terms of morality, but of effectiveness. The justice system, he said, did not want to have anything to do with the prisoners because there were too many of them, they did not know where to put them, and could not guillotine hundreds of people. According to Aussaresses's calculations more than twenty thousand people, three percent of the population of the Algiers area, far more people than could ever be tried in a court of law, were imprisoned at one time or another in the main prisoner camp (Aussaresses 2001, 35, 153–54).

Massacre

Surely one of the most iniquitous and revealing forms of evil is when its most savage blows are reserved for categories of people who could not rationally be considered an enemy of those victimizing them. Numerous victims of more than a decade of bloody massacres of innocent Moslems carried out in Algeria in the name of Islam fit that description. It is estimated that during the 1990s these massacres killed approximately two hundred thousand people, displaced a million others, caused twenty billion dollars of damage, and created tens of thousands of exiles.[2]

In the early 1990s, the cancellation of the second round of the legislative elections after the democratically elected Islamic Salvation Front won 188 of the seats (leaving 15 and 25 seats respectively to the two other parties) brought a budding democratic process to a halt in Algeria. The president was forced to resign. The victorious party was dissolved. Its leaders, activists, and sympathizers were incarcerated, subjected to tough interro-

---

[2] The facts and figures cited in this section were collected from articles published in the French press.

gation, deported to camps in the midst of the desert. Many Algerians had voted for the Islamic Salvation Front because it seemed to be espousing noble values, to be led by people of exceptional courage, strong, just, generous people who inspired admiration. They really believed in its beautiful promises, saw the choice being held out to them as one between paradise and hell, and it seemed normal and legitimate for them to choose paradise. The other parties were not perceived as proposing anything concrete.

Islamic fundamentalists reacted to the dissolution of the Islamic Salvation Front by declaring war on Algeria and proceeded to massacre after massacre of the civilian population of Algeria. In the dead of the night, howling hordes of swarthy beasts swept down upon villages to cast themselves upon entire families with sabers, axes, picks, knives, farming implements. Guns blazing and blades flying, these predators rushed from house to house, smashed open the doors, killed the men, encircled the women and children, killed them with axes and left them bathing in pools of blood. Or, men, women, and children were forced to lie down on the ground while their heads were cut off, or their throats slit open, or half open to increase the suffering. Or, mothers were struck with machetes as the predators violently grabbed the small children and threw them against concrete walls, or crushed their heads and trampled them underfoot. Told that it is easy to cut up children because their flesh is tender, the predators sliced babies and small children to pieces. The throats of mere girls were slit because they were not wearing veils. Some victims were burned or blown to pieces by bombs. The predators were known to laugh madly and joke as they killed. Heads were chopped off and mounted on stakes as trophies. Bodies were set afire. To finish the slaughter, the killers turned to attack sheep and cows so as not to leave any animals alive. The hordes would then retreat into the darkness.

Several essays anthologized in Bovy's *Gandhi* are devoted to understanding the nature and causes of the violence in Algeria. In "La symbolique de la violence dans l'imaginaire collectif algérien," (Bovy, 143–49), Naget Khadda emphasizes that the horror did not come about on its own. Before the wave of violence began, ideologists were at work feeding fanaticism, ascribing divine value to the kind of thinking that would lead to slaughter, legitimating the idea that it is acceptable to divide people into categories that make people of certain groups acceptable and others intolerable and, therefore, subject to elimination.

For years, Khadda relates, preachers in Algeria had repeated endlessly that it was necessary to demonstrate fidelity to God by purifying the earth of all infidels. For these Islamic fundamentalists, the heretical secularization of society is a punishment visited upon Moslems precisely because believers have turned away from God. The Islamic fundamentalists came to declare an entire people ungodly and apostate because they did not revolt against a government that those fundamentalists had declared ungodly and apostate. They called for the slaying of all those compromising the sacred pact against that government, of all those not contributing to its eradication, including those who voted for the Islamic Fundamentalist party and later wished to draw away from it because they could not support practices that seemed to them indefensible.

According to Khadda's understanding of the causes of the violence in Algeria, the massacres committed in the name of Islam should be seen within the context of ideas about religious purification. According to the reasoning of the fundamentalists, since secularization is a divine punishment, Moslems must find their way back to God again, must once again make themselves worthy of God's attention by eliminating those who have strayed from Islam. The infidels who have turned away from God can therefore be immolated since, in the eyes of these Islamic "theorists," they are no longer people but animals, trash. It is therefore legitimate to put them to death.

So according to that murderous logic, Khadda explains, violence is not a sin, but a kind of revelation, a divine sign, and even a lesson in the power of God. Those resorting to the violence in Algeria are not ashamed of engaging in it. It is licit. It is the way of expressing fidelity to God. What are commonly considered to be rational values, shared by all, are no longer viewed in the same light, which explains why during the massacres, children, including babies, are not spared. For the killers, the babies are no longer children, but the fruit of sin. The very zealousness with which they are cut to pieces and harmed is itself seen as an act of purification. Girls are carried off and treated like slaves because they are no longer considered human. They may be obliged to walk about naked, in order to keep them from running away, on the one hand, but also to be held up to ridicule, humiliated. One girl told of how she was forbidden to say her prayers because she was considered impure and therefore unworthy to perform pious acts. Everything is to be purified, even the cemeteries, where dead people not deemed worthy to be buried in a Moslem cemetery are to be disinterred.

Destroying One's Own

The Stalinist purges of members of the Communist Party who sincerely and innocently believed in the leaders, system, and ideologies behind the evil perpetrated against them is an example of the particularly iniquitous practice of targeting people who actually share the ideals in whose name they are victimized, of directing one's most savage blows towards groups of people in whose name the savage practices are being carried out. In the case of the Stalinist purges, those who really believed in its ideals of social justice, humanism, solidarity, a worker's paradise, fell under the blows of a system sown with internal contradictions that would one day undermine it in nonviolent ways.

In *Journey into the Whirlwind*, Eugenia Semyonovna Ginzburg describes herself as someone who in 1934 was "an ordinary woman" living "a clean and happy life full of the consciousness of having chosen the right way" and who did not have "a shadow of a doubt of the rightness of the Party line." She says that had she been ordered to die for the Communist Party "not once but three times," she would have obeyed without hesitating in the least. She considered that everything she had in the world—the thousands of books she had read, her memories of a childhood in the dawn of the revolution "such as no one has ever had before or since," her youth and endurance—had all been given to her by the Soviet system and the revolution that had transformed her world as a child (Ginzburg, 3, 138, 227, 233).

Yet, through the reversal of logic that reigned during the Stalinist regime, for which, as she put it, "when you get down to it, there is no difference between 'subjective' and 'objective,'" she was found guilty of being an agent of international imperialism, a member of a secret Trotskyist terrorist counterrevolutionary organization "dedicated to the restoration of capitalism and the physical annihilation of Party and government leaders." She herself was condemned to years of solitary confinement, then to hard labor in Siberia by Stalinist repression that eliminated "whole layers of society," weeded out "enemies of the people" who like her were "orthodox communists," members of the Party machine (Ginzburg, 32, 49, 50, 63, 137, 166, 213, 334, 418).

Also accused of Trotskyist terrorism was a woman called Grandma Nastya, "with her mild, wrinkled old peasant woman's face and her sad childlike eyes." Among her fellow prisoners was "an elderly woman who had all the marks of an impeccable member of the working class. She looked like a washer-woman, with deep-set eyes, a flat chest and a big belly, long thin arms and large hands with prominent veins" who had been charged with having "lived it up with foreigners in elegant restaurants, seduced Soviet diplomats, and wormed secret information out of them" (Ginzburg, 181, 158–59).

Unable to believe that the Soviet system would betray them, fellow prisoners were convinced that saboteurs had infiltrated the government, that they would be unmasked and set free, that if Stalin knew the truth he would not let such things happen to innocent people. Ginzburg herself concluded that the system that saw to her imprisonment was out to destroy, physically exterminate the best people in the Party, out to trick or torture them into signing confessions and papers about their subversive activities and monstrous crimes and so destroy friends, coworkers, family, acquaintances, and themselves as well. She was persuaded that it was the interrogators and judges who were the traitors. She grew accustomed to the idea that everyone that she met who was not a fellow prisoner "had only one aim: to torture and to kill." She saw those carrying out the purge as sadists who had "traveled all the way from the human condition to that of beasts," who believed that "unlike run-of-the-mill corpses, we could still be tortured physically and morally, subtly or crudely, together and separately, by night and by day." At times, she said, she "felt as though some incarnate Evil, almost mystic in its irrationality, were grimacing" at her (Ginzburg, 60, 74, 119, 182, 186, 253, 283, 318).

Decades later, in *Progress, Coexistence, and Intellectual Freedom,* Soviet dissident Andrei Sakharov judged what he called the "anti-people's regime of Stalin" in very harsh terms. He condemned it as "cruel and at the same time dogmatically narrow and blind in its cruelty," a combination "of crime, narrow-mindedness, and short-sightedness." So it was that, to borrow his words, it was "the Soviet people, its most active talented, and honest representatives, who suffered the most terrible blow" during the Stalinist purges. According to the facts available to him in the late 1960s, more than 1.2 million party members, half of the total party membership, had been arrested between 1936 and 1939 alone. Only fifty thousand of them regained freedom. The remainder were tortured during interrogation, or shot, or died in camps (Sakharov, 52–55).

Sakharov saw the "Stalinist dogmatism and isolation from real life" particularly demonstrated "in an almost serflike enslavement of the peasantry, the depriving of peasants of the most simple means of mechanization, and the appointment of collective-farm chairmen on the basis of their cunning and obsequiousness." For Sakharov, the results of this were evident: "a profound and hard-to-correct destruction of the economy and way of life in the countryside, which, by the law of interconnected vessels, damaged industry as well" (Sakharov, 53).

To demonstrate the inhuman nature of Stalinism, Sakharov's book lists some of its misdeeds. Among them figure: the ten to fifteen million people who perished in the torture chambers of the secret police from torture and execution, in camps for exiled rich peasants and so-called semi-rich peasants and members of their families and in camps that were the prototypes of the Fascist death camps in which thousands of prisoners were machine gunned; the repression of prisoners of war who survived Fascist camps who were then thrown into Stalinist camps; the anti-worker "decrees"; the criminal exile of entire peoples condemned to slow death; the unenlightened zoological kind of anti-Semitism characteristic of the Stalinist bureaucracy and Stalin personally; Stalin's Ukrainophobia; the draconian laws for the protection of socialist property that mainly served to fulfill the demands of the "slave market"; the people who died in mines, from freezing, starvation, exhausting labor, at countless construction projects, in cutting timber, building canals, or while being transported in prison trains, or in the overcrowded holds of "death ships"; during the resettlement of entire peoples (Sakharov, 52–54).

Weeding Out People

Years later Mikhail Gorbachev told the same story as seen from his perspective. In his book *On My Country and the World*, he estimated the number of Soviet citizens destroyed or victims of the Gulag system to have been in the millions. Thousands of talented generals and officers of the Soviet army were mowed down by "Stalin's terror." The whole Leninist old guard was virtually destroyed. People were "arrested for nonexistent crimes, unbreakable Bolsheviks, who had many times looked death in the eye while fighting for their ideas . . . ended up broken. They slandered and denounced themselves and their comrades, confessed to being 'enemies of the people,' criminal evildoers!" (Gorbachev, 19, 31).

After the war, Gorbachev recounts, "the system cruelly intensified ideological and political pressures. Millions of people . . . were made victims of repression. A new wave of terror swept the country. Official anti-Semitism was added to the arsenal of government techniques, and a shameful campaign against so-called cosmopolitanism was unleashed. Totalitarianism made use of every means possible, every lever of power, to shield itself from the slightest possible encroachment by the people" (Gorbachev, 31–32). Many "nationalities were subjected to wholesale repression. They were deported from their ancient homelands and resettled in remote parts of the country. Tens of thousands of these people perished in the process" (Gorbachev, 85). "Collectivization and the Gulag together destroyed the human potential of our nation; both drained the blood from the most important and vital base of our economy—agriculture—and they strengthened the dictatorial regime." The local authorities used the cruelest methods to carry out collectivization. Those who were competent and industrious, who were able to produce better than others, were destroyed. This dealt a terrible blow to the countryside and had an impact on the entire country, the consequences of which are still being felt to this day (Gorbachev, 27–28).

Gorbachev says that he learned a lot about the repression of the 1930s as a result of the fate his family suffered. He explained how he had been inspired by the simple, people that he had known whom history had maltreated and who had deserved better. The key to his dreams and ambition, the key to his conduct and his conscience, he said, were to be found in the ethics and morality of the grandfather who raised him. Panteleï, his mother's father, Gorbachev recalls, was the son of poor peasants. He had been orphaned at the age of thirteen. He espoused the revolutionary ideal, became a leader in the peasant revolutionary movement of his village, joined the Communist Party, helped organize collectivization. He was "infinitely grateful" to the USSR for having saved the peasants. He never questioned the Soviet government or its policies. He felt that the Soviet power had given him the land he farmed and had thereby saved his family. "Soviet power is OUR power," he repeatedly told Gorbachev (Gorbachev, 20; Cojean).

The whole dramatic thing about the Soviet revolution and power, Gorbachev stressed, was that that power took pity on no one. Ardent supporter of the Soviet ideal that he was, Panteleï was accused of counterrevolutionary Trotskyite activities, declared an enemy of the people, tortured many times in very cruel ways, sentenced to be shot, but finally "miraculously released." Gorbachev recalls the winter evening that Panteleï returned home. The family was seated around their big wooden table, and Gorbachev's grandfather, the only time in his life, told them about what had happened in the prison: the torture, the beatings, the electrodes, the hands crushed, the fingers jammed in the doorways. He never confessed to the deeds of which he had been accused and which were utter calumny. He came close to dying. But he never questioned Stalin. Panteleï died at an early age, his health broken by imprisonment and torture (Gorbachev, 20; Cojean).

Gorbachev also remembers his other grandfather, who was the relentless enemy of collectivization, of sharing property and harvests. It was he who saw to it that his grandson Victor was baptized Mikhail. He was accused of sabotage and condemned to forced labor in Siberia for not having respected the official plan for sowing the crops, something which Gorbachev says was impossible to do since there had been a famine the year before and he had seen three of his children die of hunger. "I have not betrayed them," Gorbachev concluded the interview, "I succeeded because I came from that world of peasants and that family, honestly believed in what I was doing" (Gorbachev, 20; Cojean).

Cleansing Society by Destroying Useless Lives

To put into practice theories expounded in *Mein Kampf* about this world belonging only to forceful "whole" persons and not to weak "half" persons, so that if "the power to fight for one's own health is no longer present, the right to live in this world of struggle ends" (Hitler, 257), once he was in the position to do so, Hitler did what he could to "burst all the absurd fetters of the so-called humanity of individuals" and to replace it with what he called "the humanity of Nature which destroys the weak to give his place to the strong" (Hitler, 132). So it was that, once he was in power, and under the cover of war, he and his minions set about devising ways to remove from the ranks of the living those who, according to their way of thinking, were useless, undesirable people.[3]

Under Hitler's leadership, the Nazi regime developed an extraordinarily broad definition of just who might fit into the category of useless, undesirable, half-people. And the longer the National Socialist Party was in power, the longer their list became. On that list came to figure members of the following (not mutually exclusive) groups: the incurably ill, syphilitics, epileptics, victims of encephalitis, tuberculosis patients, sick prisoners in camps, handicapped people, the elderly, the infirm, children in foster homes, people who had fallen into need through no fault of their own and could not pull themselves up by their own efforts, people requiring "unnecessary expenditures," the mentally ill, psychiatric patients, schizophrenics, people suffering from major depression, civilians who had suffered mental breakdowns and become disoriented after bombing raids, the mentally retarded, the congenitally feeble-minded, members of marginal social groups, maladjusted adolescents, nonconformists, homosexuals, homeless people, people unwilling to work, criminals, tramps, beggars, swindlers, peddlers, prostitutes, drunkards, the visible poor, the homeless, foreign slave laborers, those thought to pose a threat to public order and discipline, people inferior in appearance, racially "inferior" Jews, Gypsies, Poles, and other Slavs, degenerates . . . (Aly, Chroust and Pross, 13, 22, 23 43, 48–49, 58–59, 76).

The following excerpt from a 1940 report reflects attitudes taken toward such "useless," "undesirable" half-people. It declared that:

> In the many mental institutions in the Reich there are an infinite number of incurably ill patients of all kinds who are completely useless to humanity; in fact, they are nothing but a burden, their care creates endless expense, and there is no possibility that these people will ever become healthy or useful members of human society. They vegetate like animals, and are antisocial people unworthy of living; but otherwise, their internal organs are healthy and they could live on for many decades. They only take nourishment away from other, healthy people, and often need two or three times as much care. Other people must be protected from these people. (Aly 1994a, 48–49)

---

[3] The material making up this section on cleansing society by destroying "useless" people is principally drawn from essays published in *Cleansing the Fatherland* by Aly, Chroust, and Pross. In particular, the introduction by C. Pross, 1–21; "Medicine against the Useless," by G. Aly, 22–98; "Pure and Tainted Progress," by G. Aly, 156–237; "Selected Letters of Doctor Friedrich Mennecke," by P. Chroust, 238–95.

The outbreak of war in September 1939, with all the distractions that wars provide, promised cover for the implementation of Hitlerian plans to cleanse the society. So it was that from the beginning of the war, alongside the fight against foreign powers, a domestic fight to cleanse society began, a fact symbolized by the September 1, 1939 date on Hitler's authorization of euthanasia which, in Götz Aly's words in his essay "Medicine Against the Useless," "set into motion the planners' ambition and practical imagination, as well as a systematic bureaucratic procedure" (Aly 1994a, 35).

In September 1939, for example, killing units began to shoot asylum inmates by the thousands (Aly 1994a, 35). In October 1939, processing of patients in psychiatric institutions began, and a figure of sixty-five to seventy thousand people to be eliminated was established. At that time, questionnaires asking, among other things, for information on each patient's type of illness, length of stay, and ability to work were sent to various mental institutions (Aly 1994a, 22–23). This was when the organized the killing of handicapped toddlers and infants in so-called pediatrics departments began, and a list was drawn up of all asylums in the territory of the Reich in which mentally ill, epileptic, and feeble-minded people were held on more than a temporary basis (Aly 1994, 36). That fall, the Germans set a Lithuanian hospital of contagious diseases afire after having blocked all the windows and locked the doors so that no patient, doctor, or member of the staff could flee. Sixty patients and the entire medical staff were burnt alive (Faitelson, 53).

In his essay entitled "Pure and Tainted Progress," Aly writes of a file containing reports on thirty-three children and adolescents murdered on October 28, 1940. According to Aly, the reports indicate that they were not "empty husks" or "mentally dead," as their murderers later claimed in court. In some cases, they were from children from a difficult social background and were obviously put to death for scientific reasons (Aly 1994b, 224–25). Aly records the attitude that one doctor took towards collecting brains for scientific research. He was reported to have said that he had learned about what was going to be done and said: "Look here now, boys, if you are going to kill all these people, at least take the brains out so that the material could be utilized." When asked how many he could examine, he was to have answered an unlimited number, the more the better. He was to have enthused that there was wonderful material among the brains, "beautiful mental defectives, malformations, and early infantile disease," that the "thing was a beautiful mess" (Aly 1994b, 224).

The mass killing program was suspended in August 1941 and the program transformed. By then, the goal of seventy thousand victims had been exceeded by two hundred and seventy-three (Aly, 1994, 39). Aly argues that this "suspension" might more accurately be called a pause for reorganization, for the coming years would bring an ever increasing number of

groups to be included among the candidates slated for selection and possible extermination, among those new candidates were tuberculosis
patients, the elderly, the homeless, and people deemed unwilling to work.
For example, he points out, a "parallel killing program in concentration
camps . . . had already gotten away by April 1941. Its aim was to gas, by
the winter of 1944-45, all concentration camp prisoners who were unable
to work, disruptive, or simply exhausted" (Aly 1994a, 23). As Aly notes,

> The first phase of institutional killing had involved implementation of an ideo-
> logical position—extermination of supposedly worthless life, elimination of vis-
> ible suffering and visible poverty; it had been favored by the euphoria of the
> blitzkrieg. As of 1943, however, all unproductive people in general were to
> make room for those who could be 'restored to health.' The mentally ill,
> infirm, and chronically ill had become part of the overall triage. They were
> transferred and murdered whenever necessary—whenever local authorities
> needed sickbeds, blankets, sheets, stretchers, and basic medical equipment.
> (Aly 1994, 81–82)

During this latter phase of the war, Aly relates, the "asylums pompously
renamed 'clinics' and 'sanitaria' to emphasize their focus on healing, now
obviously became camps; the directors, along with the physicians and chief
physicians serving under them, turned into white-uniformed combinations
of camp-commandant and executioner" (Aly, 1994a, 89).

As the war ground on, occupants of homes for the aged became the
victims of euthanasia. In one case, after a two-day odyssey, one hundred
and fifty mainly older, bedridden people were sent to an asylum that func-
tioned as an "intermediate asylum" for gas chambers. In June 1944, Aly
recounts, instructions were given to eliminate a transport of around five
hundred little old ladies who had been bombed out. Another group of
patients who had suffered severe shocks as a result of air raids were brought
directly to a hospital and killed the same day. Toward the end of the war,
doctors more and more turned killings into "undisguised executions, using
air and gasoline injections." As Aly explains it, the "state administration's
fear of an outbreak of 'psychological epidemics,' of incalculable despair, of
people proving unresponsive to Nazi leadership and influence . . . became
the reason for forcibly committing and killing people who panicked during
large-scale attacks and fled inwardly into insanity to escape the external catastrophe." (Aly 1994a, 80, 83, 88)

According to Aly, the doctors involved saw themselves as reformers,
who in addition to "advocating anonymous, assembly line murder of
patients classified as incurable" believed that once the era of mass killing
was over, the number of chronically ill patients could be reduced still further through early, intensive therapy (Aly 1994a, 24). "Healing and
killing," Christian Pross explains in the introduction to *Cleansing the*

Fatherland, "were an integral part of selective social policy. 'Superior' citizens were to receive the best and most modern medical treatment and social services available, whereas the genetically 'inferior,' the subproletariat, children in foster homes, prostitutes, the mentally retarded, alcoholics, and the mentally ill, as well as the racially 'inferior,' Jews, Gypsies, and Slavs, were to be sterilized or killed" (Pross, 13).

The destruction of certain categories of people deemed inferior provided the funds, facilities, social guarantees for the preferred categories of "superior" people and secured a standard of living for them at the expense of those excluded. However, Proust wants to make it clear that the Nazi doctors were not tragically misled scientists seduced by Hitler, whose work could simply be explained in terms of some kind of terribly misguided, blind idealism, of murder for the sake of a higher purpose. Their diaries, letters, and publications, he points out, "contain few indications of idealism or . . . high ethical standards. Dominating these documents, instead are small-minded greed for money and privileges, careerism, and a mixture of envy, inflated self-esteem, and contempt for the so-called inferior" (Pross, 13–14).

Sick, Weak Men

It must be indicative of the intrinsically unwholesome nature of theories about supramen that it tends to be people who least resemble the model that they so passionately celebrate and would impose who espouse such ideas. It is often pointed out how far removed leading Nazis like Hitler, Goebbels, and Göring were from resembling their Aryan ideal. As for Himmler, one of the points that Padfield drives home in *Himmler: Reichsführer-SS* is how much "the unsoldierly, bespectacled Himmler," "whose physique, colouring and facial features were about as far from the Nordic ideal as was possible"; who was "to outward appearance a grotesque caricature of his own laws, norms and ideals," "must have despised himself for his short sight, awkward, unathletic body, constitutional weakness and physical ineptitude" (Padfield, 24–25, 105, 137).

Pursuing the notion that Nietzsche's "philosophy stemmed from most violent struggles against what was most deeply rooted in his self" (Gilman, 218), this is a good place to complement Nietzsche's and Hitler's theories championing healthy bodies and supramen with a realistic look at just how healthy Nietzsche was. A parallel discussion could be provided for Baudelaire. For the reality, of course, is that both men were wracked with syphilis and both of them finally lost their minds to the disease. Let us start with the year 1879-80. During that year, by Mencken's account,

Nietzsche was very ill, indeed, and for awhile he believed that he had but a short while to live. Like all such invalids he devoted a great deal of time to observing and discussing his condition. He became, indeed, a hypochondriac of the first water and began to take a sort of melancholy pleasure in his infirmities. He sought relief at all the baths and cures of Europe: he took hot baths, cold baths, salt-water baths and mud baths. Every new form of pseudo-therapy found him in its freshman class. To owners of sanitoria and to inventors of novel styles of massage, irrigation, sweating and feeding he was a joy unlimited. But he grew worse instead of better. . . . He swallowed more and more pills; he imbibed mineral waters by the gallon . . . (Mencken, 40–41)

In *Conversations with Nietzsche: A Life in the Words of His Contemporaries,* Sander Gilman collected the memories of people who had actually met Nietzsche at different stages of his life and illnesses. These pebbles can be pieced together into a mosaic to form a picture of Nietzsche's descent into malady. At the psychiatric clinic in Jena, Nietzsche himself clearly indicated that as a medical corpsman in 1870-71, he had contracted syphilis,[4] which soon afterwards manifested itself in Basel in a syphilitic infection of the retina of the eyes (Gilman, 223–25).

A person who saw Nietzsche lecture in Basel during the 1870s, when he was in his early thirties, reported how painful it was to watch him: "Equipped with the strongest eyeglasses, he sat with his face almost touching his notebook on the lectern. Slowly and laboriously, the words struggled through his lips and often his speech was interrupted by pauses. . . . sometimes he had to stop the class because the excruciating headaches that plagued him almost daily and deprived him of sleep at night became unbearable" (Gilman, 62). Another recalled how "the attacks of his ailment, the horrible head- and eye-aches . . . often forced him to lie in bed day and night in endless torment" (Gilman, 89). He impressed yet another person as being "a lonely man, suffering severely," who "strode along, bent, perhaps oppressed by physical pain." (Gilman, 99).

Ida Overbeck described Nietzsche in those days as "a severely sick man who constantly deluded himself about his dangerous condition in order to

---

[4] Asked by Nietzsche's sister to write "a critique of her brother's medical history and the unsavory controversy connected with it," in 1899, Health Commissioner Vulpius speculated that the "most obvious and likely occasion" for the "exogenous disease germs" that caused the metasyphilitic affection to have entered his system was while he was transporting influenza and diphtheria patients under unfavorable hygienic conditions during his service as a volunteer medical corpsman. Vulpius hypothesized that, to overcome his lively disgust, and probably in the belief that he was enjoying some disinfecting protection in so doing, Nietzsche smoked in the ambulance. In that case, the causal toxin could have easily been transmitted if he had ever set down his cigar to help a patient in the crowded vehicle. For, he subsequently became mortally ill with an infection of the jaws which was diagnosed as diphtheria, but might have contained an admixture of syphilis (Gilman, 257–59).

endure it. . . . He really suffered in the head. . . . every few weeks Nietzsche's exhaustion was so complete that all activity was impossible. This suffering. . . . imposed the shortest leash on him, whereas he desired the longest. . . . Finally, he lived in fantasy only with greatness" (Gilman, 109). Nietzsche was described as having left the University of Basel, "his eyesight and his stomach ruined . . . like a walking skeleton. . . ." (Gilman, 174)

He was described as a broken figure with a helpless look who aroused deep, deep pity during the ten years preceding his final breakdown in 1889 (Gilman, 126, 132). In that period of his life, Ida Overbeck often found him "without will and weakened" (Gilman, 120). In memories dated 1883, she described him as "deeply depressed by the consciousness that as a sick man he was not one of the strong, and could not say the last word to mankind; he was excluded from too much; to a certain extent he was already dead" (Gilman, 144). Another friend sometimes sat at his bedside as "he lay so sick, with his raging headaches for days on end, and vomiting constantly . . ." (Gilman, 171). Yet another recalled how, to combat sleepless nights, he numbed his feverish brain for a few hours with chloral, which was only a palliative that brought oblivion, but helped him endure the moral and physical suffering (Gilman, 179–80). One visitor recalled seeing him leaning wearily against the post of the half-opened door with a distraught expression on his pale face and speaking to him about the unbearableness of his ailment. Nietzsche described to her how, "when he closed his eyes, he saw an abundance of fantastic flowers, winding and intertwining, constantly growing and changing forms and colors in exotic luxuriance, sprouting one out of the other" (Gilman, 164).

Then came his collapse in January 1889. His condition is reported to have been quite satisfactory during the first years after the breakdown. He was "calm, participated in conversations, went on walks arm in arm with his mother, and enjoyed tolerable health." However, "little by little the individual systems of nerves were affected. His consciousness vanished more and more his limbs failed, his language became unclear" (Gilman, 244). Another person remembers Nietzsche's health as varying in those days. Sometimes, he "sat there with a strongly reddened face and eyes that flared up wildly and painfully, guarded by a keeper." He was so "cruelly tormented by disease" that "one could observe only with the deepest pity. . . . the incomparable face contorted with Laocoöntic pain, his gaze glowing with affliction . . . wound about by the serpent of the mortal disease . . ." (Gilman, 224–25).

The care that he received from his mother and sister who nursed him "with unspeakable tenderness" during his final years was described as "truly ideal," "loving, considerate." When he wanted to scream, his mother would fill his mouth with something to eat, which he then would chew and swallow while "growling dully to himself." She would lead him like a little child to church, the only place where he felt calm. His interests became those of a child again. It was reported that when he was not brooding dully to himself, he played with pennies, dolls, and other toys. He might watch a drummer boy for a long time, or locomotives, at times talking to himself "in tangled confusion." There were times that he repeated the same sentence over and over again almost for hours without interruption. He had a perfect memory for poems he had learned in childhood. "Zarathustra" had become a child (Gilman, 132, 226, 232, 233, 244, 260).

And while his sister "saw to the spread of his fame on earth," Nietzsche "sat in his chair or lay on his bed, silent and indifferent, hour by hour, week by week, year by year—his beautiful, slender, white hands crossed over his chest, occasionally muttering indistinct sounds under his mustache, which grew to fabulous size" (Gilman, 242). One visitor saw him confined to a "mattress-grave," "surrounded by all kinds of protective measures to prevent his escape" (Gilman, 260).

Of a visit in November 1897, Resa von Schirnhofer recalled, "I left sadly, pondering what thoughts and feelings might still be alive behind that impenetrable external mask in this form of life which bore the seal of human helplessness and in which every spark of mental life seemed extinguished" (Gilman, 238). Other visitors found that he completely had the appearance of a mentally ill person, with a wild, dull, stupid expression in his eyes, who "answered questions only with a stupid smile" and "reached stupidly for every shining object to try to put it into his mouth" (Gilman, 232, 234, 261). Of a visit to Nietzsche in August 1899, Ernst Horneffer recalled,

> I consider any reports that Nietzsche spoke in his last years of illness completely incredible. And if anyone says so, it must be the result of self-deception. Music made a great impression on him. When he was told that music would be played, he immediately was ecstatic and emitted ugly, unarticulated sounds, a dull, horrible groaning. After the music began his whole face was transfigured and beamed indescribably. But this expression of excessive joy was, in its sickness, no less terrible than the animalistic behavior just before. When I reflect on how the sick Nietzsche struggled for an expression and after terrible torments produced nothing else but ugly sounds, I cannot imagine that in this deep stage of mental derangement he can ever have spoken. . . . Progressive paralysis silenced him. (Gilman, 255–56)

Nietzsche's plunge into the dark night of disease is reminiscent of that of the eminent theologian of Baudelaire's "Punishment for Pride" who was punished for having declared in a burst of "satanic pride": "Jesus, little Jesus! I pushed you quite high! But if I had wished to attack you for want of armor, your disgrace would equal your glory, and you would be no more than a ridiculous fetus!" Upon this, the theologian

> immediately lost his reason. The brightness of this sun was veiled in crape. All chaos revolved in this mind. . . . Silence and night came to reside in him, as in a vault whose key is lost. From that time on he was like the beasts in the street, and when he passed without seeing anything, through the fields, without distinguishing the summers from the winters, dirty, useless and ugly like a worn out thing, he was the joy and the laughing-stock of children. (Baudelaire 1857, XVI)

Jung on the Sentiment of Inferiority

Padfield comments: "It is surely no accident that the three leaders who increased their power from the outbreak of war until the final collapse and who kept the Reich on its straight course for destruction, Hitler, Himmler, Goebbels, had the best reasons for feeling inferior" (Padfield, 269). In the wake of World War II, Jung analyzed the feeling of inferiority that he felt was characteristic of Germans and made them vulnerable to Hitler's bewitchment. For Jung, the effect that Hitler, whom Jung refers to as a "scarecrow," had on the masses could only be explained by a kind of "psychopathic inferiority" from which the entire nation suffered. The German people, Jung maintained, would never have been taken in and carried away so completely if Hitler had not been "a reflected image of the collective German hysteria" (Jung 1945, 188–89).

As Jung saw it, one reason why the Germans fell for Hitler was that, in common with the rest of the world, they failed to understand that Hitler's significance lay in something that he symbolized in every individual. Jung characterized this "something" as being the fact that Hitler "was the most prodigious personification of all human inferiorities. He was an utterly incapable, unadapted, irresponsible, psychopathic personality, full of empty infantile fantasies, but cursed with the keen intuition of a rat or a guttersnipe. He represented the shadow, the inferior part of everybody's personality, in an overwhelming degree . . ." (Jung 1946, 178).

Suggesting that it could not have been pure chance to find all these pathological features combined together in the "man who was diagnosed clinically as an hysteric, and whom a strange fate chose to be the political, moral, and religious spokesman of Germany for twelve years," Jung named some of the pathological features that he found united in Hitler's personality. Figuring on his list were: "complete lack of insight into one's own character, auto-erotic self-admiration and self-extenuation, denigration and terrorization of one's fellow men . . . , projection of the shadow, lying, falsification of reality, determination to impress by fair means or foul, bluffing and double-crossing . . . (Jung 1945, 188).

Jung characterized the hysteric as someone who "always complains of being surrounded by people who are incapable of appreciating him and who are activated only by bad motives; by inferior mischief-makers, a crowd of submen who should be exterminated neck and crop so that the Superman can live on his high level of perfection." Jung saw the very fact that hysterical people think and feel along these lines as being "clear proof of inferiority in action. Therefore, all hysterical people are compelled to torment others, because they are unwilling to hurt themselves by admitting their own inferiority" (Jung 1945, 188).

"It was certainly not the healthy elements in the German nation that led to the triumph of these pathological fantasies on a scale never known before," wrote Jung as he integrated Nietzsche's ideas and personality into his analysis of the circumstances that went into the making of the Hitler era. Some helpful conclusions, he suggested, might be drawn from what he termed "the prophetic example of Nietzsche." Jung depicted Nietzsche as someone who was "German to the marrow of his bones, even to the abstruse symbolism of his madness." According to Jung, like Nietzsche's weakness, the weaknesses inherent in the German character "proved to be fertile soil for hysterical fantasies." Jung credited what he called "the psychopath's weakness" with having prompted Nietzsche "to play with the 'blond beast' and the 'Superman'" (Jung 1945, 195).

As seen in Part One, Nietzsche himself wrote of how guilt was always sought wherever there was failure. According to him, the accompanying ill-feeling acts as the instinctively applied cure found in a new excitation of the feeling of power that comes from condemning the guilty party, who becomes a sacrifice of weak, humiliated, depressed people who want to prove that they still possess strength (Nietzsche 1881, §140). Nietzsche believed that those needing to raise themselves above their own wretchedness require those around them to be wretched, that those needing to raise themselves above their own piteousness and establish a sense of dignity and importance require other people to hector and to harm, people whose powerlessness allows them to act with impunity in a superior, irate manner in front of them (Nietzsche 1881, §369). Nietzsche wrote of how people who suffer want to find someone to blame for their suffering, of how inventive they can be when it comes to finding excuses for their pain, of how they relish their suspicions, brood about depravity, and prejudices, search their past and present looking for reasons to wallow in torturous suspicions, tear at their oldest wounds, make friends, women, children and those around them into miscreants (Nietzsche 1887, III §15).

So it was that, in his analysis of the impact that Hitler had, Jung cited Nietzsche's writings among the "symptoms of the mental change" that were taking place in Europe well before World War I. As Jung saw it, Nietzsche had announced the death of God and the advent of the Superman, whom Jung derided as a "doomed rope-dancer and fool" (Jung 1945, 196–97). For Jung, "when somebody hits on the singular idea that God is dead, or does not exist at all, the psychic God-image, which is a dynamic part of the psyche's structure, finds its way back into the subject and produces a condition of 'God-Almightiness,' that is to say all those qualities which are peculiar to fools and madmen and therefore lead to catastrophe" (Jung 1945, 196–97). As Jung explained:

> The individual's feeling of weakness, indeed of non-existence, was thus compensated by the eruption of hitherto unknown desires for power. It was the revolt of the powerless, the insatiable greed of the 'have-nots.' By such devious means the unconscious compels man to become conscious of himself. Unfortunately, there were no values in the conscious mind of the individual which would have enabled him to understand and integrate the reaction when it reached consciousness. Nothing but materialism was preached by the highest intellectual authorities. The Churches were evidently unable to cope with the new situation: they could do nothing but protest and that did not help very much. Thus the avalanche rolled on in Germany and produced its leader, who was elected as a tool to complete the ruin of the nation. (Jung 1946, 177)

Jung says that by the late 1930s, his personal observations had led him to conclude that, when the final catastrophe came, it would be far greater and bloodier than he had previously supposed. "For this theatrical hysteric and transparent imposter was not strutting about on a small stage, but was riding the armoured divisions of the Wehrmacht, with all the weight of German heavy industry behind him " (Jung 1945, 188–89).

Racism and Slaughter

Padfield writes of how Nietzsche's "language entered the German vocabulary, and men who might never have read his books spoke with his tongue, that is to say with those phrases which sank into the national consciousness because they had emerged from it" (Padfield, 33). In Padfield's estimation, especially the language used involving notions about producing a race of Supermen and "race hygiene" mingled perniciously with certain nineteenth-century ideas to create a particularly noxious effect (Padfield, 33).

Padfield cites the case of Alfred Ploetz, whose book entitled *The Fitness of Our Race* is prefaced with words taken from Nietzsche, "Upward leads our way from the Species into the Superspecies." Like Galton and his kind, Padfield explains, Ploetz viewed disease as a positive selection of those who are fit. Like them, he saw modern medicine and concerns about the health of the race as standing in fundamental contradiction. Ranking racial considerations higher than individual concerns, he proposed that racial hygiene be given priority over the health of individuals. It was assumed that the highest race was the white race, and that the highest branch of the white race was the Aryan branch. Aryans should therefore be bred into a Superspecies. "Such state-centered biological views," Padfield was careful to note, "were only Nietzschean in the sense that Nietzsche gave them their most memorable expression. Actually they permeated . . . military, political, intellectual, economic and even artistic life" (Padfield, 33–34).

One example of extreme racism is the efforts that Nazis made to destroy *Untermenschen* in Poland. A 1940 memorandum from Heinrich Himmler reveals the nature of the Third Reich's plans for that country. It indicates that Poland and its different peoples, Poles, Ukrainians, White Russians, Jews were to be broken up "into the largest possible number of parts and fragments . . . the racially valuable elements extracted from the hodgepodge," and the rest left to die (Sereny 1995, 213). The Nazi leadership considered the Poles in general to be an inferior race to be subjugated and exterminated. Shortly before launching the invasion of Poland in 1939, Hitler was to have declared:

> Our strength is in our quickness and our brutality. Genghis Khan had millions of women and children killed by his own will and with a gay heart. History sees in him only a great state builder. Thus, for the time being, I have sent to the east only my Death's Head units with orders to kill without pity or mercy all men, women, and children of Polish race or lineage. Only in such a way will we win the vital space that we need. Who still talks in our day of the extermination of the Armenians? (cited Rosenbaum, 175)

The goal of the Nazi leadership was to reduce the Polish people "to a remnant of sub-standard beings . . . a leaderless labor force capable only of furnishing Germany with casual labourers . . ." (Sereny 1995, 213; Padfield, 301). Suitable Poles who appeared to have Germanic blood and children who were "racially valuable" would be candidates for germanization. The Polish leadership, nobility, officers, clergy, teachers, educated classes would be liquidated (Gorska and Wojtatowicz 2000). The remainder of the population would only be allowed a basic education. They would learn to do simple calculations, how to write their names, "to obey Germans and to be honest, industrious and trustworthy." They would not need to learn to read.

Excerpts from the diary of the German anatomist Hermann Voss, dean of the Medical Department of the "Reich" University of Posen after the conquest of Poland, are published in *Cleansing the Fatherland* (Voss, 99–155). In his diaries, Voss consigned his ideas about the Polish people to paper. For instance, he wrote: "The Polish people are multiplying twice as fast as the Germans, and that is decisive! The much more primitive Slavic peoples will devour the German people, which do not multiply fast enough by far" (Voss, 105). "I think one should look at this Polish question without emotion, purely biologically. We must exterminate them, otherwise they will exterminate us. And that is why I am glad of every Pole who is no longer alive" (Voss, 105–6, 128). "The Polish people must be exterminated, or there will be no peace here in the East" (Voss, 127).

In 1939, the Gestapo took over the cremation oven in the cellar of Voss's anatomical institute for their exclusive use (Voss, 127). Of the cellar and crematorium, Voss wrote in his diaries:

> Yesterday I viewed the cellar for corpses and the cremation oven that is also located in the cellar. This oven was built to eliminate parts of bodies left over from dissection exercises. Now it serves to incinerate executed Poles. The gray car with the gray men—that is, SS men from the Gestapo—comes almost daily with material for the oven. Because it was not in use yesterday, we could look into it. It contained the ashes of four Poles. How little remains of a human being when everything organic has been burned! Somehow looking into such an oven is very comforting. (Voss, 130)

The entry to Voss's diary for July 5, 1942 tells of a party for medical students. Voss contributed bones to be given as prizes in an anatomy guessing game. Voss described the first prize as "a very nice skull." Jósef Jendykiewicz, porter of the *Collegium Anatomicum*, described how Voss acquired his skulls: "The heads of transported victims were thrown into a basket like turnips and brought in the elevator to the third floor for maceration. Here they were prepared and later used in our institute of anatomy" (Voss, 144n.). In his memoirs, Albert Ponsold, a non-Nazi doctor of forensic medicine at Posen recalled:

> At police headquarters in Posen, I happened to pass through a room in which Polish resistance fighters were being interrogated—two young men and a woman, apparently students. The officers sat around causally, one on the table, as if it was nothing important. When I saw a truck standing in front of the anatomical institute the next morning and asked what had been brought by, the driver pulled back the hood and revealed a horrifying sight: the three Poles beheaded, their heads between their feet. (Voss, 136n.)

According to witnesses, the oven was often used day and night and could hold four to six bodies, or, if quartered, up to ten bodies. The cremation process took some four hours. According to records, almost 5,000 bodies of Poles and Jews murdered by the German police and judicial authorities were cremated between 1939 and 1945 (Voss, 130n.).

Voss's diaries show entries like these: "The Poles they shoot are brought here at night and cremated. If one could only incinerate the whole Polish pack!" (Voss, 127); or "The Poles are quite impudent at the moment, and thus our oven has a great deal to do. How nice it would be if we could drive the whole pack through such ovens! (Voss, 130); or "Yesterday, two wagons full of Polish ashes were taken away" (Voss, 132).

On October 31, 1941, Voss noted that the "institute received its first corpses: five executed Poles, one of them a woman" (Voss, 125n.). On March 10, 1942, he described this dissection exercise: "Nineteen corpses were dissected. Seven of them come from the Polish period, the rest had almost all been executed. . . . In addition to the usual muscle and joint dissections, dissections of the breast, stomach, and sex organs were also made. The dissections of the organs of the executed persons were the loveliest I have ever seen in a dissecting room" (Voss, 135).

Polish Jews were to be completely eliminated. It was Joseph Stroop's job to root out "*Untermenschen*" from the Warsaw ghetto. The Jews were putting up strong resistance and withdrawing at the last moment through attics or underground passageways. To trap them, Stroop had the sewer system flooded, but they responded by blowing up the valves of the damgates. Stroop then had the buildings burned down to force the Jews out into the open and to prevent reoccupation. He reported how: "Jews in masses—whole families—already gripped by the flames, leaped from windows or attempted to let themselves down with bedsheets tied together. Provision had been made to liquidate these as well as the other Jews immediately. . . ." (Padfield, 449).

He finally concluded that "the only way and the method of last resort to force the this riff-raff and *Untermenschtum* to the surface" was to burn down the buildings systematically, block by block. He reported that only "after the streets and all the courtyards on both sides were ablaze did the Jews, some alight themselves, emerge from the block, attempting to save themselves by leaping from windows and balconies to the street. . . . Again and again we saw that despite the great fire-danger Jews and bandits chose rather to return in to the fire than fall into our hands" (Padfield, 449).

In prison after the war, Stroop enthusiastically described his work to destroy the Warsaw ghetto. Apparently, he worked himself into a state of great excitement and began jumping around his cell imitating the actions of SS soldiers firing upon Jews. He is recorded as having described a "monstrous" uproar, "burning houses, smoke flames, flying sparks, whirling bed feathers, the stench of singed bodies, thunder of guns, cracking grenades, the glow of fire, Jews with their wives and children leaping from windows and burning houses . . . they appeared everywhere in windows, on balconies, on the roofs and ledges. Some shot, others sought to escape . . . (Padfield, 449–50).

Lecturing Miklós Horthy, the Hungarian head of state in March 1944, Hitler is recorded as having said that in Poland, "if the Jews there did not *want* to work, they were shot. If they *could* not work, they were treated like tuberculosis bacilli with which a healthy body may become infected. This is not cruel if one remembers that even innocent creatures of nature, such as hares and deer when infected, have to be killed so that they cannot damage others. Why should the beasts who wanted to bring us Bolshevism be spared more than these innocents?" (cited Sereny 1995, 420).

Mass Executions

Most people would be surprised upon finding the words: "Beautiful conspiracy to organize for the extermination of the Jewish Race" jotted down in Baudelaire's *Mon cœur mis à nu* (Baudelaire 1949, 101). Of course, literally speaking, Baudelaire was writing there of the beauty of a *conspiracy*, that is of a *plan*. He was not writing of the beauty of the actual work of killers really voluptuously gratifying their instincts of aggression, carnage, and destruction upon victims who are real people whom they actually see moving, breathing, then collapsing, whose blood, fragments of bones and of brain they see flying in all directions, even landing on their themselves, dirtying their faces and clothes, victims whose screams and moans ring in their ears stimulating them to attack their victims with ever greater ferocity.

In comparison, it is precisely the point of this section on "Mass Executions" and the following one on "Extermination" to write about those realities, to look at just how beautiful actually trying to exterminate a people can really be by looking at the most outstanding example of this that humanity has yet known, the work of Hitler and his minions to annihilate the Jewish people. The Nazi leadership itself resorted to words like *'ruthless'*, *'merciless'*, *'barbaric'*, *'crude'*, *'gruesome'* to qualify the extermination work described below. In the next section, entitled "Extermination," I shall look at the "kinder, gentler," "final" solution that they ultimately adopted.

To begin with, it is important to point out that the idea of exterminating the Jews was not as unheard of, unforeseeable, and literally unthinkable as it may now seem that it was, or as many may now want it to seem that it was. It figures in the writings of Baudelaire, Nietzsche, and Hitler, all three. There is the scribbling by Baudelaire cited above. And Nietzsche, for example, wrote of talk in his time of leading the Jews to the slaughter, as sacrificial lambs for all possible public and inner wrongs (Nietzsche 1878, I §475). As Weaver Santaniello points out, the very fact that Nietzsche " wrote about and against Jewish extermination . . . leads one to strongly suspect that the intent to destroy the Jews was already formulated during Nietzsche's time" (Santaniello 1997, 43).

Hitler left little to the imagination in *Mein Kampf*, where he railed and railed against the "nonsense and madness" that the Jewish gang of Marxists had been "funneling into the masses" (Hitler, 168). He wrote that with World War I "the time had come to take steps against the whole treacherous brotherhood of these Jewish poisoners of the people. . . . to deal with them summarily without the slightest consideration for any screams and complaints that might arise. . . . to exterminate mercilessly the agitators who were misleading the nation. . . . All the implements of military power should have been ruthlessly used for the extermination of this pestilence," he said (Hitler, 169). He considered that:

> The soul of the people can only be won if along with carrying on a positive struggle for our own aims, we destroy the opponent of these aims. The people at all times see the proof of their own right in ruthless attack on a foe, and to them renouncing the destruction of the adversary seems like uncertainty with regard to their own right if not a sign of their own unright. . . . The nationalization of our masses will only succeed when, aside from all the positive struggle for the soul of our people, their international poisoners are exterminated. . . . Anyone who wants to free the German blood from the manifestations and vices of today, which were originally alien to its nature, will first have to redeem it from the foreign virus of these manifestations. Without the clearest knowledge of the racial problem and hence of the Jewish problem there will never be a resurrection of the German nation. (Hitler, 338–39)

Jacob Kaplan, Great Rabbi of France during World War II, whose name appears on the cover of the wartime edition of the French translation of *Mein Kampf*, saw the handwriting on the wall. In 1938, he lucidly saw that the Nazis had "but one step to make, only one, for the racist program to be carried out point by point: violent extermination or death through starvation" (Kaplan 1952, 71).[5]

With the advent of World War II, the Nazi leadership was fully cognizant that the distractions, distortions, confusions, powers that wartime inevitably affords offered them opportunities to proceed in a radical, thorough way to a definitive solution of the Jewish problem. "Thank God," Joseph Goebbels confided in his diary in March 1942, "the war offers us possibilities that would have been barred to us in peacetime. These we must now use." He wrote of the situation being ripe to engage in a "life

---

[5] See also Schwarzfuchs 1998, *Aux prises avec Vichy, Histoire politique des Juifs de France (1940–1944)*; Kaplan 1952, *Les Temps d'Epreuve*; Kaplan 1984, *N'oublie pas*; Kaplan 1995, *Justice pour la foi juive, Dialogue avec Pierre Pierrard*.

and death battle between the Aryan race and the Jewish bacillus." The Jews were to be out of Europe, if necessary, by applying the most brutal means, he stressed (Fraenkel, 273–74; Sereny 1995, 350).

Goebbels acknowledged that in the course of solving the problem numerous personal tragedies would occur, but he saw that as being unavoidable. He admitted that the procedures to be used were barbaric and that there would not be much left of the life of the Jews, but deemed that they had earned the catastrophe that they were experiencing. He believed that one could not allow any sentimentality to prevail and that the process would have to be expedited with cold ruthlessness. He was convinced that he and his cohorts were be performing an invaluable service to humanity, that the burden that Nazis were taking upon themselves would prove to be to the benefit and good fortune of those who would come afterward.

Numerous accounts of the barbaric procedures that Goebbels alluded to in his diaries have survived. Here, I shall use *Heroism and Bravery in Lithuania 1941–1945* by Alex Faitelson, a survivor of the attempts to exterminate the Jews of the Kovno ghetto, to piece together a detailed account of how members of his family and other "poisoners of the people" met their deaths.[6]

At the end of October 1941, Faitelson recalls, the SS informed the Jewish Council of the ghetto that the authorities had decided that Jews without jobs were to be transferred since food could not be distributed indifferently to everyone. All the Jews of the ghetto, without exception, including children, the sick, were to leave their homes and gather on a certain square on the fateful day at six in the morning. People remaining in their apartments after six o'clock would be shot on sight.

On the eve of the roundup the ghetto was consumed with anxiety. In the morning, Faitelson and his family dressed by five-thirty and left the house. It was still dark outside and half raining and half snowing. At nine o'clock, in a show of force, the German and Lithuanian police encircled the people grouped on the square. Men went to verify that no one had remained at home.

Then the selection process began. Young people, small families, those who were properly dressed were to go to the left. Families were separated. Elderly people, people who seemed sick, as well as large, poorly dressed, or dirty families and people who did not belong to any work group were directed with a whip to the right. They were then lined up, surrounded by the police, and led away. Snow began to fall lightly and pile up. It was terribly cold, and people were hungry. During the selection process, the com-

---

[6] This account is pieced together from pages 58–70, 203–4, 224, 228–29, 233 of Faitelson 1999. Since only the French edition was available to me, some of the vocabulary, for example, the code names, might differ somewhat from those found in the English edition.

mandant ate sandwiches, drank coffee, told jokes as he screamed and used his whip to put people into place. The next morning at dawn, the police led columns of those who had been directed to the right to the Ninth Fort where prisoners of war had dug enormous pits.

A Nazi report recorded what took place then. Eighty men of the Gestapo arrived at the fort accompanied by about fifty policemen. They were ordered to take the positions assigned to them. One section occupied posts along the pits that had been dug and placed heavy machine guns on these posts. Another encircled the outside of the fort to prevent escapes. Ten men came at regular intervals to escort people to the pits. At a certain distance from the pits, the people were told to undress and move in the direction of the pits. They were then pushed into the pits and forced to lie down to be shot. Anyone who refused to obey the order to lie down was beaten into submission. The women carried babies in their arms and took the other children by the hand. The first groups were shot in pits full of water. The later groups were obliged to climb into the pits and to lie down on the cadavers of those who had just been shot to await their own deaths.

The guards insulted their victims as they shot and killed them. All day long one heard the moans and cries of the victims, the crying of the women, and the cries of small children. At the same time there was a sort of gathering among the Jews in the courtyard. Speeches were made exhorting those who were waiting to go to their deaths with their heads held high. Others cried slogans advocating the organization of a revolutionary fight for freedom. These activities helped maintain order, the Nazi report noted, because the people listened to the speeches, while most of the others prayed in spite of unceasing tears.

Towards the evening the collective slaughter came to an end. The pits were full. The victims were covered with dirt. In the midst of those who were dead were children, men, and women who were still alive. They were lying under cadavers and moaning. Many people covered with blood tried to climb out of the pits and attempt to escape, but the guards caught them and forced them back into the pits where they finished them off with bullets.

Originally among those directed to the left, Faitelson was imprisoned in the fort at a later time, when the Nazis were working to obliterate the traces of the slaughter by having prisoners in chains unearth and burn the bodies of those who had been slaughtered. So it was that those prisoners were obliged to participate in the unearthing and burning of those closest to them . . . their children . . . their brothers . . . their sisters . . . their parents, to help the killers make the proof of their murders vanish.

The prisoners' feet were girdled with a chain locked with a rivet. The chains prevented them from taking normal steps and hurt their leg bones. They were provided with buckets, rakes, and picks and escorted by two officers with machine guns to what the Nazis called the "battlefield," which was about 100 by 200 yards and enclosed by a wall three yards high. The pit was about 100 by 2.5 yards and about three yards deep.

A guard tower had been set up with a guard with a machine gun. Several guards armed with machine guns and automatic rifles watched as the work began to extract the corpses from their tombs. A bulldozer created piles of ashes from those extracted from the pit. From time to time fumes rose from the earth and the putrid odor of rotten flesh invaded the place. That was when the bulldozers attained the level of the cadavers.

Code names were assigned to each job in the battlefield. "Excavators" removed the upper layer of clayey soil. Then "gravediggers" arrived with buckets to uncover the "dolls." The smell of rotten flesh caught them by the gorges and dizzied them. One just simply could not breathe. A sensation of revulsion made them nauseous. The Germans obliged prisoners who suffered from nausea and revulsion merely upon seeing the decomposing bodies to lie down on the ground, bend over the dead people, and breathe the nauseous odor for five to ten minutes in order to accustom themselves to the horrible odor of rotting bodies.

In one almost empty tomb, the people had not all had been killed outright. Many of them had only been wounded. The dead were found upright, their eyes open, filled with surprise, fright, mouths half open as if they were alive, or as if they had fallen asleep from fatigue. Those with their mouths open seemed to have tried to breathe. In other cases, the bodies had putrefied. Mothers were hugging their babies in their arms, as if they were trying to protect them. There were fists raised in the air as if crying out for vengeance. All were mixed together and seemed to form a single mass. Some pits contained only children and babies piled one upon the other.

Then came the "carriers" who, with the help of long poles with hooks at the end raised the "dolls" to the surface of the pit. The "draggers" had the difficult job of separating the corpses and bringing them up in parts to the surface of the ditch. Those who transported the corpses, or parts of corpses, to the fire had to take them barehanded to the "checkers." The limbs of the dead oozed a strange grease and it was difficult to carry them barehanded.

The "checkers" looked for objects of value among the "dolls," in particular diamonds, jewels, or money. They extracted gold teeth and dentures from their mouths. The objects that they found were placed in a box watched by the guards. After the "checkers" had done their work, the "carriers" came with stretchers to load the "dolls" two by two onto stretchers to take them to the place where the fire had been set. Then a new pile of "dolls" was prepared for the fire.

The burning of the bodies took place in a great fire set near the pit. A group of "firemen" tended the fire, which was arranged in layers. A layer of combustible fuel was placed on a grill made of rails, then a layer of cadavers, then a layer of wood and a layer of "dolls," all arranged in a square. The head "fireman" recorded the number of "dolls" brought to the fire, and when there was an appropriate number, fuel was poured onto the pile and the lower layer of wood was set afire. A sort of ditch was dug around the fire in which the fuel and body fat drained off. The air was permeated with the smell of burnt flesh.

The lighting of the fire marked the end of the day's work. In the evening, the body burners were lined up into two columns, counted several times, and led back to their quarters. Their chains were removed. The fire burned all night long. The next day the grinders came to crush anything remaining of the bones. Gold teeth, jewelry, coins were taken from the ashes, which were cast to the wind.

Extermination

Although the efforts of Hitler and his minions to annihilate Jewry stands as the most outstanding example of an attempt to exterminate a people that humanity has known, the notion of exterminating a people is, of course, by no means limited to Hitler's endeavors. For instance, in "Our Struggle," Martin Luther King alludes to an actual handbill that "was circulated at a White Citizens Council meeting stating that Negroes should be 'abolished' by 'guns, bows and arrows, sling shots and knives'" (King 1956, 6). In his *The Philosophy of Nietzsche* of 1908, Mencken alludes to "a clear-headed and vigorous, if slightly theatrical southerner," who had "courageously voiced the instinctive conviction" that the injunction to love one another "must be disregarded, and that the white race, to preserve itself, must pronounce upon the black race and set out to execute— as gently as possible, but still with unalterable firmness—a sentence of extermination" (Mencken, 292).

Now, it is of course fine to speak about being gentle, but firm, but realistically speaking, just how gentle is exterminating, or trying to exterminate, millions, even thousands, or hundreds of people ever really going to be? In his autobiography, Commandant of Auschwitz Rudolf Hoess, who said (Hoess, 173) that he

> had to see everything. . . . had to watch hour after hour, by day and by night, the removal and burning of the bodies, the extraction of the teeth, the cutting of the hair, the whole grisly, interminable business. . . . had to stand for hours on end in the ghastly stench, while the mass graves were being opened and the bodies dragged out and burned . . . had to look through the peephole of the gas-chambers and watch the process of death itself, because the doctors wanted me to see it,

acknowledged that it was not always easy to drive people into the gas chambers (Hoess, 140). For instance, he recalls how people "would suddenly give the most terrible shrieks while undressing, or tear their hair, or scream like maniacs" (Hoess, 168). The Commandant of Sobibor death camp put buckets along the way to the gas chambers because people defecated as they were forced by SS men with whips to run to the place of their deaths or to stand waiting for those ahead to be dead when the gassing mechanism broke down (Sereny 1974, 149, 161, 165).

Besides, it is fair to ask just what unalterable firmness in exterminating people realistically involves, another area in which the implementation of Hitler's Final Solution certainly represented a historical breakthrough. When repeatedly asked how he and his men could go on watching the extermination process and how they were able to stand it, Hoess said that he invariably answered that the "iron determination" with which they had to carry out Hitler's orders "could only be obtained by a stifling of all human emotions" (Hoess, 173).

In his well-known October 6, 1943 Posen speech, Hitler's determined henchman Himmler directly addressed the matter of the hard decision that had to be taken to have Jewish people disappear from the face of the earth. And he acknowledged that "the brief sentence 'The Jews must be exterminated'" was easy to pronounce, but the demands placed on those who have to put it into practice were "the hardest and the most difficult in the world." He also thought that he could say that, though "the danger was great and ever present," it was being "carried out without damaging the minds or spirits" of their men and leaders. One had to engineer a route between growing cruel and heartless and no longer respecting human life, or becoming soft and succumbing to weakness and nervous breakdowns, he realized. He thought that it could later be considered whether the German people should be told about this, but that for the time being it was better for the SS to carry the responsibility "for an achievement, not just an idea," and then take the secret with them to their graves (cited Sereny 1995, 389–92).

In his autobiography, Hoess remarked how: "Many members of the *Einsatzkommandos*, unable to endure wading through blood any longer, had committed suicide. Some had even gone mad. Most of the members of these *Kommandos* had to rely on alcohol when carrying out their horrible work" (Hoess, 164–65). Even someone as abnormal as Himmler is reported to have suffered from the sight of such executions. It was reported that he was:

> driven to a open field, in the middle of which two graves had been dug. . . . a twelve-man firing squad was drawn up by one of them. The victims . . . would be brought up in batches, and those waiting would not hear the shots. A truck

drove up with the first batch, 'ragged forms, mostly young men, some with tears running down their cheeks', two of whom, while being hustled from the lorry to the grave, threw themselves down, 'clasping their police escorts around the knees, pleading for their lives'. . . . The Jews were driven to the grave and made to lie down on the earth bottom on their stomachs. . . . Himmler . . . was gazing down at the victims, both arms folded across his chest, his lips pressed tightly together, his dark brows lifted. The police Captain brought the execution squad to the ready: twelve carbine barrels pointed down. 'Fire!' The salvo ripped out, followed by a rattle of bolts, and another salvo, and another. . . . Wolff watched Himmler jerk convulsively and pass his hand across his face and stagger. . . . Himmler's face was almost green; he took out a handkerchief with trembling hands and wiped his cheek where a piece of brain had squirted up on to it. Then he vomited. . . . He stayed while the next truck loads were despatched, then . . . had the face to give the squad a talk on the sacred necessity of their tasks—hard as it was—which according to other participants strengthened them in their resolve to do their duty . . . (Padfield, 342–43)

Padfield speculates that it may even have been that this demonstration led him to decide him that another method had to be found (Padfield, 343). There are numerous indications that the Nazi leadership considered the mass murder by the gassing that has left such an indelible mark on people's consciences to be a "kinder, gentler," relatively humane, civilized way of killing people by "granting them a mercy death," in comparison to the kind of slaughter described above. In 1941 and 1942, one hundred of the Nazi regime's experts on mercy killings were donated to the "final solution of the Jewish question," including the original commandants of the death camps Belzec, Sobibor, and Treblinka (Aly, 1994a, 23).

Rudolf Hoess, who described himself as a man who "had a heart and . . . was not evil," who "unknowingly . . . was a cog in the wheel of the great extermination machine created by the Third Reich" (Hoess, 205), told of his reaction the gassing of some Russian prisoners. He wrote:

Protected by a gas-mask, I watched the killing myself. In the crowded cells death came instantaneously the moment the Cyclon B was thrown in. A short, almost smothered cry, and it was all over. During this first experience of gassing people, I did not fully realize what was happening, perhaps because I was too impressed by the whole procedure. . . . I had always thought that the victims would experience a terrible choking sensation. But the bodies, without exception, showed no signs of convulsion. The killing of these . . . prisoners did not cause me much concern at the time. The order had been given, and I had to carry it out. I must even admit that this gassing set my mind at rest, for the mass extermination of the Jews was to start soon. . . . Now we had the gas, and we had established a procedure. I always shuddered at the prospect of carrying out extermination by shooting, when I thought of the vast numbers concerned, and of the women and children. . . . I was therefore relieved to think that we were to be spared all these bloodbaths, and that the victims too would be spared suffering until their last moment came. It was precisely this which had caused me the greatest concern when I had heard Eichmann's description of Jews being mown down by the Special Squads armed with machine-guns and machine pistols. Many gruesome scenes are said to have taken place, people running away after being shot, the finishing off of the wounded and particularly of the women and children. (Hoess, 164–65)

Hannah Arendt speculated that none of the "various language rules, carefully contrived to deceive and to camouflage had a more decisive effect on the mentality of the killers than this first war decree of Hitler, in which the word for 'murder' was replaced by the phrase 'to grant a mercy death'" (Arendt, 108). Eichmann, she wrote, "claimed more than once that his organizational gifts, the coordination of evacuations and deportations achieved by his office, had in fact helped his victims; it had made their fate easier. If this thing had to be done at all, he argued, it was better that it be done in good order" (Arendt, 190).

Arendt deemed that Eichmann failed to understand the question as to whether the "directive to avoid 'unnecessary hardships' was not a bit ironic, in view of the fact that the destination of these people was certain death anyhow" because it was "still anchored in his mind that the unforgivable sin was not to kill people but to cause unnecessary pain." She speculates that the new method of gassing must have indicated to him "a decisive improvement in the Nazi government's attitude toward the Jews, since at the beginning of the gassing program it had been expressly stated that the benefits of euthanasia were to be reserved for true Germans. As the war progressed, with violent and horrible death raging all around . . . the gassing centers in Auschwitz and Chelmno, in Madjanek and Belzek, in Treblinka and Sobibor must actually have appeared the 'Charitable Foundations for Institutional Care' that the experts in mercy death called them," Arendt writes (Arendt, 108–9).

Beyond Good and Evil?

Based on interviews with Franz Stangl, commandant of the extermination camps of Sobibor and Treblinka, Gitta Sereny's book *Into that Darkness: An Examination of Conscience* provides a wealth of details about just how kind and gentle carrying out an unalterably firm sentence of extermination is. In her preface, she explains that she thought "it essential, before it became too late, to try at least once, as far as possible unemotionally and with an open mind, to penetrate the personality of a man who had been intimately involved with the most total evil our age has produced." She saw this as a chance to evaluate "whether evil is created by circumstances or by birth, and to what extent it is determined by the individual himself or by his environment" (Sereny 1974, 13).

A composite picture of the extermination process at Treblinka and Sobibor can be put together from Sereny's interviews with Stangl and others who worked there. Richard Glazar, who was chosen to be a worker Jew at Treblinka, recalls that, even when the first signs of it were apparent, envisaging the full, or even partial, extent of the horrors to come under Nazism was all but impossible in Czechoslovakia.[7] In September 1942, he was told to report to the exhibition hall in Prague. His family was upset, but no one had any idea at all what to expect or what was in store for him.[8] His group stayed in the hall for two or three days and waited. Rumors of every kind circulated, and there was a fear of uncertainty, but no physical fear. One morning they were counted and sent to Theresienstadt and then to Treblinka (Sereny 1974, 172–75).

Glazar says that the journey was not "particularly rough, or frightening." His group traveled in relative comfort on a passenger train supervised by police in green uniforms. At Treblinka, they found a green fence, barracks, and heard what sounded like a farm tractor at work. Glazar was delighted to see what looked to him like a farm and felt glad to be going to do work he knew something about. They were politely asked to disembark at their leisure in an orderly fashion. "Medical orderlies" were present to "care for" the old and sick. On the platform were men with blue armbands without insignias who spoke German in a very strange way. One carried an unusual leather whip, like something for big animals. There were loud announcements, but nobody did anything to them. Everything was

---

[7] The following books tell how the Jewish leadership in France grew aware and reacted to the threat: Simon Schwarzfuchs 1998; Kaplan 1952; Kaplan 1984; Kaplan 1995. Maurice Szafran's biography of the politician Simone Veil (*Simone Veil, Destin*, 1994) tells of her deportation to Auschwitz.

[8] It is hard now to think that people had no idea what to expect, but there is ample evidence that many did not. Schwarzfuchs (293–95) tells of how, in about mid-1943, Rodolphe Helbronner, president of the central consistory of the Israelites of France gassed in Auschwitz in November 1943, learned of the existence of the gas chambers and mass executions of Jews from a copy of a typed letter from the papal nuncio in Munich. He initially found the revelations unimaginable. He and other Jewish leaders sent the information to de Gaulle and decided not to tell the Jewish community about it. The desire not to bring despair to those with relatives in internment camps or already deported prevailed. It was reasoned that that by that time, all those who could were in hiding. In his autobiography Joseph Rovan (p. 194 and note), an engineer of Franco-German reconciliation and secret Jew in Dachau, writes that although he was fairly high in the French Resistance, he did not know anything about the extermination camps and at the time of his deportation in July 1944 no one in France suspected that the Nazis sent their enemies arrested in foreign countries to concentration camps.

fairly restrained. The arrival of western European Jews at the death camps was designed to be "at no time grossly alarming" (Sereny 1974, 148, 176).

For the purpose of lulling people into the belief that they had come to a genuine transit camp, the commandant had ordered the construction of a false railway station, replete with a false clock with painted numerals, and hands that never moved, ticket windows, timetables, and painted arrows pointing the way to Warsaw and other cities. A camp street was built. Things were painted in beautiful, garishly bright colors. Flowers and evergreen shrubs were planted. There was a gas station with flowers around it. Wooden benches dotted the landscape "like a luxury spa." New fences were erected. The forest was cleared. A zoo was installed with "any number of marvelous birds" and benches and flowers. Glazar referred to this as "a whole macabre fakery" (Sereny 1974, 148, 166, 200, 219).

Glazar followed the crowd. Men were directed to the right, women and children to the left. The women and children disappeared into a barrack and the men were told to undress. One of the SS men told them in "a chatty sort of tune" that they were going into a disinfection bath and would afterwards be assigned a job. Clothes could be left in a pile on the ground where they would find them again later on. Documents, identity cards, money, watches and jewelry were to be kept with them. There was no time from the moment they were taken in there to talk to anyone, or to take stock of what was happening. They had no idea at all what the whole installation was about (Sereny 1974, 176–77).

The Nazis, Sereny explains in her book, "recognized the capacity of the Western Jews individually to grasp the monstrous truth and individually to resist it, and therefore ordered that great pains be taken to mislead and calm them until, naked, in rows of five and running under the whiplash, they had been made incapable of resistance" (Sereny 1974, 199). Her book contains an account of a special transport of 24,000 rich Bulgarians from Salonika who arrived with 720,000 kilograms of belongings, who, even in April 1943, with three million or so dead in camps in Poland, still did not have a clue of what awaited them, and arrived as full of illusions as Glazar's group of Czechs had six months earlier (Sereny 1974, 213–14).

Such precautions were not in general deemed necessary for most eastern Jews. Stanislaw Szmajzner remembered how he arrived in Sobibor in May 1942 with several members of his family in a freight train without windows, sanitary facilities, light, air, and filled with so many people that they had to stand up one against the other. The captives urinated, defecated, and vomited. The weakest died standing up. He recalls that the first thing he saw when the door of his car was pushed open was "two guards with whips who began shouting and hit out blindly at those who stood in front, who as the immediate target of the whips, jumped off as quickly as they could. All was perfectly planned to get people out of the cars with no delay. . . . the hurry, the noise, the fear and confusion were indescribable. . . . I saw a line of SS officers and they were shooting. . . . The purpose was to get us all to run in one direction . . ." (Sereny 1974, 122).

From the moment the train stopped, Sereny remarked, eastern Europeans saw "guards with their whips lining the platform, the SS drawn up behind them; all this deliberate, to provoke instant dread and foreboding. They were literally whipped out of the trains, and hurried and harried until the moment of their death" (Sereny 1974, 148). It was presumed that eastern Jews "up to a point—expected terror. All that was needed here was to create mass hysteria. 'They arrived, and they were dead within two hours,' Stangl said. And these two hours were filled with such an infinity of carefully devised mass violence that it robbed these hundred thousands of any chance to pause, or think" (Sereny 1974, 199).

Sereny describes the area adjoining the disembarkation ramp as no larger than a medium-sized football ground and "cunningly divided by means of blind fences into squares and corridors, with many narrow 'doors' from one square into another," to allow "the systematic separation of the arriving deportees, usually without arousing their suspicion" (Sereny 1974, 115, 202). The first selections were made. The victims stripped in the undressing barracks, left their clothes, had their hair cut off if they were women, and were internally searched for hidden valuables. The *Himmelfahrtsstrasse* (Sereny translates this "Road to Heaven") led out from the exit from the undressing area. It was a wide path through which the naked prisoners were forced to run to the "baths." When the gassing mechanism was not working properly, they were condemned to stand there, sometimes in the biting cold, for hours at a time waiting for those ahead to die. The children's naked feet often froze to the ground so that their mothers had to tear them loose when the whipping on both sides of the path began to drive them on (Sereny 1974, 149, 164–65).

An SS man waited at the door to the gas chambers to drive the people in with a whip, day after day. He was drunk most of the time. Lime pits were initially used to dispose of the corpses. Then enormous iron racks called "the roasts" were constructed, each one of which could hold several hundred stacked-up bodies. They were used for the incoming transports and to burn thousands of partly decomposed corpses dug up by excavators and either thrown into "the roasts" or carried on stretchers. "We always had to run," testified one of the survivors of this death camp detail, "and we had to be careful never to carry just one adult corpse, but always to add a couple of children—otherwise it would have looked as though we were shirking" (Sereny 1974, 164–65, 220–21).

When asked whether it would it be true to say that he got used to the exterminations, Stangl replied that one did actually become used to it. He said that it took him months before he could look them in the eyes, that he "repressed it all by trying to create a special place: gardens, new barracks, new kitchens, new everything; barbers, tailors, shoemakers, carpenters." He said that there were hundreds of ways to take one's mind off it and he took advantage of all of them. "In the end," he confessed, "the only way to deal with it was to drink. I took a large glass of brandy to bed with me each night and I drank. . . . of course thoughts came, but I forced them away. I made myself concentrate on work, work and again work" (Sereny 1974, 200). The undressing barracks were the worst place in the camp for him Stangl admitted. "I avoided it from my innermost being; I couldn't confront them; I couldn't lie to them; I avoided at any price talking to those who were about to die: I couldn't stand it." Sereny sensed that for Stangl, once the people were in the undressing barracks, once they were naked, they were no longer human beings and he avoided witnessing the transition at any price (Sereny 1974, 203).

Stangl confided that on a trip after the war, his train stopped near a slaughterhouse. He remembered,

> The cattle in the pens, hearing the noise of the train, trotted up to the fence and stared at the train. They were very close to my window, one crowding the other, looking at me through that fence. I thought then . . . that's just how the people looked, trustingly, just before they went into the tins. . . . I could not eat tinned meat after that. Those big eyes . . . which looked at me, not knowing that in no time at all they'd all be dead. . . . They were cargo. . . . I rarely saw them as individuals. . . . It was always a huge mass. I sometimes stood on the wall and saw them in the tube. But—how can I explain it—they were naked, packed together, running, being driven with whips . . . (Sereny 1974, 201)

He said that he thought that he had begun to see them as cargo in Treblinka when he had stood "next to the pits full of blue-black corpses. It had nothing to do with humanity—it couldn't have; it was a mass—a mass of rotting flesh." He said that he thinks that he unconsciously began thinking of them as cargo when he was asked what they should do with that "garbage." When asked whether or not he had been in a position to stop the nakedness, the whips, the horror of the cattle pens, he replied: "No, no, no. This was the system. . . . It worked. And because it worked, it was irreversible" (Sereny 1974, 201).

When asked what was the difference for him between hate and a contempt that results in thinking of people as cargo. He answered that it did not have anything to do with hate. "They were so weak; they allowed everything to happen—to be done to them. They were people with whom there was no common ground, no possibility of communication—that is how contempt is born. I could never understand how they could just give in as they did. Quite recently I read a book about lemmings, who every five or six years just wander into the sea and die; that made me think of Treblinka" (Sereny 1974, 232–33).

Stangl told Sereny a story in a manner that came to represent to her the starkest example of a corrupted personality she had ever encountered. One morning, one of the worker Jews, Stangl recalled, knocked on the door of his office. He asked permission to speak with Stangl. He explained that his eighty-year-old father had arrived that morning and wanted to know whether there was anything Stangl could do. Stangl responded that it was really impossible to save an eighty-year-old man, but would give him unofficial permission give his father a meal in the kitchen and then take him to what was called the *Lazarett*, a fake hospital where old people and sick people were shot instead of gassed. It consisted of a shell of a small, roofless building with a Red Cross painted on the front. People were taken there to be killed and for no other reason. There was an earthen wall running almost the length of the building with a pit on the other side. The victims were helped to undress, then had to sit on that wall, were shot, in the neck and dropped into the continually burning pit. In the afternoon, with tears in his eyes, the man returned to Stangl's office to thank him for his magnanimity. Sereny says that she thinks that the only reason she was able resume her conversations with Stangl after hearing that story was that she had come "to realize that for a man whose view was so distorted that he *could* tell that story in that way, the relatively simple terms 'guilt' or 'innocence,' 'good' or 'bad' no longer applied" (Sereny 1974, 165, 190, 207–8).

Baudelaire's Meditation on a Corpse

Radical evil, be it in Europe, Rwanda, Cambodia, Algeria, the Soviet Union, Liberia, the Congo, Burundi, Sierra Leone, Iraq . . . often leaves a trail of dead bodies and otherwise destroyed lives in its wake. So in concluding this part about the reality of evil, it is appropriate to let dead bodies have their say. We can begin with a famous poem by Baudelaire, who fancied that he might be thought of by others as the "Prince of Corpses" (Pichois, 380):

"A Corpse"

Remember the object we saw, my soul,
That beautiful summer morning so mild:
At the turning of a path, a foul corpse
On a bed strewn with pebbles,
Legs in the air, like a lewd woman,

Afire, and oozing poisons,
Nonchalantly and shamelessly opened
Her belly full of fumes.
The sun beamed down on this rottenness,
As if to cook it just right
And to render unto great Nature hundredfold
All that she had joined together;
And the sky was watching that superb carcass
Blossom like a flower.
The stench was so strong, that you believed
You would fall unconscious onto the grass.
The flies buzzed over this putrid belly,
From which strode battalions
Of larvae flowing like a thick liquid
All along the living rags of clothing.
All that fell, rose like a wave,
Or shot out scintillating.
One might have said that the corpse, puffed up with some
hesitating breath
Was living by multiplying.
And this world produced a strange music,
Like running water and the wind,
Or the grain of a winnower with a rhythmic movement
Shakes and turns in the winnow.
The forms faded away and were no more than a dream,
A rough sketch slow to be realized,
On a forgotten canvas, and that the artist finishes
From memory only.
Behind the rocks a restless bitch
Was looking at us with an angry eye,
Watching for the moment to take again from the skeleton
The bit she had let go of.
—And yet you will be like this refuse,
Like this horrible putrefaction,
Star of my eyes, sun of my self,
You, my angel and my passion!
Yes! So you will be, o queen of graces,
After the last sacraments,
When you go beneath the grass and wealth of flowers,
To mold among the bones.
Then, o my beauty! Tell the vermin
Who will devour you with kisses,
That I safeguarded the form and divine essence
Of my decomposed love! (Baudelaire 1857, XXIX)

Meditating on Piles of Corpses

Jacques Sommet, a political philosopher and one of the 2,579 priests in the Nazi concentration camp Dachau (Kammerer, 70), has written of his search for meaning in what he experienced there and the spiritual evolution that it forced him to undergo. Of particular interest are his reflections on his experiences of pure evil as destruction and his meditations on Dachau's piles of corpses (Sommet 1987, 58–147).

The first phase of Father Sommet's reflections on radical evil begin in the few days that he spent in the leaded train car that took him to Dachau. He came to view his journey across the countryside in those closed boxes as a symbol, as a central point of crystallization for reflections on "God and evil in a pure, or almost pure, state." One hundred and ten captives were stuffed into a car designed for "forty people, eight horses." The doors were locked from the outside and the small openings that were meant to allow the animals to breathe were closed shut. The prisoners were walled in. The summer heat fast became asphyxiating. Once crammed into that box, the captives were in total darkness in broad daylight. They had to stand for four days. The conditions were physically intolerable, the dehydration unbearable. No one touched food because everyone was thirsty and there was nothing to drink. Then the convoy started to linger interminably at the border. They cried out for water. Without opening the door, the guards only responded only by sprinkling the car with hoses. The watering just dampened the heat and made conditions worse (Sommet 1987, 67–68).

After three days the captives were worn out from exhaustion. A sort of decomposition set in. People, Father Sommet noted, change rapidly in such degrading circumstances. Some were unable to control their terror. Others lost their minds. No matter what their life had been in the resistance movement and in prison, many were lost. They remained buried in that human mass closing in upon itself. Human relationships were utterly destroyed. Communication stopped. No relationship could seriously develop. One was alone. Just being completely indiscriminately jumbled in with other people in that way was a kind of aloneness. One could speak of a hell, Father Sommet reflects, but there was another hell to come afterwards (Sommet 1987, 67–68, 121).

Father Sommet remembers having experienced all this as a kind of descent into an impaired state of consciousness. You slip on a slope and you fall without knowing how, and you skid more and more quickly, with no end in sight. The first phase is quite conscious. You try to cope. During the second phase, you are tired, under a great deal of strain, drained. During the third phase, you are only conscious of being shaken in a crate. Towards the end, he lost consciousness several times. Finally, he could not stand up any longer and he collapsed in a corner. When they arrived, he was half conscious. One had no sense of where one was (Sommet 1987, 68–69).

Seven or eight people died of asphyxiation. A genuine metamorphosis had taken place in the rest. Their faces were empty, hollow. People had lost several pounds, grown skeletal. They gave one another astonished looks. They had undergone an ordeal of individual, subjective destruction, had become only a disintegrated lump, without prospects for the future. The world was no longer the same (Sommet 1987, 68–71, 122).

They had crossed a threshold before even entering the camp. Before that ruinous train ride, Father Sommet explains,

> I would not have been so inclined to think of evil as pure destruction. I entered into a universe without any relationship to other people. I passed through a place that is in and of itself utterly destructive. It did not finish its work. It might have. It was physically destructive. One does not see anything there that could enable someone to survive for very long. It was the destroying of human relationships. Practically speaking, all prior ties were liquidated. And you do not start up others during that time. You plunge into gratuitous destruction. What you experience has no connection with the political causes espoused, social or political guilt that one might have. Things are radically out of proportion. During those few days there was also the evil that illness is. A strange thing, if you like, it was the universe itself, organized by people, that I experienced as outstripped by what I would call the mystery itself of evil. The activity of evil goes beyond any plan, be it of imprisoning people, of stymieing enemies, of executing others, of purifying a situation. A kind of destruction is at work that is a kind of gratuitousness, gratuitousness turned upside down! Because gratuitousness can be a grace. But there, it was destruction for the sake of destruction, beyond any apparent reason, any motive, or justification. (Sommet 1987, 122)

That period of utter aloneness without human contact brought Father Sommet to resituate himself with regard to what, because there was nothing else, he calls *God alone.* There was nothing, and there was the experience of God, or rather there were two things: human experience and the experience of God in the raw state. He found that the only possible alternative, and one which proved quite a good one in that situation, was in the relationship to God. "Abandonment to the incomprehensibility of God remained supremely possible," he explains.

> Because against that destructive universe, that very God, who is the transcendent God, dwells in this world, dwells in what remains of life . . . despite everything escapes the clutches of that destruction because unable, from certain angles, to do anything there. God offers himself as the possibility that I have to say yes or no to what is destroying me. That is the very experience of freedom. Everything is doomed to be destroyed, and yet I can say no to this destruction. If I am destroyed, I shall be destroyed as a body. But in this destruction, noth-

ing can force my mind, my freedom, to say the opposite of what I am saying. (Sommet 1987, 122–23)

Arriving at Dachau after that devastating journey, Sommet remembers the first day of quarantine, before any human relationships had built up. A bit of sun was shining at the foot of a watchtower at the top of which was a man wearing a helmet with the skull insignia of the SS and armed with a machine gun. That fellow, Sommet reflected, is utterly afraid of being sent to Russia and is ready to do anything to escape that fate. In a certain way, he wanted to say:

> "I am the winner." The universe of destruction seemed to me there in its violence and yet beset with great fragility. That armed, leather clad SS man, that metallic order, that adulterated conscience, finally that construction, was a deconstruction. Such as I am here, he can do nothing against me. They have done everything they could. They have practically robbed me of my body. The rest I find intact. I can freely say: "I believe in God." I can freely say: "Long live life!" While he up there is already destroyed by his destruction. He can shorten the life of my body, but it will end in any case. That is part of my life as a human being. That man can no longer even say a word to me. He is isolated in his power, and I continue to think what I am and even do so a bit more than before. (Sommet 1987, 123)

Each morning during the typhus epidemic, piles of cadavers were gathered on the doorsteps of the barracks, and each day carts filled with corpses dangling like broken marionettes traversed the central thoroughfare to be transformed into cinders that went to nourish the fields. Like some absurd incense, Sommet says, the faint odor of their burning bodies left an indelible memory. Yet, daily life continued to unfold under wretched circumstances, a bit like a hospital where terminally ill patients die, but the life of the establishment nevertheless carries on (Sommet 1987, 111, 125–26).

Father Sommet writes of the collective significance of these deaths, for "in this group of people who were trying to live, the very ones who were dying in their midst were witnesses both to the point up to which one must go and of the grandeur of what they were doing." The excessiveness of what was overpowering them, of what was being imposed upon them, that in the name of which they were beaten, martyred, terrorized, made their lives into a kind of protest" (Sommet 1987, 111). In the camp's dead, Sommet saw

> a great number of people who, in spite of everything, died to witness to the indignity of what overpowered them and to the dignity of what they were. . . . This kind of test is another sign that what is inhuman cannot succeed in triumphing over people because there are always people who manage to manifest

their goodness. Yes, some manifested their goodness there, some their courage, some their *joie de vivre*, the naiveté of living simply to the end. After all, this heap of people did not commit suicide. That already raises the question. That is already affirming the meaning of something. So many people die who have perhaps never positively reflected about everything that is involved in their lives; and in times of trial, before lives given up in such a senseless way, they tried to live to the end, more or less maladroitly, more or less adroitly. Does that not mean that the path they trod has some meaning for them? If not it has no *raison d'être*. (Sommet 1987, 110)

Hope, Father Sommet is prepared to affirm, "rests first of all in the encounter with death. People are apparently abandoned by life: they die . . . . Yet, in spite of everything, it is within people's reach to live death as an affirmation of life" (Sommet 1987, 110).

In the face of the evil he was experiencing, Sommet took heart in the example of "people who believed it possible and reasonably right always to be supportive of the least among them at any cost to themselves and acted accordingly. The mere fact that life organized itself when it was supremely impossible, the mere fact that people, including the most doomed, were treated with a certain amount of respect and dignity, and were so in an environment made to debase them, is a kind of victory, of light, even if there is not any immediate effectiveness in it. . . . Accepting to live that as being the truth," Sommet reflects, "is to accept it upon its terms, to accept to disappear. To accept peacefully, patiently, hour after hour, to disappear" (Sommet 1987, 125).

In writing that, Father Sommet was particularly thinking of the example of those who unconditionally chose to risk their own lives to care for doomed victims of typhus by going to live in their barracks "to live as living people in order to help the dying die as living people . . . to share the life of dying people in such a way that their dying moments were truly a fight for life" (Sommet 1987, 106). He says that that fidelity to the fraternal, incomprehensible God that he witnessed in those who unconditionally served their doomed fellows taught him a new fidelity, a fidelity to what he called the people of the piles of corpses (Sommet 1987, 127).

When the fences came down at the end of the war, Father Sommet did not leave the camp immediately. He went to the place where they burned the dead. He found himself before a pile of cadavers. There he meditated amid the piled up, broken up corpses, bodies, amid the human remains of broken lives in the presence of those who were not there. There had been misery and death in the camp before, but the crisis-filled final weeks before the camp was liberated brought about an intensification of misery and death on a massive scale. It was the corpses heaped up at the end of the camp that spoke to him as the deepest expression of evil. He considered the earlier stages of his experience of evil to have been "outdone, or van-

quished. . . . Here they were overflowing. They were irrationality extant
. . . a sign of the satanic, of the destruction that kills blindly, of a collective
cancer at work" (Sommet 1987, 111, 126–27).

Some of those people, he reflected, had perhaps been cared for in their
dying moments, "but nine out of ten had died without that experience. It
was therefore the failure of a life. That spectacle of bodies," he considered,
"had both a cruel and tender side. As if the humanity that had disappeared
took on a concrete face, though that face was disfigured. Those dead people were in positions of abandonment, in several senses of the word abandon. It was not only terrifying, but it was that too" (Sommet 1987, 126).

Father Sommet says that he felt overwhelmed "by the silence of their
presence, which was a kind of silent, immense speech. While they were
freedom vanquished in what it was accomplishing, they continued to say
. . . that the price of freedom goes by way of that. Those dead people who
were there, freedom vanquished in their bodies, were a reminder . . . that
the failure of their existence was indicative of the price that freedom and
dignity demand" (Sommet 1987, 127). For Father Sommet, those corpses
were a kind of protest in the name of life. "Because, while they, those abandoned bodies could not do anything, they had come to that by doing
something, or being constrained to do something, constrained to be
deserving, constrained to leave their lives in an adventure that was not simply one of making daily choices every about what feels good and does not
feel good" (Sommet 1987, 112).

Those piles of dead people challenged Sommet to find answers to the
questions they raised. It took him a long time to perceive and learn to
express a meaning. Before this evil as the seeming historical failure of
everything that had gone on before, he found himself asking in protest
what meaning any past, however brilliant, could have before this reality of
failure, what could be said, and what could be done. In that human adventure there were people who had escaped, did not experience either the
opportunity or the risk of interpersonal relationships.

There was something paradoxical in his meditation on the cadavers,
Sommet concluded. Being there as stacks of bodies was a failure, but they
spoke to him of the "failure of an adventure, of the adventure of destruction," for the failure in question

> was not utter annihilation. It was both a sign and a protest. . . . The executioner
> could not eliminate them. The bodies were there and they were the sign of
> something. That was not nothing. It did not lie with Hitler and his to make
> them disappear. They had only been able to kill. That is not the same thing.
> Some were burned and their ashes cast to the wind. That did not happen to all
> of them. The piles of corpses existed. Those were the cadavers of people who
> exhausted the forces of the adversary who did not have the time to eliminate
> them to the point of reducing them to ashes. (Sommet 1987, 127)

He could not escape asking questions about the relationship between life, death, and the future of society. "Where," he asked, "were the others?" Not the victims he helped to die, but the masses of other people who would not have been able to know the duty of continuing to be present to people, or who were never conscious of this duty? He saw that question as putting forward the absolute weight that the problem of dignity has in interpersonal relationships and it gnawed away inside him unanswered for a long time as something upon which light had to be shed in spite of everything (Sommet 1987, 126–27).

Those corpses, Sommet came to see, had two kinds of companions. There were people like him who had gone through the same ordeal and were not dead, and there were the generations to come who might not remember or might not know what had happened. If these dead people did not have any progeny, he reflected, if the universe was finite, then failure would have had the last word. But because they did have children, and he was between the two, those mountains of apparent failures obliged him to take his place between them and the future. There remained the task of taking up what had been attempted through these dead people. This task had failed momentarily in their bodies, but not in terms of the significance of what they had done and of which they were the meaningful presence. He was a witness. He was a bridge between them and the future (Sommet 1987, 128).

What was God present, incomprehensible, immediate, saying to them, saying through them? Sommet did not interpret his experience as a message about the absence of God, or of abandonment by God, but rather one of the mystery of the hidden God. If he had cause to feel scandalized by extreme evil, he thought that it was perhaps because he had not sufficiently listened to what God expected. He saw Dachau as still being only one gauge of human suffering and death and his own job as being to try to understand, through that human suffering and death, marks of human contempt, hardships, weaknesses, betrayals, and hatred for one another, to understand through all that human suffering and death the risk that love as an opportunity, and not simply as human defeat, can run. The piles of corpses taught him that

> divine life was also running all throughout that share of disfiguration and destruction, for there is not only the failure of the individual, there is the betrayal of friends by friends, contempt of the adversary, the violent fist striking the face of a child, there are also those great failures, more or less conscious, that were expressed by those stacks of cadavers, those piles of corpses. Either that opportunity does not exist, or that massive dying was still telling me something of what people should have, could have been. (Sommet 1987, 130–31)

Sommet says that he has sufficiently participated in the fight of people who give their lives to know how hard it is to give one's life with purity and justice. "Where people give their lives and do it with justice, honesty, integrity, is where the power of suffering and dying is truly effective. If no one suffers and dies with sufficient purity, then people are victims. They do not suffer and die in a way that transforms their history" (Sommet 1987, 131–32).

"*Violence is rarely intelligent*" (Sommet 1987, 64, my emphasis).

PART THREE

And from Reality to Theory

Not everyone enjoys the spectacle of cruelty as Nietzsche said, not even secretly,—or hypocritically, as Baudelaire suggested. Some people are genuinely sickened and revolted by evil, even to the point of being willing to risk their lives, their chances for health and well-being, to put an end to it. History, past and present, is replete with illustrations of this.

So the question that arises in the wake of the recitation of the cruel litany of Part Two is: Is one obliged to accept the evil depicted there as the inevitable realizations of the kinds of evil glorified, beautified, idealized, justified through the ideas of the likes of Baudelaire, Nietzsche, and Hitler? Are we to leave evil the last word? Is there an alternative?

Sigmund Freud, for one, considered that people needed "education to reality"(Freud 1927, 233) and that in "reality, there is no such thing as 'eradicating' evil" (Freud 1915, 68). Many, however, have gone to quite the other extreme. "By saying non-violence," stressed the French peace activist Jean Goss,[1] "I begin by refusing a fatality of violence, that is, of evil. The evil in me, the evil around me is not inevitable" (Houver, 1).

Mohandas Gandhi, to take one of the most notable examples, endeavored to show that the "way of purging the world of evil" was to "try to overcome evil by good, anger by love, untruth by truth, violence by nonviolence" (Gandhi 2002, 91). He believed that people face two alternatives: "The one is that of violence, the other of nonviolence; the one of hatred, the other of love; the one of disorder, the other of peace; one that is demonic, the other Godly. . . . As they are incompatible with each other, the fruit . . . that would be secured by following the one would necessarily be different from that which would be secured by following the other. . . . We shall reap what we sow" (Gandhi 2002, 104).

Gandhi further believed that it "should be an essential of real education that a child should learn that in the struggle of life, one can easily conquer hate by love, untruth by truth, violence by self-suffering" (Gandhi 2002, 88). He believed that in the hands of the teacher, nonviolence should "take the form of the purest love, ever fresh, an ever gushing spring of life expressing itself in every act. Ill will cannot stand in its presence. The sun of nonviolence carries all the hosts of darkness such as hatred, anger, and malice before itself. Nonviolence in education shines clear and far and can no more be hidden, even as the sun cannot be hidden by any means" (Gandhi 2002, 127).

---

[1] Jean Goss (1972–1991) and his wife Hildegard Goss-Mayr (1930–), who holds a doctorate in philosophy from Yale University, work together for peace through the Movement for International Reconciliation. Her father was one of Europe's first nonviolent activists.

From Reality to Theory

Proponents of eradicating evil through non-violent means typically underscore how thoroughly planted in reality their approach is. Goss utterly rejected the idea that nonviolence is "for saints and naive idiots; 'reality' . . . for realists and violent people" (Houver, 96). Love, he insisted, "is not a cloud wandering high up in the sky. It's hands, faces, hearts; it's Life there where you are, immediately" (Houver, 104).

Dr. Martin Luther King, famous for his work to end segregation in the United States, did not consider himself a "doctrinaire pacifist," but someone who "tried to embrace a realistic pacifism" (King 1960a, 61). He affirmed that true "nonviolent resistance is not unrealistic submission to evil power. It is rather a courageous confrontation of evil by the power of love, in the faith that it is better to be the recipient of violence than the inflictor of it, since the latter only multiplies the existence of violence and bitterness in the universe, while the former may develop a sense of shame in the opponent, and thereby bring about a transformation and change of heart" (King 1959a, 44). According to King, the nonviolent approach "first does something to the hearts and souls of those committed to it. It gives them new self-respect; it calls up resources of strength and courage that they did not know they had. Finally it reaches the opponent and so stirs his conscience that reconciliation becomes a reality" (King 1960a, 60). So, the answer King found was to "face violence if necessary, but refuse to return violence. If we respect those who oppose us, they may achieve a new understanding of the human relations involved" (King 1956, 7).

In "Pilgrimage to Nonviolence" (King 1960a, 54–62), in words that really turn Hitler's theory about the need to resort to violence and physical terror on its head, King told of how the world picture and philosophy that became the unshakeable basis of his action for the rest of his life had taken shape within him. He told of how he had verified what he had learned from reality and had used reality to test his theories. Before he came upon the life and teachings of Gandhi, King said of his search for "a method to eliminate social evil," he had "almost despaired of the power of love in solving social problems," had felt that when racial groups and nations were in conflict "a more realistic approach" was necessary (King 1960a, 58).

However, as he delved deeper, King came to see that the "Gandhian method of nonviolence was one of the most potent weapons available to people in their struggle for freedom" (King 1960a, 58–59). The reality of his own earliest experiments with nonviolence, King said, finally served to clarify his thinking more than all the books he had read. "As the days unfolded," he recalled, "I became more and more convinced of the power of nonviolence. Living through the actual experience of the protest, nonviolence became more than a method to which I gave intellectual assent; it became a commitment to a way of life. Many issues I had not cleared up intellectually concerning nonviolence were now solved in the sphere of practical action" (King 1960a, 59). King considered nonviolence really to be the "most potent weapon available to the Negro in his struggle for justice" (King 1967b, 175).

Gandhi insisted that nonviolence was "no wooden or lifeless dogma, but a living and a life-giving force" (Gandhi 2002, 127). He said that Tolstoy had furnished him "a reasoned basis" for his nonviolence" and Thoreau's "Duty of Civil Disobedience" had provided him with "scientific confirmation of what he was doing" (Gandhi 2002, 169), but that experience was "the real school" (Gandhi 2002, 174). At one point, Gandhi said that he had "been practicing with scientific precision nonviolence and its possibilities for an unbroken period of over fifty years," that he had "applied it in every walk of life—domestic, institutional, economic, and political" and knew of no single case in which it had failed (Gandhi 2002, 120).

What Experience Has Taught Proponents
of Nonviolence

Gandhi said that his "study and experience of nonviolence" had proved to him "that it is the greatest force in the world. It is the surest method of discovering the truth and it is the quickest because there is no other. It works silently, almost imperceptibly, but nonetheless surely. It is the one constructive process of nature in the midst of incessant destruction going on about us" (Gandhi 2002, 100).

"Human experience," professed Gandhi, "is that as good comes out of good, only evil comes out of evil. Retaliation cannot end violence. If humanity is to rise above violence there is no alternative but to adopt nonviolence. Love alone can conquer hatred . . ." (Gandhi 2002, 125). "Humanity has to get out of violence only through nonviolence," he believed. "Hatred can be overcome only by love. Counter-hatred only increases the surface as well as the depth of hatred" (Gandhi 2002, 146). "Hatred ever kills. Love ever dies. Such is the vast difference between the two. What is obtained by love is retained for all time. What is obtained by hatred, proves a burden in reality, for it increases hatred" (Gandhi 2002, 159). Gandhi said that after decades of experience, his faith in these ideals grew stronger day after day (Gandhi 2002, 125).

"Violence keeps itself going through violence," agreed Goss (Houver, 96). "The logic of violence is implacable; from one murder you make another," he stressed (Houver, 74). "Every time we use violence we are prisoners of violence; there is no break in the chain. Every time we live on love we break a link in the chain of violence" (Houver, 121).

When one is concerned about justice, brotherhood, and truth, Martin Luther King stressed along the same lines, one can never advocate violence: "For through violence you may murder a murderer but you can't murder murder. Through violence you may murder a liar but you can't establish truth. Through violence you may murder a hater, but you can't murder hate. Darkness cannot put out darkness. Only light can do that" (King 1967b, 176). As Sigmund Freud, himself no believer in the efficaciousness of nonviolence, observed: violence "cuts all the common bonds between the contending peoples, and threatens to leave a legacy of embitterment that will make any renewal of those bonds impossible for a long-time to come" (Freud 1915, 65).

The Russian hermit Leo Tolstoy reasoned that the "more people you murder, the smaller the chance of saving yourselves from your chief enemy: the hatred people feel towards you. By your crimes you only increase this hatred tenfold and make it more dangerous to yourselves" (Tolstoy 1908, 222). He considered it "apparent that evil deeds committed by the governing powers in order to rid themselves of their visible enemies gather twice or even ten times as many invisible enemies, who are far more angry" (Tolstoy 1908, 224), for "all those you strangle with ropes and shoot above graves dug out by men still living had and have fathers, brothers, wives, sisters, friends and like-minded followers, and if these executions spare you from those who are buried in the graves they generate, not only among those who were close to them, but among strangers too, twice as many enemies, twice as pernicious as those you have killed and buried in the earth" (Tolstoy 1908, 222). "Apart from increasing the number of your enemies and their hatred, through those you execute, these very executions increase, even among men who are perfect strangers to yourselves and your enemies, that feeling of cruelty and immorality you think you are combating with these executions. For these executions are not performed automatically by the papers which you write in your law courts and ministries. People are executed by other people" (Tolstoy 1908, 222–23). As Gandhi pointed out: "behind the death-dealing bomb there is the human hand that releases it, and behind that still, is the human heart that sets the hand in motion" (Gandhi 2002, 179).

Proponents of nonviolent methods of eradicating evil also emphasize that nonviolent actions "can never adopt the methods of violent action; they would head ineluctably for the same goals as violence: the destruction of man, death and evil," that nonviolence represents "the definitive break in the crazy spiral of violence" (Houver, 74). If revolutionaries of whatever party, Tolstoy argued, permit murder for the attainment of their aims, "their crimes are just as immoral and cruel as the activities of the government. And they therefore lead to the same awful consequences as do the evil-doings of the government: the animosity, bestialization and corruption of the people" (Tolstoy 1908, 224).

Martin Luther King addressed "the danger that those of us who have lived so long under the yoke of oppression, those of us who have been exploited and trampled over, those of us who have had to stand amid the tragic midnight of injustice and indignities" would be tempted to respond "with hate and bitterness." If we retaliate with hate and bitterness, he taught, the future will only be a duplication of the past. He called upon African Americans to use love and justice to "blot out the hate and injustice" of the past. He said that the reason that he believed so firmly in nonviolence to combat what he called the "glaring evil" of segregation (King 1957, 24) was that: "Violence never solves problems. It only creates new and more complicated ones. If we succumb to the temptation of using violence in our struggle for justice, unborn generations will be the recipients of a long and desolate night of bitterness, and our chief legacy to the future will be an endless reign of meaningless chaos" (King 1957, 20). "The way of violence leads to bitterness in the survivors and brutality in the destroyers. But, the way of nonviolence leads to redemption and the creation of the beloved community" (King 1959a, 43).

Mikhail Gorbachev on Going from Theory to Reality and from Reality to Theory

In *On My Country and the World,* Mikhail Gorbachev, the engineer of what former CIA director Robert Gates has called "one of the most far-reaching, and bloodless, political revolutions in history" (Gates, 447), studies the implications of several interrelated realities (ex. Gorbachev 84, 171, 175, 188, 189, 216, 248) that led him to call for "a profound and critical reexamination" not only of the problems confronting the Soviet Union, "but a rethinking of all realities—both national and international" (Gorbachev, 58), for the "new thinking" that brought about the stunning change of course of what his counterpart in the United States famously called "the evil empire."

In that book, Gorbachev condemns the socialism of the Soviet Union as having been "distorted, deformed, and incomplete" (Gorbachev, 15). The Bolshevik model of socialism was defective, he considered, because "it was a crudely schematic model based on ideological principles and standards that could not withstand close examination" (Gorbachev, 18). He condemned Stalin's interpretation of those principles and standards as "a quasi-religious doctrine based on intolerance and ruthless suppression" that "deepened their harsh and dogmatic character" (Gorbachev, 18). "By its very nature, wherever it might arise and in whatever garments it might be vested, totalitarianism cannot exist without a harsh ideological and political system, a set of stereotypes that distort reality . . .," he maintained (Gorbachev, 172).

Problems of internal development in the Soviet Union, Gorbachev explains in that book, "were ripe, even overripe, for a solution. New approaches and types of action were needed to escape the downward spiral of crisis, to normalize life, and to make a breakthrough to qualitatively new frontiers" (Gorbachev, 56). "Conditions had grown ripe —not only economically but also politically and psychologically—for a fundamental change . . ." (Gorbachev, 24). He believed that the Soviet Union "had grown ripe for a profound restructuring" well before the mid-1980s, but if the restructuring had not begun when it did, "an explosion would have taken place in the USSR, one of tremendous destructive force" (Gorbachev, 60), for history teaches "that when the times are ripe for change and the government refuses or is unable to change, either society starts to decay or a revolution begins" (Gorbachev, 5).

An analogous problem afflicted Soviet foreign policy, Gorbachev considers, for it too lie in concepts that "rested on a dogmatic world outlook" (Gorbachev, 172). According to him, a "hard core of ideological constructs ultimately determined the behavior of the USSR on decisive questions of international relations" (Gorbachev, 65). He saw the prevailing conceptions of the world and its developmental trends, and of the Soviet Union's place and role in the world as based "on dogmas deeply rooted in our ideology, which essentially did not permit us to pursue a realistic policy" (Gorbachev, 59).

He believed that those dogmas "had to be shattered and fundamentally new views worked out" (Gorbachev, 59). The time had come, he believed, "for everyone to gradually learn to live together, based on the realities of a modern world that was constantly changing according to certain basic regularities inherent in it" (Gorbachev, 178). "International relations had to be freed of ideologies" (Gorbachev, 189). He believed that "earlier attempts to refine or modernize Soviet foreign policy, taking the world's realities into account . . . were inconsistent and, most important, were not reinforced by appropriate changes in the very conception of the fundamental principles of state policy" (Gorbachev, 177).

The Reality of Power in the Nuclear Age

The realities of life in the nuclear age have won many a convert to the cause of nonviolence, have brought many to sense along with Martin Luther King that the "choice today is no longer between violence and nonviolence. It is either nonviolence or nonexistence" (King 1960a, 61). "If we assume," King observed, "that mankind has a right to survive then we must find an alternative to war and destruction. In a day when sputniks dash through outer space and guided ballistic missiles are carving highways of death through the stratosphere, nobody can win a war" (King 1960a, 62). "War is not the answer. Communism will never be defeated by the use of atomic bombs or nuclear weapons," King preached. America's best defense against communism is a positive revolution of values, "to take offensive action in behalf of justice," to engage in "a positive thrust for democracy" (King 1967a, 149).

"In this age of the atom bomb," Gandhi said in the late 1940s, "unadulterated nonviolence is the only force that can confound all the tricks put together of violence" (Gandhi 2002, 146). "Nonviolence is a mightier weapon by far than the atom bomb" (Gandhi 2002, 148). He believed that the world has no other really effective remedy to offer than the way of nonviolence (Gandhi 2002, 89), that it was the only weapon that could save the world (Gandhi 2002, 145), "the greatest force at the disposal of humanity. It is mightier than the mightiest weapon of destruction devised by the ingenuity of humanity" (Gandhi 2002, 96). In 1938, before the advent of the atom bomb, he had noted:

> It is open to the great powers to take up nonviolence any day and cover themselves with glory and earn the eternal gratitude of posterity. If they or any of them can shed the fear of destruction, if they disarm themselves, they will automatically help the rest to regain their sanity. But then these great powers have to give up imperialistic ambitions and exploitation of the so-called uncivilized nations of the earth and revise their mode of life. It means complete revolution. Great nations can hardly be expected in the ordinary course to move spontaneously in a direction the reverse of the one they have followed and according to their notion of value, from victory to victory. But miracles have happened before and may happen even in this very prosaic age. Who can dare limit God's power of undoing wrong? (Gandhi 2002, 187)

Gorbachev lucidly saw that the nuclear age inevitably dictated new political thinking (Gorbachev, 177, 174). Profound reflection on the possible consequences of the use of weapons of mass destruction forced him, he explains, to draw three theoretical-political conclusions of prime importance: (1) "the nature of modern weaponry leaves no country any hope of defending itself by purely military and technical means"; (2) "politics based on the use of force is doomed"; (3) "security under contemporary conditions . . . can only be mutual . . . universal" (Gorbachev, 192).

Taking the new realities into account, Gorbachev's "new thinking" tackled the subject of "a world without armaments, a world without wars" from two angles. It recognized: on the one hand, the inadmissibility of nuclear war and its deadly consequences and the need to renounce military methods in general as a means of resolving conflicts; and on the other hand, that rational goals could not be achieved by use of force, but only by renouncing power politics. This meant that a "transition had to be made to a nuclear-free world and a world without violence" (Gorbachev, 248). "Governments had to renounce approaches involving the use of force, fraught with the danger of the destruction of millions of people, if not the entire human race" (Gorbachev, 174).

Gorbachev is aware that some justify "war as an inevitable evil rooted in the very depths of human nature—an evil that the human race can never eliminate" and that this even seems to be confirmed by history (Gorbachev, 248). He also acknowledges that "the tradition of power politics and of solving problems by armed force is deeply rooted in the consciousness of individuals and entire nations" (Gorbachev, 249). However, he lucidly points out that "the experience of the entire era since World War II shows that not a single armed conflict has given its participants or, above all, its initiators any serious political dividends" (Gorbachev, 191). To support his contention, one need only consider the fact that the great American military victories of the Reagan era, a period of massive military buildup for the United States, were Grenada and Panama.

Meanwhile, back in Washington, the Reagan administration was so engrossed in its "glorious crusade" to "counter the awesome Soviet missile threat" of President Reagan's evil empire speech, so bent on engaging in a dangerous, expensive acceleration of the arms race that it was slow to perceive Gorbachev's dramatic change of course and the degree of change that he was bringing about, did not at first notice that the other runner was dropping out of the race (Gates, 263, 446, 550, 565–66, 575).

So while the Reagan administration was hard at work unleashing its aggressive impulses in a massive military buildup, Gorbachev was clearing a path to a nuclear-free world that would make it possible to "break through the seemingly impregnable wall of old ideas and the policies of hatred, intolerance, and mutual rejection that corresponded to those ideas" (Gorbachev, 194–95, 216). He considers that it was precisely the Soviet Union's new foreign policy orientation that allowed it "to take a principled position, to insist that aggression was unacceptable, no matter who the aggressor might be" (Gorbachev, 204). He considered that: "the Soviet Union was willing to find a way to arrive at genuinely democratic and peaceful international relations. In the West, particularly in the United States, no such willingness existed" (Gorbachev, 210).

Attacking with the Truth

Philosophers of nonviolent responses to evil will be quick to see links between Sigmund Freud's conviction that in "reality, there is no such thing as 'eradicating' evil" (Freud 1915, 68) and his talk of "the immense advantages to be gained by the practice of lying and deception" (Freud 1915, 62–63).

Gandhi acknowledged having been "overwhelmed" by the "independent thinking, profound morality, and the truthfulness" evident in the theories of Leo Tolstoy (Gandhi 1927-29, 136). Gandhi claimed that he had "not a shadow of a doubt that there is no power superior to the power of truth and nonviolence in the world" (Gandhi 2002, 145). He called lying "the mother of violence" (Gandhi 2002, 104). In *An Autobiography or The Story of My Experiments with Truth*, he wrote: "Truth is like a vast tree, which yields more and more fruit, the more you nurture it. The deeper the search in the mine of truth, the richer the discovery of the gems buried there . . ." (Gandhi 1927-29, 206). He says there that it had been his ceaseless effort to describe truth as it has appeared to him and in the precise manner in which he had arrived at it. He had hoped in so doing that this might bring faith in Truth and the lack of desire to harm or do violence to any living being, the will to nonviolence to waverers (Gandhi 1927-29, 452–53). "Truthful people cannot long remain violent. They will perceive in the course of their search that they have no need to be violent and they will further discover that so long as there is the slightest trace of violence within, they will fail to find the truth they are seeking" (Gandhi 2002, 104).

Martin Luther King defended the same principle in his Nobel Prize acceptance speech when he affirmed that "unarmed truth and unconditional love will have the final word in reality. That is why right temporarily defeated is stronger than evil triumphant" (King 1964, 111). Earlier, he had declared: "There is something in this universe that justifies Carlyle in saying, 'No lie can live forever'" (King 1957, 23). He stressed that "truth pressed to earth will rise again. . . . no lie can live forever . . . you still reap what you sow . . . the moral arm of the universe is long but it bends toward justice . . . the Lord . . . has loosed the fateful lightning of his terrible swift sword. His truth is marching on" (King,1965, 124).

As Hildegard Goss-Mayr has explained: "The effectiveness and the strength of direct actions is conditioned by how much truth penetrates through them and deeply affects people who were, at first indifferent" (Houver, 107). "Non-violent action is fundamentally creative. It makes each particular individual discover the latent forces of truth within himself and put them into action with imagination and initiative" (Houver, 105). "The reality of this love, the experience we can have of this truth, this liberty within ourselves, is the only force we can set against violence"

(Houver, 118). "Has not truth shown itself to be the power of the poor?" she asks (Goss-Mayr, 238).

Partisans of nonviolent solutions to evil are perfectly realistic about the extent to which hypocritical, lying behavior is shortsighted and ultimately proves to be one of the most effective means of bringing an end to precisely what one says that one is intent upon preserving. So people fighting evil by nonviolent means have prescribed truthfulness and behavior that brings the deepest values of their adversaries to the fore. They realistically see the power of criticism emanating from within and of the violence of people's own bad consciences in particular.

Jean Goss explained that the nonviolent activist "attacks the person in front of him with truth. The other one has a choice: he accepts that truth or he kills. There's nothing in between. There we have the aggressivity of non-violence. It really attacks man in his deepest and strongest parts: his conscience, his heart, his reason, his being" (Houver, 12). "If we refuse to heap burning coals onto our enemies, that is, to set fire to their consciences with our own capacity for loving, they will never realize what they are doing. . . . Even if you cut them off, the heads of violence will grow again and again" (Houver, 28).

Nonviolence, King saw, offers a method by which one can fight the evil with which one cannot live. "It offers a unique weapon which, without firing a single bullet, disarms the adversary. It exposes his moral defenses, weakens his morale, and at the same time works on his conscience" (King 1961, 79). As Tolstoy realized, people who "know that they are not behaving as men should behave . . . are afraid, and tell lies and try to bring evil upon themselves in order not to see the truth. They stifle the truth that exists within them and which appeals to them, and they suffer, unceasingly, from the most cruel of all torments: the sufferings of the soul" (Tolstoy 1908, 197).

Gandhi's, Tolstoy's, King's, and Goss and Goss-Mayr's affirmations stand in stark contrast to the "new language" of Nietzsche's *Beyond Good and Evil,* where Nietzsche says that he is fundamentally disposed to maintain that it is the falsest judgments that are most indispensable because renouncing false judgments would be renouncing life itself, would be a negation of life. According to Nietzsche, a philosophy that dares to admit untruth as condition of life positions itself beyond good and evil (Nietzsche 1886, §4).

Sowing the Seeds of One's Own Destruction

Martin Luther King referred to the "way of nonviolence" as "the method which seeks to implement the just law by appealing to the conscience of the great decent majority who through blindness, fear, pride, or irrationality have allowed their consciences to sleep" (King 1960b, 69). In "Our Struggle," he spoke of how in "their relations with Negroes, white people discovered that they had rejected the very center of their own ethical professions. They could not face the triumph of their lesser instincts and simultaneously have peace within" (King 1956, 4).

King saw the seeds of the destruction of racial inequality in the United States sown in America's Declaration of Independence and Constitution and so in his quest to bring an end to segregation, he set about arousing America's conscience (King 1968b, 202). His famous dream was "deeply rooted in the American dream that one day this nation will rise up and live out the true meaning of its creed—we hold these truths to be self-evident, that all men are created equal" (King 1963b, 104). King was displaying perfect lucidity about the self-destructive nature of hypocrisy and the vulnerable position into which hypocrites put themselves when he insisted that: "All we say to America is, 'Be true to what you said on paper'"(King 1961, 80).

King said that when he saw students throughout the South sitting-in at lunch counters, he "knew that as they were sitting in, they were really standing up for the best in the American dream. And taking the whole nation back to those great wells of democracy which were dug deep by the Founding Fathers in the Declaration of Independence and the Constitution" (King 1968b, 202). He wrote of how we "must work assiduously and with determined boldness to remove from the body politic this cancerous disease of discrimination which is preventing our democratic and Christian health from being realized. Then and only then," he maintained, "will we be able to bring into full realization the dream of our American democracy—a dream yet unfulfilled. A dream of equality of opportunity, of privilege and property widely distributed . . ." (King 1960b, 71). He said that if he lived in any totalitarian country, he could perhaps understand the denial of freedom of assembly, freedom of speech, freedom of the press because a commitment had not been made to that (King 1968b, 197).

Two months before he was shot to death, King reminded the United States that: "God did not call America to do what she's doing in the world now. God didn't call America to engage in a senseless, unjust war, [such] as the war in Vietnam. And we are criminals in that war. We have committed more war crimes than any nation in the world, and I'm going to continue to say it. And we won't stop it because of our pride, and our arrogance as a nation" (King 1968b, 188). In "A Time to Break Silence," King had cited message of the Buddhist leaders of Vietnam: "It is curious that the Americans who calculate so carefully on the possibilities of military victory, do not realize that in the process they are incurring deep psychological and political defeat. The image of America will never again be the image of revolution, freedom and democracy, but the image of violence and militarism" (King 1967a, 145).

Confirmation of King's point is found in *In Retrospect: The Tragedy and Lessons of Vietnam* by Robert McNamara, secretary of defense under John F. Kennedy and Lyndon Baines Johnson. In that book, McNamara explains his conviction that "the United States of America fought in Vietnam for eight years for what it believed to be good and honest reasons" and those of the Kennedy and Johnson administrations who participated in the decisions on Vietnam acted according to what they thought were the country's principles and traditions and made their decisions in light of those values (McNamara, xvi, 333).

In spite of those good intentions, McNamara came to feel obliged to concede "with painful candor and a heavy heart" that although "we sought to do the right thing—and believed we were doing the right thing" by fighting in Vietnam, hindsight had proved that they were wrong. The Vietnam war "caused terrible damage to America" (McNamara, xvi) and shattered the political unity of American society (McNamara, 319). "A nation's deepest strength," he recognizes "lies not in military prowess, but, rather, in the unity of its people. We failed to maintain it" (McNamara, 323).

McNamara describes the effect that the antiwar sentiment directed at him from many sources had upon him as secretary of defense. The dissenters, he remembers, often targeted him as a symbol of America's "war machine." He was picketed and hooted. During one week in June 1966, faculty and students at both Amherst College and New York University walked out as he received honorary degrees (McNamara, 252). What disturbed him most during his visits to university campuses, he says, visits "was the realization that opposition to the administration's Vietnam policy increased with the institution's prestige and the educational attainment of its students." To his consternation, the percentages of those protesting his presence rose with the level of academic distinction and some "of the largest and most intense campus demonstrations occurred at premier institutions" (McNamara, 253–54).

In a particularly memorable passage of the book, McNamara recalls how at one point in his "his long process of growing doubt about the wisdom of our course," Jackie Kennedy "erupted in fury and tears and directed her wrath" at him. He was overwhelmed by her feelings. He writes that she "had grown very depressed by, and very critical of, the war," and finally had grown "so tense that she could hardly speak." Suddenly she "exploded" and began literally beating on his chest, demanding that he "do something to stop the slaughter!" (McNamara, 257–58).

McNamara's encounters with protesters grew louder and uglier (McNamara, 258). The incidents upset him and had a damaging effect on his family (McNamara, 258). He recalls the Soviet poet Yevtushenko having once said to him: "They say you are a beast. But I think you are a man" (McNamara, 258–59). McNamara finally came to the conclusion and told Johnson "point-blank that we could not achieve our object in Vietnam through any reasonable military means, and we therefore should seek a lesser political objective through negotiations" (McNamara, 313). McNamara resigned in February 1968. President Johnson did not seek reelection in 1968.

Breeding Lilacs Out of Dead Ground

Gandhi once observed that "you can wake a man only if he is really asleep; no effort that you may make will produce any effect upon him if he is merely pretending to sleep" (Gandhi 1927-29, 412). And there is good reason to believe that, say, Hitler and Stalin were not asleep, that they were unconscionable, that they had their eyes wide open and were perfectly aware of the evil that they were bent on accomplishing, even pleased beyond belief to see themselves succeeding in accomplishing reprehensible deeds beyond their wildest hopes.

The Soviet activist Andrei Sakharov astutely observed that Nazism: "lasted twelve years in Germany. Stalinism lasted twice as long in the Soviet Union. There are many common features but also certain differences. Stalinism exhibited a much more subtle kind of hypocrisy and demagogy, with reliance not on an openly cannibalistic program like Hitler's but on a progressive, scientific and popular socialist ideology" (Sakharov, 52).

According to Sakharov's analysis, Stalinism's subtle kind of hypocrisy and demagogy and reliance on a progressive, scientific and popular socialist ideology effectively "served as a convenient screen for deceiving the working class, for weakening the vigilance of the intellectuals and other rivals in the struggle for power, with the treacherous and sudden use of the machinery of torture, execution, and informants, intimidating and making fools of millions of people, the majority of whom were neither cowards nor fools" (Sakharov, 52). Such observations yield important insight into why the Soviet regime had a longer life than Nazism, yet sowed the seeds of its destruction in a way that made it one day ripe for nonviolent dissolution.

Standing on Sakharov's shoulders, Gorbachev saw the Soviet system as abusing the faith of the people in the high ideals of socialism, so that when "the ineffectiveness of the system became obvious and the promises of a better life proved deceptive, people lost confidence in the government and the party. The growing gap between the government and the system was the fundamental cause of the weakening of the system" (Gorbachev, 24).

Gorbachev saw Russia as a country whose capable people were "paralyzed by the dictates of the party" and how this "inevitably resulted in apathy, anemia, loss of initiative, and the extinguishing of social energy . . ." (Gorbachev, 31). Soviet society seemed to him to have become "ossified" and to be "creeping toward the abyss" (Gorbachev, 34). He has written that:

> The incentive to work efficiently disappeared, as did people's desire to participate in a socially conscious way in public affairs or to take any kind of initiative aside from criminal activity. Political conformism and a primitive leveling psychology took deep root. The stagnation in society was fraught with serious consequences that actually began to make themselves felt in literally all areas. (Gorbachev, 34)

Through his efforts, Gorbachev considers: "Apathy and indifference toward public life were overcome. . . . Society awakened" (Gorbachev, 56); the Soviet people, "quickly and actively" supported the new course.

Applying Social Pressure to Revolutionize Social Ideas

Proponents of nonviolence have seen the extent to which the power of unconscionable individuals can be very considerably diminished, if not annihilated, by an appeal to the consciences of sincere people. Gandhi saw in nonviolence "a force, which, if it became universal, would revolutionize social ideas and do away with despotisms and the ever growing militarism under which the nations of the West are groaning and are being almost crushed to death . . ." (Gandhi 2002, 88). He maintained that: "In the dictionary of nonviolence, there is no such word as 'enemy.' Even for the supposed enemy, nonviolent persons will have nothing but compassion in their heart. They will believe that no one is intentionally wicked, that there is no person but is gifted with the faculty to discriminate between right and wrong, and that if that faculty were to be fully developed, it would surely mature into nonviolence. They will therefore pray to God that God may give the supposed enemy a sense of right and bless that person" (Gandhi 2002, 114).

Tolstoy drew particular attention to "the tremendous power of public opinion, which is one hundred times more effective in protecting people from all kinds of violence than are gallows and prisons" (Tolstoy 1908, 216). "It was not government decrees that abolished child-beating, torture and slavery," he maintained, "but a change in people's consciousness that called for the necessity of these decrees" (Tolstoy 1908, 200). Tolstoy believed that the delusion that one was behaving well and justly by exerting influence over others was being destroyed for both rulers and their opponents, that not even the most powerful men were any longer convinced of it. Both parties, he considered, "try through every kind of argument to convince themselves that violence is useful and necessary, while knowing in the depth of their hearts that their acts of cruelty only achieve a semblance of what they want—and that only a temporary one which, in reality, distances them from their aims rather than drawing them closer" (Tolstoy 1908, 163–64).

Writing fifty years after violent revolution had begun to transform Russia, in *Progress, Coexistence, and Intellectual Freedom*, Andrei Sakharov engaged in an internal critique of the practices of the Soviet Union. He called Stalin's "pseudo-socialism of terroristic bureaucracy, a socialism of hypocrisy and ostentatious growth that was at its best a quantitative and one-sided growth involving the loss of many qualitative features" (Sakharov, 66). He said that he considered that the assertion commonly made by Soviet propaganda that "the Soviet Union has something just, entirely in the interests of the working people" contains "half-truths and a fair amount of hypocritical evasion" (Sakharov, 74).

In the book, Sakharov observed that by the late 1960s nonviolent pressures had actually done more to improve the conditions of the working class than bloody revolution would have. He explained that "the facts suggest that there is real economic progress in the United States and other capitalist countries, that the capitalists are actually using the social principles of socialism, and that there has been real improvement in the position of the working people" (Sakharov, 74). His "basic conclusion about the moral and ethical character of the advantages of the socialist course of development of human society" was that the social progress of the twentieth century had only been made possible by the competition with socialism and the pressure of the working class, and that only this would insure the rapprochement with the capitalist world (Sakharov, 78).

Sakharov considered that the "socialist world should not seek to destroy by force the ground from which it grew," but "should ennoble that ground by its example and other indirect forms of pressure and then merge with it" (Sakharov, 78–79). The rapprochement that he envisioned would "rest not only on a socialist but on a popular, democratic foundation, under the control of public opinion, as expressed through publicity, elections, and so forth" (Sakharov, 79).

Of course, it is a most incredible fact that since Sakharov wrote these words, and in no small measure thanks to his own nonviolent protests, the Soviet Union, that superpower called the "evil empire" by those most intent on countering it through armed force, has undergone radical, unexpected, nonviolent transformation. "An obvious sign that the times were ripe for changes," the transformer Gorbachev writes, "was the activity of the dissidents. They were suppressed and expelled from the country, but their moral stand and their proposals for changes (for example, the ideas of Andrei Sakharov) played a considerable role in creating the spiritual pre-conditions for perestroika" (Gorbachev, 55). He particularly credits the Prague Spring of 1968 with having "sowed the seeds of profound thought and reflection" (Gorbachev, 55) and cites the importance of Willy Brandt's "Eastern policy" and the search for new avenues toward social progress by those who were called Euro-Communists" (Gorbachev, 55).

Planting Lethal Seeds

In *From the Shadows: The Ultimate Insider's Story of Five Presidents and How They Won the Cold War*, former CIA director Robert Gates addresses the role that the cultivation of fundamental contradictions inherent in the Soviet system (which he calls "a truly evil empire") ultimately played in uprooting it. In a chapter entitled "Planting Lethal Seeds," he makes a point of stressing the extent to which the "efforts of Gerald Ford and Jimmy Carter to plant and nurture the seeds of change on behalf of human rights in the East, and to challenge the communist governments' treatment of their own people . . . gave heart, resolve, and courage to those inside the Soviet 'prison house of nations,' people who would challenge not just governments' treatment of their citizens but the legitimacy and very existence of those governments" (Gates, 96).

Gates particularly stresses how Carter's human rights campaign and public support of Sakharov "further served to highlight the contrast between Soviet declaratory policy and repression of its own citizens" and how the Carter administration's "covert actions in Eastern Europe and the Soviet Union contributed to undermining the legitimacy of the Soviet regime in the eyes of its own citizens" (Gates, 536). He also lauds the CIA's efforts to bring to Soviet citizens "the words of their own dissidents" and to help "many in the Soviet elite and in the scientific and technical community to grasp the backwardness of the Soviet Union and the contrast between their government's words and its deeds," which "contributed to the erosion of the myths that had sustained the Soviet government at home" (Gates, 536).

According to Gates's analysis, the Soviets liked dealing with Richard Nixon and Henry Kissinger because they "never tried to cause the Soviets trouble at home, to question seriously their internal policies or the legitimacy of their rule" (Gates, 85). In contrast, Gates considers,

the Carter administration waged ideological war on the Soviets with a determination and intensity that was very different from its predecessors. . . . Carter had, in fact, changed the long-standing rules of the Cold War. Through his human rights policies, he became the first president since Truman to challenge directly the legitimacy of the Soviet government in the eyes of its own people. And the Soviets immediately recognized this for the fundamental challenge that it was: they believed he sought to overthrow their system. . . . The Soviet leaders knew the implications for them of what Carter was doing, and hated him for it. . . . While Carter's human rights policies were derided at home as naïve and counterproductive, in later years Soviet dissidents would be virtually unanimous in their praise of those policies and the importance to the democratic dissidents of the publicity those policies brought to their cause." (Gates, 95–96)

Citing Walter Lippmann's comment that we all "plant trees we will never get to sit under," Gates maintains "that the propaganda and covert endeavors of the Carter administration's human rights policies produced their share of the tiny fissures in the Soviet structure that ultimately helped bring about its collapse" (Gates, 95), that the "fragile seeds of change planted between 1975 and 1978, so scorned and controversial at the time, would bear lethal fruit and help destroy an empire that was more vulnerable than either its own rulers or the West understood at the time" (Gates, 96).

Curbing the Power of Evildoers through Nonviolent, Noncooperation with Evil

The theories and actions of proponents of nonviolent responses to evil are also entirely realistic about the fact that leaders of political and religious groups are dependent on their following and that sincere followers have often been duped into cooperating with evil by means of what seemed to be beautiful, even good ideas.

Martin Luther King saw in noncooperation with evil an effective means of facing "vicious and evil enemies squarely." As he pointed out: "There is more power in socially organized masses on the march than there is in guns in the hands of a few desperate men. Our enemies would prefer to deal with a small armed group rather than with a huge, unarmed but resolute mass of people" (King 1959b, 52). From "this form of struggle more emerges that is permanent and damaging to the enemy than from a few acts of organized violence" (King 1959b, 53). "Basic to the philosophy of nonviolence," he preached, "is the refusal to cooperate with evil. There is nothing quite so effective as a refusal to cooperate economically with the forces and institutions which perpetuate evil in our communities" (King 1966, 133).

Gandhi taught that "we should not forget that even evil is sustained through the cooperation, either willing or forced, of good people. . . . In the last resort we can curb the power of the evildoers to do mischief by withdrawing all cooperation from them and completely isolating them" (Gandhi 2002, 98). "And at the back of the policy of terrorism," he considered, "is the assumption that terrorism if applied in a sufficient measure will produce the desired result, namely, bend the adversary to the tyrant's will. But supposing a people make up their mind that they will never do the tyrant's will, nor retaliate with the tyrant's own methods, the tyrant will not find it worth his while to go on with his terrorism" (Gandhi 2002, 122).

Before Gandhi, Tolstoy had pointed out that

> the violence the rulers do to the oppressed is not the direct, spontaneous violence of the strong over the weak, or the majority over the minority. . . . The violence of the rulers is upheld in the only way the violence of the minority over the majority can be: by the fraud which cunning, quick-witted people established long ago, as a consequence of which people, for the sake of small but instant gain, deprive themselves not only of greater profits but of freedom, and expose themselves to the most cruel sufferings. (Tolstoy 1908, 177)

Tolstoy lamented the fact that the oppressed "no longer see the connection between their oppression and their participation in violence" (Tolstoy 1908, 179), do not see that the suppression of violence would deprive those in power of the "possibility of living in the way they do" and "expose all the age-old injustice and cruelty of their life" (Tolstoy 1908, 177).

In face of the question as to what "hundreds, thousands, let us say hundreds of thousands of insignificant, powerless, isolated people [could] do against the vast number of men who are bound to the State and equipped with all the powerful weapons of violence" (Tolstoy 1908, 195), Tolstoy suggested that one "would think it would be the working people, receiving no advantage from the violence exercised over them, who would eventually see through the deceit in which they are entangled and, having once done so, free themselves in the most simple and easy way by ceasing to participate in the violence which can only be done to them by virtue of their participating in it" (Tolstoy 1908, 178).

Tolstoy thought that it "would seem such a simple thing for the working people to realize this and to finally say to those they regard as their leaders: 'leave us in peace! If you, emperors, presidents, generals, judges, bishops, professors and other learned men need armies, navies, universities, ballets, synods, conservatoires, prisons, gallows and guillotines, do it all yourselves and leave us in peace because we need none of it, and we no longer wish to participate in all these useless, and above evil deeds!'" (Tolstoy 1908, 179). Tolstoy realized that such a struggle seemed "not only unequal but impossible," but believed that its outcome was "as little in doubt as the outcome between the struggle between the darkness of night and the light of dawn" (Tolstoy 1908, 195).

Goss-Mayr has explained that it was the poor who taught her and her husband Jean Goss about nonviolence. The poor, she and her husband had learned, had discovered nonviolence out of necessity. "To kill effectively," she has explained,

> you need arms, and arms are never in the hands of the poor, always in the hands of the rich. . . . In their struggle they don't want to provoke the violence of the authorities. If they use violence the authorities' violence will always be there to crush them, and it will always be stronger. . . . Developing a theory of armed revolution, as Che Guevara and Camillo Torres did in their time, is the privilege of the rich and of intellectuals. They had moved away from the reality of the people. (Houver, 4)

"One must not underestimate the subversive, revolutionary and at the same time liberating and healing power of nonviolence," Goss-Mayr concludes her book *Oser le combat non-violent*. "Of course, a liberation movement that rejects violence, which respects even the enemy, and which is based on truth and justice represents, for dictators, a particularly dangerous threat, not only because of its immense power of attraction, but again because such a movement is the most difficult to stifle as soon as the bloody repression nakedly striking unarmed people shows the whole world the contempt for people that characterizes these regimes" (Goss-Mayr, 137).

A Creative Force in the Universe

It has been argued above that by arousing and attacking people's consciences, by laying bare contradiction, lies, and hypocrisy, by applying social pressure, by forcing a rethinking of old practices in terms of new realities, by noncooperation with evil, nonviolence can and has been an entirely realistic, powerful way of transforming evil situations. In these cases, it is really the evildoers themselves who plant the seeds of their eventual ruin; they end up reaping what they have sown. Eroded by inner contradiction, evil practices have actually withered away. It is very much to the credit of nonviolent movements, small and large, that many more of them have proved fruitful than could ever be done justice to in these pages.

However much such arguments still fly in the face of ordinary intuitions about the effectiveness of violent responses to evil, they are nevertheless framed in natural, humanistic, even logical terms. They do not rely on universal metaphysical, supernatural, spiritual, or religious principles. Indeed some nonviolent movements act on purely humanitarian grounds. Nonetheless, in studying the philosophy of nonviolence, one must face the fact that rather many of the most formidable foes of violence appeal to the existence of necessary universal metaphysical, supernatural, and spiritual principles to explain the thought provoking efficacy of their undertakings.

Mohandas Gandhi maintained that the "first and last shield and buckler of nonviolent persons will be their unwavering faith in God" (Gandhi 2002, 114). He maintained that in the last resort nonviolence "does not avail to those who do not possess a living faith in the God of love" (Gandhi 2002, 115), that it "succeeds only when we have a living faith in God" (Gandhi 2002, 124). Goss declared that "if we cut ourselves off from that source of love which is Jesus, truth, justice, love, everything we do will dry up like rotten wood. The only force that can unify man is love; everything else cuts him into bits, and plants division in him and incites war" (Houver, 104).

Gandhi said that he felt God pervade every fiber of his being (Gandhi 2002, 160) and that his own experience was that whenever he had acted nonviolently he had "been led to it and sustained in it by the higher promptings of an unseen Power" (Gandhi 2002, 124). "Supplication, worship, prayer are not superstition," he insisted; "they are acts more real than the acts of eating, drinking, sitting or walking. It is no exaggeration to say that they alone are real, all else is unreal" (Gandhi 1927-29, 80). It was his "conviction that the root of evil is want of a living faith in a living God" (Gandhi 2002, 188). He believed that "the very existence of the world in a broad sense depends on religion. All attempts to root it out will fail" (Gandhi 2002, 190).

King recommended that: "When our days become dreary with low-hovering clouds of despair, and when our nights become darker than a thousand midnights, let us remember that there is a creative force in this universe willing to pull down the gigantic mountains of evil, a power that is able to make a way out of no way and transform dark yesterdays into bright tomorrows. Let us realize that the arc of the moral universe is long but it bends toward justice" (King 1967b, 179).

Aware that some people believe firmly in nonviolence, but do not believe in a personal God, King was himself convinced: that "the universe, is under the control of a loving purpose and that in the struggle for righteousness man has cosmic companionship. Behind the harsh appearances of the world there is a benign power" (King 1960a, 62, 23); and that "every person who believes in nonviolent resistance believes somehow that the universe in some form is on the side of justice. That there is something unfolding in the universe whether one speaks of it as an unconscious process, or whether one speaks of it as some unmoved mover, or whether someone speaks of it as a personal God" (King 1958, 32).

Limning the True and Ultimate Structure of Reality

Gandhi and King, to give two examples, even considered a nonviolent approach to evil to be instrumental in limning the true and ultimate structure of reality, in arriving at the truth, and in proving the existence of God and of God's active intervention in the world. Such bold, philosophical claims merit consideration.

In Gandhi's case, he affirmed that "when you want to find Truth as God, the only inevitable means is love, that is nonviolence" (Gandhi 2002, 73). He believed that to "see the universal and all-pervading Spirit of Truth face to face one must be able to love the meanest of creation as oneself" (Gandhi 1927-29, 452–53) and that he would never know God if he did not "wrestle with evil and against evil even at the cost of life itself" (Gandhi 2002, 72).

No one, Gandhi declared, "who has faith in a living God need feel helpless or forlorn" (Gandhi 2002, 164). In his autobiography, Gandhi explained that when he was young he did not know the essence of religion or of God and how God worked in us, but that, although he did not yet feel that he had grasped its entire meaning and only "richer experience" could help him have a fuller understanding, he knew that the phrase *God saved me* had acquired a deeper meaning for him. He said, that in all his trials of a spiritual nature, as a lawyer, in conducting institutions, and in politics he could say that God had saved him (Gandhi 1927-29, 80). When every hope was gone, when helpers had failed and comforts flown, he said that he found that help arrived somehow, from he knew not where (Gandhi 1927-29, 80, 387).

In parallel fashion, King too wrote of how his experience of the power of nonviolence had made God profoundly real to him, of how he had "become more and more convinced of the reality of a personal God" (King 1960a, 61). Earlier in his life, he once recalled, the idea of a personal God had been "little more than a metaphysical category" that he had found "theologically and philosophically satisfying," but he had grown "more and more convinced of the reality of a personal God." God had become "a living reality . . . validated in the experiences of everyday life" (King 1960a, 61). He told of having come to experience an inner calm and to know resources of strength in the midst of outer dangers that only God could give, of often having "felt the power of God transforming the fatigue of despair into the buoyancy of hope" (King 1960a, 61). He felt that, in their struggle, he and those struggling alongside him had "cosmic companionship" and that the belief that the universe was on the side of justice was one of the things that kept them together (King 1958, 32).

King said that when he spoke of love, he was not speaking of some sentimental and weak response, but of "that force which all of the great religions have seen as the supreme unifying principle of life. Love is some-how the key that unlocks the door which leads to ultimate reality" (King 1967a, 150). King saw "a new age coming into being, with a new struc-ture of freedom and justice" (King 1957, 19). He believed that "the fact that this new age is emerging reveals something basic about the universe. It tells us something about the core and heartbeat of the cosmos. It reminds us that the universe is on the side of justice. It says to those who struggle for justice, 'You do not struggle alone, but God Struggles with you'" (King 1957, 23).

Tolstoy on Undermining the Entire Existing Order of the World

Leo Tolstoy taught that the "precise and definite meaning given to the doctrine of love and the guidance resulting from it" inevitably undermined "the entire existing order of the world," inevitably involved "a complete transformation of the established structure of life" among all the nations of the world (Tolstoy 1908, 201, 174).

He considered love to be "metaphysically the origin of everything, practically the highest law of human life, i.e. that which under no circum-stances admits of exception" (Tolstoy 1908, 172). He believed that the true love that "denies itself and transfers itself to another, is the awakening within oneself of the highest universal principle of life." For him, love was "only true love and affords all the happiness it can give when it is simple love, free from anything personal, from the smallest drop of personal bias towards its object. And such love can only be felt for one's enemy, for those who hate and offend" (Tolstoy 1908, 230).

Tolstoy emphasized that in all ancient religious teachings, those of "the Egyptian sages, the Brahmins, the Stoics, the Buddhists, Taoists and oth-ers," "amicability, pity, mercy, charity and love in general are considered the chief virtues" (Tolstoy 1908, 172) and that in that the most superior religious teachings the recognition "that love is a necessary and happy aspect of human life . . . reached the point where love towards every living thing was advocated, and even recompense of good for evil" (Tolstoy 1908, 172).

He was convinced that Christian teaching, in its true meaning, offered a clearer, more precise expression of the basis of human life and of the guiding of conduct inevitably ensuing from it than had been felt and vaguely expounded in earlier religions (Tolstoy 1908, 172–74). According to him, the "true meaning" of the Christian teaching lie in the recognition that the "essence of human life is the ever-growing manifestation of the source of everything, indicated in us through love; and, therefore, that the essence of human life and the highest law governing it is love" (Tolstoy 1908, 172).

For Tolstoy, Christian theory inevitably undermines the entire existing order of the world because it alone acknowledges that love is metaphysically the origin of everything and highest law of human life, which under no circumstances admits of exception and teaches that it even be applied to enemies who hate, wrong, offend, and curse us (Tolstoy 1908, 172–74, 201). Christian teaching, he stressed, "ruled out any form of violence and consequently could not but condemn the whole structure of the world founded on violence" (Tolstoy 1908, 175).

Tolstoy saw the explanation as to why love was the supreme law of life as having been especially clearly expressed in two of Christ's sayings:

> Beloved let us love one another: for love is of God; and everyone that loveth is born of God and knoweth God. . . . No man hath seen God at any time. If we love one another, God dwelleth in us, and his love is perfected in us. . . . God is love, and he that dwelleth in love dwelleth in God and God in him. (I John IV, 7, 8, 12, 16)

> We know that we have passed from death unto life, because we love the brethren. He that loveth not his brother abideth in death. (I John III,14) (Tolstoy 1908, 173)

Tolstoy interpreted these words to mean that "what we call 'our self', or our life, is really the divine principle, limited in us by our body, and manifesting itself as love, and that therefore the true life of each man, divine and free, expresses itself as love" (Tolstoy 1908, 173).

Tolstoy stressed that in addition to explaining in a clear way why love was the supreme law of life, Christ had indicated a series of actions in which people had to engage or not engage as a consequence of accepting this teaching as the truth (Tolstoy 1908, 173). Tolstoy found the guidance for conduct flowing from this interpretation of the law of love to be expressed in especially clear and precise terms in the fourth commandment of the Sermon on the Mount, verse 38 of the fifth chapter of St Matthew's gospel: "You have heard that it hath been said: An eye for an eye, a tooth for a tooth (Ex. XXI, 24). But I say unto you, That ye resist not evil'" (Tolstoy 1908, 173).

Tolstoy considered that the ensuing admonition in verses 39 and 40 of the Sermon on the Mount that one should turn one's other cheek to whomever might smite one on one's right cheek and that one should let anyone who would sue one at the law and take away one's coat have one's cloak also, "clearly and definitively stated that there are, and can be, no circumstances when it is be permissible to deviate from the very simple and vital requirement of love: not to do to others that which you would not have them do to you . . ." (Tolstoy 1908, 173–74).

Tolstoy considered that, by referring straightforwardly to the usual false reasons given to justify breaking the law of love in reaction to behavior on the part of others, the last commandment of the Sermon on the Mount, expressed in a particularly clear and exact way the inadmissibility of justifying such transgressions:

> Ye have heard that it hath been said, 'Thou shalt love thy neighbor and hate thine enemy' (Leviticus XIX, 17–18), 'But I say unto you, Love your enemies, bless them that curse you, do good to them that hate you, and pray for them which spitefully use you and persecute you; That ye may be the children of your Father which is in heaven: for he maketh his sun to rise on the evil and on the good, and sendeth rain on the just and on the unjust. For if ye love them which love you, what reward have ye? Do not even the publicans do the same? And if ye salute your brethren only, what do ye more than others? Be ye therefore perfect, even as your Father which is in heaven is perfect. (Matt. V, 43–48) (Tolstoy 1908, 174)

It was Tolstoy's conviction that violence performed against one could never justify violence on one's part (Tolstoy 1908, 174), that the "acceptance of the need to oppose evil with violence is nothing other than the justification people give to their habitual and favourite vices: vengeance, avarice, envy, ambition, pride, cowardice and spite" (Tolstoy 1908, 216).

Tolstoy on Penetrating the Essence of the Human Soul

As Jean Goss, once explained: "Someone who commits himself to non-violence is obliged to plumb his own depths, with all the dizzying drops and suffering this inevitably entails. . . . As long as our non-violence doesn't arise from the depths we will be tossed about by . . . mirages. . . . Renouncing the 'spiritual self' leads inevitably to . . . fanaticism and destruction" (Houver, 48).

It was not, Tolstoy said, "reasoned conclusions" that had convinced him, or could irrefutably convince others, of the truth of nonresistance, of the "blindness of those who believe in the necessity and inevitability of violence" and the "inevitability of non-resistance," but only peoples' awareness of their spirituality, "the basic expression of which is love" (Tolstoy 1908, 230). He considered that having "penetrated the essence of the human soul, we see that it works in such a way that responding to evil with evil makes it suffer, whereas responding to evil with love leads to the highest attainable bliss" (Tolstoy 1908, 230), for it is actually "love, true love, which comprises the essence of man's soul; that love which is revealed in

Christ's teaching, and excludes even the suggestion of any kind of violence" (Tolstoy 1908, 230).

Tolstoy considered that, however "strange these things may sound to someone who has not felt this," the "supreme bliss is my love for others, and not only for those who love me, but as Christ said, for those who hate me, offend me, and commit evil against me. . . ." He maintained that it was so and that when one thought about it and experienced it, one could only be surprised that one had ever failed to understand it (Tolstoy 1908, 230). He thought that "the injunction to love not those who love us, but those who hate us, is not an exaggeration, nor an indication of possible exclusions, but simply a directive for that opportunity and possibility of receiving the supreme bliss that love can give" (Tolstoy 1908, 230).

Tolstoy was persuaded that power lies in human consciousness, that only essential inner activity could improve people's lives (Tolstoy 1908, 201). He maintained that a "better life can only come when the consciousness of men is altered for the better; and therefore, those who wish to improve life must direct all their efforts towards changing both their own and other people's consciousness" (Tolstoy 1908, 201). All "external changes of life's forms that are not founded on shifts in consciousness not only fail to improve people's situation but, by and large, worsen it" (Tolstoy 1908, 200), he warned.

Tolstoy considered that the "profession of Christianity in its true meaning, including nonresistance to evil, frees men from all external power. But it not only frees them from external power, it also gives them the possibility of attaining those improvements of life which they vainly seek through altering the external forms of life, whereas changes in life's external forms are always a consequence of shifts in consciousness"; he believed that "life is only improved as far as it is based on modified consciousness. . . . that is to the extent that in people's consciousness the law of violence is exchanged for the law of love" (Tolstoy 1908, 200).

For Tolstoy Christian doctrine represented a step forward in human consciousness:

> based on the fact that all the former religious and moral teachings on love, while compelled to admit the virtue of love in human life, yet allowed the possibility of certain situations whereby the fulfilment of the laws of love ceased to be obligatory and could be suspended. And as soon as the law of love ceased to be the highest, immutable law of human life, all it's beneficence disappeared, and the teaching of love was reduced to eloquent homilies and words which were non-obligatory and left the whole way of the life of the nations as it was before the doctrine of love appeared: that is based on violence alone . . . (Tolstoy 1908, 174–75)

Tolstoy believed that the difference between what went on in the pre-Christian world and what goes on in the Christian world today is that in those days the truth that Christ expressed so clearly that violence exercised by some over others cannot unite and can only separate people and that there was no basis to the claim that violence used by some over others could be useful and unifying had been completely concealed from the people, whereas today it has become more and more apparent. Tolstoy predicted that "as soon as people realize that the violence of some over others, apart from being the cause of their suffering, is irrational, those who used to bear their oppression quietly, immediately become provoked and embittered by it" (Tolstoy 1908, 163).

So Tolstoy considered that the way out of oppression, for both oppressors and oppressed "consists in one thing: in mankind accepting the true meaning of Christ's teaching, which has been concealed from them and which is still unknown to the majority of people, together with the guidance for conduct that flows from it and which excludes violence" (Tolstoy 1908, 164). Salvation from the enslavement in which the people find themselves could be "achieved only through Christianity, by substituting the law of violence for the law of love" (Tolstoy 1908, 199). Tolstoy concludes that "Christ said that He conquered the world, and indeed He did. Evil, however dreadful it is, no longer exists, because it no longer exists in people's consciousness" (Tolstoy 1908, 202).

Tolstoy and King Contra Nietzsche

Tolstoy's theories are, obviously, in all points diametrically opposed to those of Nietzsche who was intent upon undermining the entire existing order of the world in quite the opposite way and who condemned in no uncertain terms precisely what Tolstoy considered to be the true sense of Christianity.

Tolstoy characterized the "unfortunate Nietzsche, who has lately become so famous" (Tolstoy 1893, 145) as "a daring, but limited and abnormal German, suffering from power mania" (Tolstoy 1902, 111), who has declared that "he is convinced that self-renunciation, meekness, submissiveness and love are all vices that destroy humanity" (Tolstoy 1902, 111). Tolstoy dismissed Nietzsche's works as "some disjointed writings, striving after effect in a most sordid manner," which neither "in talent nor in their basic argument . . . justify public attention." He found it lamentable that "all the so-called educated people are praising the ravings of Mr N, arguing about him, elucidating him, and countless copies of his works are printed in all languages" (Tolstoy 1902, 111).

Tolstoy condemned Nietzsche's theories as a doctrine "of egotism and cruelty, sanctioning the ideas of personal happiness and superiority over the lives of others, by which they live" (Tolstoy 1902, 112), while the whole world knew "that virtue consists in the subjugation of one's passions, or in self-renunciation," "virtues that restrain and condemn the animal side" (Tolstoy 1902, 112), something which Tolstoy considered to be "an eternal supreme law towards which all humanity has developed, including Brahmanism, Buddhism, Confucianism and the ancient Persian religion" (Tolstoy 1902, 111).

In "Where Do We Go From Here," Martin Luther King used Nietzsche as an example of a philosopher who had gotten "off base." One of the great problems of history, King explained, has been that the concepts of love and power have usually been contrasted as polar opposites, so that love had come to be identified with a resignation of power, and power with a denial of love (King 1967b, 172). It was that kind of misinterpretation, King maintained, that had caused Nietzsche, who King refers to as the "philosopher of the will to power," to reject the Christian concept of love. And it was the same kind of misinterpretation that had brought Christian theologians to reject Nietzsche's philosophy of the will to power in the name of the Christian idea of love (King 1967b, 172). King himself believed that the "call for a world-wide fellowship that lifts neighborly concern beyond one's tribe, race, class and nation is in reality a call for an all-embracing and unconditional love for all men." He stressed that that "oft misunderstood and misinterpreted concept—so readily dismissed by the Nietzsches of the world as a weak and cowardly force—has now become an absolute an absolute necessity for the survival of man" (King 1967a, 150).

King believed that America had this matter wrong and confused and that it was important to get it right. There is nothing wrong with power if power is used correctly, he maintained, but one has to see that "power without love is reckless and abusive, and love without power is sentimental and anemic. Power at its best is love implementing the demands of justice, and justice at its best is power correcting everything that stands against love." King believed that it was "precisely this collision of immoral power with powerless morality" that was constituting the major crisis of the time and was leading people "to seek their goals through power devoid of love and conscience" and to advocate "the same destructive conscienceless power" that they abhor in others (King 1967b, 172–73).

Freud on the Impossibility of Eradicating Evil

For Hildegard Goss-Mayr: "Evil and injustice can only be overcome by the strength of justice and love. Love for one's enemies and love for God" (Houver, 121). Gandhi argued that "belief in nonviolence is based on the assumption that human nature in its essence is one and therefore unfailingly responds to the advances of love" (Gandhi 2002, 122). According to Gandhi: "Love is a rare herb that makes a friend even of a sworn enemy, and this herb grows out of nonviolence. What in a dormant state is nonviolence becomes love in the waking state. Love destroys ill will" (Gandhi 2002, 158).

Nothing could be more different from such convictions than Sigmund Freud's theories about evil and violence. Indeed, the thoughts, words, and deeds of partisans of nonviolence are so diametrically opposed to those of Freud that presenting his theories in contrast to theirs helps bring important issues to the fore.

For Freud, the deepest essence of human nature consisted of instinctual impulses that aim at the satisfaction of certain primal needs (Freud 1915, 68). He taught that there are only two kinds of human instincts: erotic or sexual ones, which seek to preserve and unite; and, aggressive or destructive instincts, which seek to hate, destroy, and kill (Freud 1933, 355–56). For him, the erotic instincts represented the effort to live; he referred to the aggressive or destructive instincts as death instincts. (Freud 1933, 357). He counted "incest, cannibalism and lust for killing" among the "instinctual wishes" that are "born afresh with every child" (Freud 1927, 189).

Freud considered that people were only too ready to disavow the truth that "men are not gentle creatures who want to be loved, and who at the most can defend themselves if they are attacked" (Freud 1930, 302). For him, the "countless cruelties in history and in our everyday lives" vouched for the existence and strength of a lust for aggression and destruction (Freud 1933, 357); he held that there was "no use in trying to get rid of men's aggressive inclinations . . . no question of getting rid entirely of human aggressive impulses" (Freud 1933, 358).

Freud believed that all the impulses that society condemns as evil were similar in all people, were of a primitive kind and neither good nor bad (Freud 1915, 68), that one "must not be too hasty in introducing ethical judgements of good and evil" (Freud 1933, 356). He held that neither of the two instincts was "any less essential than the other" (Freud 1933, 356) and that neither was ever capable of operating in isolation. One was always accompanied, or alloyed "with a certain quota from the other side," which modified its aim or, in some cases, enabled it to accomplish that aim (Freud 1933, 356). He considered it obvious that the satisfaction of destructive impulses was facilitated by their admixture with others of an erotic and idealistic kind (Freud 1933, 357).

Freud saw the phenomena of life as arising from the concurrent or mutually opposing action of both kinds of instincts (Freud 1933, 356). In harmony with Nietzsche's convictions that, "*in themselves*, injuring, raping, exploiting, exterminating (*Vernichten*) can naturally not be unjust inasmuch as in its basic functions life essentially functions by injuring, raping, exploiting, exterminating and can by no means be thought of without that quality" (Nietzsche 1887, II §11), and that all good things on earth end up canceling themselves out (Nietzsche 1887, II §10), Freud considered the lust for aggression and violence to be at work in every living creature, striving to bring it to ruin and to reduce life to its original condition of inanimate matter. The organism, he maintained, preserves its own life by destroying an extraneous one (Freud 1933, 357).

Although Freud believed that there was no use in trying to get rid of human aggressive impulses (Freud 1933, 358), he did say that his theory of instincts made it easy to find ways of indirectly combating war. "If willingness to engage in war is an effect of the destructive instinct," he reasoned, "the most obvious plan will be to bring Eros, its antagonist, into play against it. Anything that encourages the growth of emotional ties between men must operate against war." According to his theories, these emotional ties could be of two kinds: they could be relations resembling those towards a loved object, though not with a sexual aim, such as "love thy neighbor as thyself;" or they could be by means of identifications that lead people to share important interests and produce community of feeling (Freud 1933, 359).

However, Freud considered that the ethical injunction to love thy neighbor as thyself could not be reasonably fulfilled and that "nothing else runs so strongly counter to the original nature of man" (Freud 1930, 300, 303). He saw human beings as creatures for whom their neighbor is "not only a potential helper or sexual object, but also someone who tempts them to satisfy their aggressiveness on him, to exploit his capacity for work without compensation, to use him sexually without his consent, to seize his possessions, to humiliate him, to cause him pain, to torture and to kill him." In circumstances favorable to cruel aggressiveness, Freud stressed, the instinct for hatred and destruction "manifests itself spontaneously and reveals man as a savage beast to whom consideration towards his own kind is something alien" (Freud 1930, 302).

What, Freud objected, if our neighbors are strangers to us and if they cannot attract us by any worth of their own or any significance that they may already have acquired for our emotional lives? It would then be hard for us to love them, he concluded. He even held that it would be wrong for us to do so because our love is valued by all our own people as a sign of our preferring them, and it is an injustice to them for us to place a stranger on a par with them. He feared that if we were to love them with a universal love merely because they too are inhabitants of this earth, "like an insect, an earthworm or a grass-snake," then only a small amount of our love would fall their share (Freud 1930, 299-300). "Not merely," Freud states, is the stranger in general unworthy of my love; I must honestly confess that he has more claim to my hostility and even my hatred. He seems not to have the least trace of love for me and shows me not the slightest consideration. If it will do him any good he has no hesitation in injuring me, nor does he ask himself whether the amount of advantage he gains bears any proportion to the extent of the harm he does to me. . . . He thinks nothing of jeering at me, insulting me, slandering me and showing his superior power; and the more secure he feels and the more helpless I am, the more certainly I can expect him to behave like this to me. (Freud 1930, 300)

Whereas Gandhi believed that to be truly nonviolent we must love our adversaries and pray for them even when they hit us (Gandhi 2002, 121), the injunction to "love one's enemies," unsurprisingly, aroused even stronger opposition in Freud than the idea of loving strangers (Freud 1930, 300–301). He called it "an excellent example of the unpsychological proceedings of the cultural super-ego" and "impossible to fulfil." He maintained that "such an enormous inflation of love can only lower its value, not get rid of the difficulty" (Freud 1930, 337). Cannibals, he says, that are known to have "a devouring affection" for their enemies and only devour people of whom they are fond (Freud 1921, 135).

Freud on Reality and Religion

In addition, Freud judged the kinds of religious ideas that sustained Gandhi, Tolstoy, King, or Jean and Hildegard Goss to be "foreign to reality" (Freud 1930, 261). For Freud, religion comprised "a system of wishful illusions together with a disavowal of reality, such as we find in an isolated form nowhere else but in amentia, in a state of blissful hallucinatory confusion" (Freud 1927, 227). He saw religious ideas as being but "illusions, fulfilments of the oldest, strongest and most urgent wishes of mankind," and the secret of their strength as lying in the very strength of human desires to "exorcize the terrors of nature . . . reconcile men to the cruelty of Fate, particularly as it is shown in death, and . . . compensate them for the sufferings and privations which a civilized life in common has imposed on them" (Freud 1927, 197; 212). Religious ideas, he maintained, were "not precipitates of experience or end-results of thinking" (Freud 1927, 212); they were all "illusions and insusceptible of proof," some of which were "so improbable, so incompatible with everything we have discovered about the reality of the world, that we may compare them . . . to delusions" (Freud 1927, 213).

Freud saw the technique of religion as consisting "in depressing the value of life and distorting the picture of the real world in a delusional manner—which presupposes an intimidation of the intelligence." He saw it as fixing people "in a state of psychical infantilism and drawing them into a mass-delusion. . . . But hardly anything more" (Freud 1930, 273). Among the illusions that religion sustains, according to Freud, are that:

> Everything that happens in this world is an expression of the intentions of an intelligence superior to us, which in the end, though its ways and byways are difficult to follow, orders everything for the best. . . . Over each one of us there watches a benevolent Providence . . . the same moral laws which our civilizations have set up govern the whole universe as well, except that they are maintained by a supreme court of justice with incomparably more power and consistency. In the end all good is rewarded and all evil punished. . . . And the superior wisdom which directs this course of things, the infinite goodness that expresses itself in it, the justice that achieves its aim in it—these are the attributes of the divine being or beings who also created us and the world as a whole. (Freud 1927, 199)

Freud considered our civilization to be built upon such illusions and the maintenance of human society to be based on most people's believing in the truth of such doctrines. He believed that if people were taught that there was no almighty and all-just God, no divine world order, and no life beyond the grave, they would not feel obliged to obey the precepts of civilization; they would follow their asocial, egoistic instincts and seek to exercise their power without inhibition or fear, and the chaos banished through the work of thousands of years of civilization would be the result (Freud 1927, 216–17).

Gandhi Contra Hitler

In 1938, Gandhi judged that Hitler's Germany was "showing to the world how efficiently violence can be worked when it is not hampered by any hypocrisy or weakness masquerading as humanitarianism" and "how hideous, terrible, and terrifying it looks in its nakedness." Gandhi said that he believed that the "tyrants of old never went so mad as Hitler seems to have gone." Gandhi described Hitler as one acting with religious zeal to propound "a new religion of exclusive and militant nationalism in the name of which any inhumanity becomes an act of humanity to be rewarded here and hereafter," a crime that he was visiting "upon his whole race with unbelievable ferocity" (Gandhi 2002, 164).

Gandhi wrote letters to Hitler. On July 23, 1939, describing himself as someone who had "deliberately shunned the method of war not without considerable success," Gandhi addressed a brief letter to Hitler in which he appealed to him as the one person in the world who could prevent a war that might reduce humanity to the savage state. Gandhi warned Hitler that no one had "a monopoly on the science of destruction" and that some power would certainly improve on his method and beat him with his own weapon (Gandhi 2002, 179).

In a letter addressed to Hitler on December 24, 1940, which the British government did not allow to be delivered or made public, Gandhi again appealed to Hitler to make an effort for peace. This time Gandhi described himself as one whose own "business in life has been for the past thirty-three years to enlist the friendship of the whole of humanity by befriending humanity, irrespective of race, color, or creed." He expressed his hope that Hitler would have the "time and desire to know how a good portion of humanity who have been living under the influence of that doctrine of universal friendship view" his actions (Gandhi 2002, 179, 181).

Gandhi warned Hitler that he was leaving no legacy to his people of which they would feel proud and that they could not "take pride in a recital of cruel deeds, however skillfully planned." Gandhi wrote that he was aware that Hitler's view of life regarded his acts as virtuous, but that his writings and pronouncements, and those of his friends and admirers left no room for doubt that many of those acts were "monstrous and unbecoming of human dignity," especially in the eyes of people who believed in universal friendliness and had learned to see acts of spoliation as degrading to humanity (Gandhi 2002, 179–81). Gandhi informed Hitler that he himself had discovered in nonviolence a force which, if organized, could "without a doubt match itself against a combination of all the most violent forces in the world" and could "be used practically without money and obviously without the aid of the science of destruction" that Hitler had "brought to such perfection" (Gandhi 2002, 181).

The Nazi persecution of the Jews did not seem to Gandhi to have had any parallel in history and he conceded that if "there ever could be a justifiable war in the name of and for humanity, a war against Germany, to prevent the wanton persecution of a whole race, would be completely justified" (Gandhi 2002, 164). Gandhi could not, however, advocate war. Beginning in the 1930s, he addressed himself to Jews undergoing Nazi persecution. Drawing attention to the fact that Hitler had not come across organized nonviolent resistance on an appreciable scale, if at all, but had always found ready response to the violence that he had used. Gandhi advised Jews that there was a way for them to resist the "organized and shameless persecution" to which they were being subjected, "to preserve their self-respect and not to feel helpless, neglected, and forlorn." They need not feel helpless, Gandhi suggested, if they chose to take the nonviolent way (Gandhi 2002, 121–22).

Gandhi believed that "if the Jews can summon to their aid the soul power that comes only from nonviolence, Hitler will bow before the courage which he has never yet experienced in any large measure in his dealings with people, and which, when it is exhibited, he will accept is infinitely superior to that shown by his best storm troopers" (Gandhi 2002, 167). He considered that the "exhibition of such courage is only possible for those who have a living faith in the God of Truth and Nonviolence (Love)" (Gandhi 2002, 167).

Gandhi says that if he were a Jew born in Germany and earned his living there, he would claim Germany as his home "even as the tallest Gentile German may" and would challenge him to shoot him or cast him in the dungeon. He says that he would refuse to be expelled or to submit to discriminating treatment and would not wait for fellow Jews to join him in civil resistance, but would have the confidence that in the end the rest would be bound to follow his example. He believed that if one Jew, or all Jews, were to accept the prescription he was proposing, they could not be worse off than they were then and the suffering voluntarily undergone would bring them an inner strength and joy (Gandhi 2002, 165). He wrote that he was

> convinced that if someone with courage and vision can arise among them to lead them in nonviolent action, the winter of their despair can in the twinkling of an eye be turned into the summer of hope. And what has today become a degrading manhunt can be turned into a calm and determined stand offered by unarmed men and women possessing the strength of suffering given to them by Jehovah. It will be then a truly religious resistance offered against the godless fury of dehumanized people. The German Jews will score a lasting victory over the German Gentiles in the sense that they will have converted the latter to an appreciation of human dignity. They will have rendered service to fellow Germans and proved their title to be the real Germans as against those who are today dragging, however unknowingly, the German name into the mire. (Gandhi 2002, 166)

Gandhi was prepared to acknowledge, however, that it was highly probable that if a Jewish Gandhi were to arise in Nazi Germany, he or she "could function for about five minutes and would be promptly taken to the guillotine." He did not, however, believe that that would disprove his own case or shake his belief in the efficacy of nonviolence (Gandhi 2002, 168). As he told Hitler: "In nonviolent technique . . . there is no such thing as defeat. It is all 'Do or Die' without killing or hurting" (Gandhi 2002, 181).

As for Hitler, in *Mein Kampf* he says, unsurprisingly, that even as a boy he was no pacifist and all attempts to educate him in that direction had come to nothing (Hitler, 158). He said that any "unspoiled, healthy boy . . . feels like throwing up when he hears the tirades of a pacifist 'idealist'" and is ready to give his life for the ideal of his nationality. He protested "against the visions of the pacifist windbag who in reality is nothing but a cowardly, though camouflaged egoist, transgressing the laws of development" (Hitler, 299).

The Power of Self-Sacrifice

The readiness to suffer, even to give one's life, for one's enemy is one of the principal planks of nonviolent philosophy. As Jean Goss explained: "Not only does non-violence demand that we love our enemies, but it is also based on the love of enemies. It goes even further. The non-violent person gives his life for his enemies" (Houver, 26).

In Gandhi's words: "The eternal law for undoing wrong and injustice is that you have to be prepared to suffer cheerfully at the hands of all and sundry, and you will wish ill to no one, not even to those who may have wronged you" (Gandhi 2002, 119). "Nonviolence in its dynamic condition means conscious suffering. It does not mean meek submission to the will of the evildoer, but it means putting one's whole soul against the will of the tyrant" (Gandhi 2002, 101). "Suffering injury in one's own person is of the essence of nonviolence and is the chosen substitute for violence to others," Gandhi taught (Gandhi 2002, 93). According to him, the prayer of nonviolent persons "for themselves will always be that the spring of compassion in them may ever be flowing and that they may ever grow in moral strength so that they may face death fearlessly (Gandhi 2002, 114).

Martin Luther King, who stood on Gandhi's shoulders (King 1959a, 39–48), realized that when one is a victim of broken promises, "confronted with blasted hopes, and the dark shadow of deep disappointment," that the only alternative may be to present one's very body as the means of laying one's case before people's consciences (King 1963a, 86). King saw that in passively resisting injustice, one must face acts of cruelty and violence, that it

> will mean suffering and sacrifice. It might even mean going to jail. If such is the case we must be willing to fill up the jail houses. . . . It might even mean physical death. But if physical death is the price that some must pay to free their children from a permanent life of psychological death, then nothing could be more honorable. Once more it might well turn out that the blood of the martyr will be the seed of the tabernacle of freedom. (King 1957, 26)

For King, the defense of those in his movement must be "to meet every act of violence toward an individual Negro with the facts that there are thousands of others who will present themselves in his place as potential victims" (King 1957, 26). He believed that such "dynamic unity," "amazing self-respect," "willingness to suffer," and "refusal to hit back" would soon cause their oppressors to become ashamed of their own methods, would force them to stand before the world and God splattered with the blood and reeking with the stench of their Negro brothers (King 1957, 27). King realized that there was "no easy way to create a world where men and women can live together," but considered that if such a world was created that would "be accomplished by persons who have the courage to put an end to suffering by willingly suffering themselves rather than inflict suffering on others" (King 1966, 134). He said that he had found that every attempt to end nonviolent protests of his movement:

> by intimidation, by encouraging Negroes to inform, by force and violence, further cemented the Negro community and brought sympathy for our cause from men of good will all over the world. The great appeal for the world appears to lie in the fact that we. . . . have adopted the method of nonviolence. In a world in which most men attempt to defend their highest values by the accumulation of weapons of destruction, it is morally refreshing to hear five thousand Negroes in Montgomery shout 'Amen' and 'Halleluh' when they are exhorted to 'pray for those who oppose you,' or . . . conclude each mass meeting with 'Let us pray that God shall give us strength to remain nonviolent though we may face death'. (King 1956, 11)

King affirmed that "God still has a way of wringing good out of evil. History has proven over and over again that unmerited suffering is redemptive" (King, 1963c, 116). He affirmed that there "is something in this universe that justifies James Russell Lowell in saying:

> Truth forever on the scaffold
> Wrong forever on the throne
> Yet that scaffold sways the future
> And behind the dim unknown stands God
> Within the shadows keeping watch above his own. (King 1957, 23)

According to Gandhi, a person intent on fighting evil through nonviolent means, "gives up the body in the certain faith that if anything would change his opponent's view, a willing sacrifice of the body must do so. . . . Indeed victory lies in the ability to die in the attempt to make the opponent see the Truth . . ." (Borman, 83). He argued that:

> When a lump of earth is broken into dust, it mixes with water and nourishes plant life. It is by sacrificing themselves that plants sustain every kind of animal life. Animals sacrifice themselves for the good of their progeny. The mother suffers unbearable pain at the time of childbirth, but feels only happy in that suffering. Both the mother and the father undergo hardships in bringing up their children. Wherever communities and nations exist, individual members of

those communities or nations have endured hardships for the common good. (Gandhi 2002, 153)

Gandhi described himself to Hitler as someone determined to make British rule "impossible by nonviolent non-cooperation. . . . based on the knowledge that no spoiler can compass his end without a certain degree of cooperation, willing or compulsory, of the victim. Our rulers may have our land and bodies, but not our souls. . . . For, if a fair number of men and women be found in India who would be prepared without any ill will against the spoilers to lay down their lives rather than bend the knee to them, they would have shown the way to freedom from the tyranny of violence" (Gandhi 2002, 180). "If sufficient food is given to the tyrant, a time will come when he will have had enough. If all the mice in the world held a conference together and resolved that they would no more fear the cat but all run into her mouth, the mice would live," reasoned Gandhi (Gandhi 2002, 122).

Gandhi realized that a large cause might require many self-sacrificial deaths to achieve the conversion of opponents. He said that he could "conceive the necessity of the immolation of hundreds, if not thousands, to appease the hunger of dictators who have no belief in nonviolence. Indeed, the maxim is that nonviolence is the most efficacious in front of the greatest violence. Its quality is really tested only in such cases. Sufferers need not see the result during their lifetime" (Gandhi 2002, 168). He said that it was not because he placed a low value on life that he joyfully countenanced thousands voluntarily losing their lives, but because he knew that, in the long run, it results in the least loss of life and ennobles those who lose their lives and morally enriches the world because their sacrifice (Gandhi 2002, 93; Borman 82, 88). "Sufferings of the nonviolent have been know to melt the stoniest hearts" (Gandhi 2002, 167), Gandhi pointed out in defense of his teachings.

In his memoirs, Commandant of Auschwitz Rudolf Hoess provided a memorable example of victims running into the arms of their captors. Hoess says there that of the many religious fanatics that he had met in his life, the Jehovah's Witnesses who stubbornly refused to undertake military service or do any work connected with the war surpassed anything he had seen. Afraid that they would undermine military morale by religious means, the Nazis condemned Witnesses who took such stands to death (Hoess, 95–98).

Hoess recalled two especially fanatical Witnesses who refused to do any work having any connection with the military. They had been frequently flogged, but "underwent this punishment with joyous fervor that amounted almost to a perversion" and "begged the commandant to increase their punishment." When told that they would be executed, "they went almost mad for joy and ecstasy, and could hardly wait for the day of the execution. They wrung their hands, gazed enraptured up at the sky and constantly cried: 'Soon we will be with Jehovah! How happy we are to have been chosen!' A few days earlier they had witnessed the execution of some of their fellow-believers and they could hardly be kept under control, so great was their desire to be shot with them." Hoess had found their frenzy painful to watch. They had to be forced back to their cells. He writes:

> When their time came, they almost ran to the place of the execution. They wished on no account to be bound, for they desired to be able to raise their hands to Jehovah. Transformed by ecstasy, they stood in front of the wooden wall of the rifle-range, seemingly no longer of this world. . . . Their faces completely transformed, their eyes raised to heaven, and their hands clasped and lifted in a prayer; they went to their death. All who saw them die were deeply moved, and even the execution squad itself was affected. (Hoess, 95–96)

Hoess found that Witnesses went to their death filled "with a strangely contented, . . . almost radiant, exaltation." Suffering and even dying for Jehovah being their coveted aim, they willingly submitted to all hardships. He was touched by the care they bestowed on one another, the way they helped and comforted one another in any way possible whenever they could. Himmler and other Nazi officials were even known to instruct SS-men to display comparable fanatical and unshakeable faith in the National Socialist ideal and Adolf Hitler, to tell them that only when all SS-men believed their own philosophy as fanatically would Adolf Hitler's State be permanently secure, that a *Weltanschauung* could only be established and permanently maintained by fanatics utterly prepared to sacrifice their egos for their ideals (Hoess, 95–98).

Tolstoy taught that "as well as the noose, the gallows, spies, prisons, rifles, rifle-butts, etc., there are spiritual forces that are extremely strong and far more powerful than any sort of gallows or prison" (Tolstoy 1908, 222). Immortalized in art by Francis Poulenc and Georges Bernanos, the execution of the Carmelites of Compiègne also illustrates the theories about self-sacrifice discussed above.

During the Reign of Terror during the French Revolution, sixteen Carmelite sisters daily offered themselves as victims to divine justice for the restoration of peace to France and to the Church. On July 17, 1794, they went to the guillotine singing "Let's climb the scaffold high, let's give God the victory" to the tune of the *Marsellaise* (Bush 1999). Although it is impossible to establish any real causal relationships between such immolations and any successes they appear to have achieved, given the nature of Gandhi's, King's, and Tolstoy's convictions it is important to note out that the Reign of Terror came to an end ten days after they were sacrificed.

Many have concluded that the spectacle the Carmelites created did its share to stop the bloodbath (Bush, 1999). Had not that architect of the Reign of Terror Maximilien de Robespierre himself just pointed out on May 7th of that year that "innocence on the scaffold makes the tyrant on his triumphal chariot turn pale?" (Robespierre 1794b, 316).

In 1938 Gandhi thought that even if Britain, France, and America were to declare hostilities against Germany, the "calculated violence of Hitler" might "even result in a general massacre of the Jews by way of his first answer to the declaration of such hostilities." But he suggested that if the Jewish mind could be prepared for voluntary suffering, even the massacre he had imagined "could be turned into a day of thanksgiving and joy that Jehovah had wrought deliverance of the race even at the hands of the tyrant" (Gandhi 2002, 165).

The Jews, Gandhi declared, "have not been actively nonviolent or, in spite of the misdeeds of the dictators, they would say, 'We shall suffer at their hands; they know no better. But we shall suffer not in the manner in which they want us to suffer'" (Gandhi 2002, 121). "If even one Jew acted thus," Gandhi considered, "he or she would save his or her self-respect and leave an example which, if it became infectious, would save the whole of Judaism and leave a rich heritage to humanity besides" (Gandhi 2002, 121).

In the person of Edith Stein, we have an instance of a German Jew doing what Gandhi advised. In a text that was published on the internet, Edith Stein wrote from the Carmelite monastery in Cologne on February 2, 1934 of drawing down God's grace and mercy on a humanity submerged in sin and need in a "time, when the powerlessness of all natural means for battling the overwhelming misery everywhere has been demonstrated so obviously, and an entirely new understanding of the power of prayer, of expiation, and of vicarious atonement has again awakened." "The sight of the world in which we live, the need and misery and an abyss of human malice," she wrote, "again and again dampens jubilation over the victory of light. The world is still deluged in mire." "Only someone whose spiritual eyes have been opened to the supernatural correlations of worldly events can desire suffering in expiation" (Stein 1934; Stein 1999).

In March 1939, Edith Stein offered herself to the heart of Jesus as a "sacrificial expiation for the sake of true peace." On July 11, 1942, the Christian churches of Holland notified Nazi officials that they would proclaim Sunday July 26 "a day of atonement and prayer" and read to their congregations a letter proclaiming that they were "deeply shocked by the measures being taken against the Jews in the Netherlands." The text goes on to say that they had "become aware with horror of the new regulations by which men, women and children and entire families are to be deported. . . . Because of the suffering this will cause tens of thousands of people, knowing that these measures contradict the deepest moral conscience of the Dutch people, but above all because these measures violate everything we are commanded by God as right and just, the churches must urgently appeal to you not to carry out these measures . . ." (Bourlet, 86–87).

Not heeding warnings of reprisals made by Nazi officials, the statement of protest was read from every Catholic pulpit in Holland. Nazi officials reacted by an order to deport all Catholic Jews in Holland. Approximately 700 Catholic Jews were arrested in early August, among them Edith Stein and her sister Rosa, then living in a Carmelite convent in Holland. They were gassed in Auschwitz forthwith (Bourlet, 86–87).

Again, no causal relationship can be established between immolation and the events following in their wake, and there is not really any point in trying to establish one. But within the context of a study of the claims made in this section about confronting evil through self-sacrifice, subsequent events, be they coincidental, really should not go unmentioned. In this case, it should be noted that the beginning of the end of Hitler's *Reich* came in the wake of the beginning of the implementation of the Final Solution in 1942. As Alan Bullock notes: "At the moment when the tide turned in the autumn of 1942 Hitler was undisputed master of the greater part of continental Europe, with his armies threatening the Volga, the Caucasus and the Nile." "By the autumn of 1942," however, "the German advance at Stalingrad, as well as in the Caucasus and North Africa, had been brought to a standstill. . . . The climacteric had been passed, and for the first time . . . the initiative passed out of Hitler's hands, never to return" (Bullock, 628–29).

In keeping with Gandhi's conviction that the greater the purity, the greater the power because greater channeling of spiritual forces would be Pope Pius XII's efforts to marshal spiritual power in the war against evil. On October 31, 1942, in Portugal (where his words were not subject to censorship), in what he called "this tragic hour of human history," he committed, entrusted, consecrated "the entire world torn by violent discord, scorched in a fire of hate, victim of its own iniquities" to the Immaculate Heart of Mary. He implored her to be "moved to pity in the face of so many material and moral disasters; by so many afflictions, which agonize fathers and mothers, brothers, innocent babes;" to be "moved to compassion in view of so many lives cut off in the very flowering of youth, so many bodies mangled by the horrible slaughter, so many tortured and afflicted souls;" to "obtain for us peace from God" and "those graces which can convert human hearts in an instant, those graces which prepare for, promote, and insure peace;" and to "grant to this war-stricken world the peace which the nations desire: peace in the truth, in the justice, and in the charity of Christ" and "a cessation of this conflict and true peace of soul" (Pius XII 1942, 202–4).[2]

By all accounts, right from the beginning, November 1942 was a disastrous month for Hitler and the real beginning of the end of his war. It was the month of Rommel's defeat at El Alamein, the Allied landings in North Africa, and the launching of the Soviet's huge winter offensive (Toland, 722–28; Sereny 1995, 363). Albert Speer, who as Hitler's minister of armaments saw Hitler at least twice a week, and often daily, said of Hitler that "as of that November he became a changed man." "Until that awful winter of 1942," Speer recalled, he "had rarely heard him rage, or even raise his voice in arguments. . . . But now, visibly exhausted, his body bent over with fatigue and his voice hoarse, his anger and bitterness . . . became quite awful . . ." (Sereny 1995, 364).

Hitler on Combating Spiritual Ideas by Violent Means

Paradoxically, and surely to the satisfaction of proponents of nonviolent responses to evil, the theories of evil of the theorists of Part One of this book can be interpreted in ways that actually support theories about the real power of nonviolence. In particular, Hitler and Nietzsche both wrote, even eloquently and compellingly, of the power of nonviolence, a fact that given the main arguments of this book surely bears closer examination. So, let us look at some of the theories of Part One in the light of the apparently antithetical theories of Part Three.

Adolf Hitler knew what it was to be down and out and powerless to act. In *Mein Kampf*, he gave explicit descriptions of this and of how it sharpened his sense of human psychology, of how he won his understanding of the human psyche and his ability see through illusions by being on the bottom (Hitler, 3–37). He could not claim to be a member of the master class, so made he made claims to be a member of the master race.

In a very interesting passage of *Mein Kampf* (Hitler, 170–72), Hitler asks whether spiritual ideas can be exterminated by the sword, whether philosophies can be combated by the use of brute force. His answers directly address realities recognized in the theories of the proponents of nonviolence studied above.

He says that in pondering these questions, he had discovered that the following principle emerged: "Conceptions and ideas, as well as movements with a definite spiritual foundation, regardless whether the latter is false or true, can, after a certain point in their development, only be bro-

---

[2] Pope John Paul II consecrated the world to the Immaculate Heart of Mary on March 25, 1984, an interesting moment in the history of the Soviet Union.

ken with technical instruments of power if these physical weapons are at the same time the support of a new kindling thought, idea, or philosophy" (Hitler, 170).

Hitler argues there that the "application of force alone without the impetus of a basic spiritual idea as a starting point, can never lead to the destruction of an idea and its dissemination . . . for experience shows that such a blood sacrifice strikes the best part of the people" because "every persecution which occurs without a spiritual basis seems morally unjustified and whips up precisely the more valuable parts of a people in protest" and this "results in an adoption of the spiritual content of the unjustly persecuted movement." He observed that this often takes place "simply through a feeling of opposition against the attempt to bludgeon down an idea by brute force" and as "a result the number of inward supporters grows in proportion as the persecution increases" (Hitler, 170).

The "complete annihilation of the new doctrine," Hitler avers, "can be carried out only through a process of extermination so great and constantly increasing that in the end all the truly valuable blood is drawn out of the people or state in question" (Hitler, 170–71), and the consequence of this is "that, though a so-called 'inner' purge can now take place, it will only be at the cost of total impotence. Such a method will always prove vain in advance if the doctrine to be combated has overstepped a certain small circle . . ." (Hitler, 171).

So, Hitler admits that "nearly all attempts to exterminate a doctrine and its organizational expression, by force without spiritual foundation are doomed to failure, and not seldom end with the exact opposite of the desired result" (Hitler, 171) because the "very first requirement for a mode of struggle with the weapons of naked force is and remains persistence . . ." (Hitler, 171). For, he considered, "as force wavers . . . not only will the doctrine to be repressed recover again and again, but it will also be in a position to draw new benefit from every persecution, since, after such a wave of pressure has ebbed away, indignation over the suffering induced leads new supporters to the old doctrine, while the old ones will cling to it with greater defiance and deeper hatred than before, and even schismatic heretics, once the danger has subsided, will attempt to return to their old viewpoint" (Hitler, 170).

Although rooted in many of the same realities recognized by proponents of nonviolence, Hitler's theories were, of course, designed to meet ends quite opposite theirs. So his answer to his questions about exterminating spiritual ideas with the sword, about combating philosophies by the use of brute force is that the very first prerequisite for success ultimately lies only in the steady and constant application of force which itself "can always and only arise from a definite spiritual conviction" (Hitler, 171).

Hitler concluded that any "violence which does not spring from a firm, spiritual base, will be wavering and uncertain" (Hitler, 171). Any attempt to combat a philosophy with methods of violence," he decided, "will fail in the end, unless the fight takes the form of attack for a new spiritual attitude. Only in the struggle between two philosophies can the weapon of brutal force, persistently and ruthlessly applied, lead to a decision for the side it supports" (Hitler, 172). Fighting "against a spiritual power with methods of violence remains defensive . . . until the sword becomes the support, the herald and disseminator, of a new spiritual doctrine" (Hitler, 172). This, he maintained, was the reason for the failure of the struggle against Marxism up to that point.

Hitler reasoned that any "philosophy . . . fights less for the negative destruction of the opposing ideology than for the positive promotion of its own. Hence its struggle is less defensive than offensive. It therefore has the advantage even in determining the goal, since this goal represents the victory of its own idea" (Hitler, 172). Recognizing the difficulty of determining when the negative aim of the destruction of a hostile doctrine is to be regarded as achieved and assured, Hitler considered that the philosophy's offensive will be more systematic and also more powerful than the defensive against a philosophy because the attack and not the defense is what is decisive (Hitler, 172).

The Power of the Ascetic Ideal

Nietzsche also gave good reasons to take into account, and even to fear, that flower power is more powerful than it seems. In *The Philosophy of Nietzsche*, H. L. Mencken asked how people who are called a lunatics or fools for throwing away their money, crippling themselves with drink, or turning away from their opportunities differ "from the ideal holy man of our slave-morality—the holy man who tortures himself, neglects his body, starves his mind and reduces himself to parasitism, that the weak, the useless and unfit may have, through his ministrations, some measure of ease" (Mencken, 107).

Though Mencken offered this "argument of the actual facts of existence—however unrighteous and ugly those facts may be" (Mencken, 107) in support of Nietzsche's theories, Nietzsche's own protestations against the meaning and power of the ascetic ideal reveal a deeper comprehension of the actual facts of existence than Mencken's do. Such protestations can serve to explain the power of the ascetic ideal that Nietzsche, and Gandhi, would be the first to acknowledge.

For Nietzsche, the ascetic ideal ruined health and taste. Part Three, of *On the Genealogy of Morals*, one half of the book, is entirely devoted to understanding the significance of the ascetic ideal, what it lets one divine, what lies behind it, underneath it, concealed in it, that of which it is the tentative, indistinct expression overloaded with question marks and misunderstandings. He writes of the monstrosity of its disastrous impact. He inquires into the power of this ideal, asks precisely what the monstrosity of its power signifies, why so much ground has been yielded to it, why greater resistance has not been put up to it (Nietzsche 1887, III §23).

In *Beyond Good and Evil*, Nietzsche had ventured an answer. Up until his time, he noted, the most powerful people of the world had bowed down before holy people, as before the enigma of self-mastery and deliberate extreme privation. They did so, he concluded, because they sensed in them that superior force that wishes put itself to the test in such mastery. Ascetics display a strength of a will in which the powerful recognize their own strength and domineering inclinations, and which they know how to revere. In revering saints, the powerful revere a part of themselves, Nietzsche concluded. Besides this, the appearance of holy people, decrepit and pitiful, arouses suspicion. Such a monstrosity of denial, of counternature would not be desirable without reason. The reason for it, the powerful have suspected, is that perhaps there is a very great danger about which ascetics would like to be better apprised. In short, the powerful of the world acquired a new fear of ascetics. They sensed a new power, a strange, yet untamed enemy in them. It was the will to power that forced them to stop before saints and to question them (Nietzsche 1886, §51). The ascetic ideal does not submit to any power, Nietzsche wrote well before Gandhi's time, but rather believes in its priority over any power (Nietzsche 1887, III §23).

The Powerless Declare War

Paradoxically, Nietzsche's vociferous protests about how the values he despised and wished to transvaluate had taken root themselves plainly speak of the power of nonviolence. Reflecting on the implications of the claims he made about the victories of Judeo-Christian morality, one finds astonishing affirmations on his part that, when interpreted from the perspective of nonviolent activists, actually serve to buttress Gandhi's convictions that the "power at the disposal of nonviolent persons is always greater than they would have if they were violent" (Gandhi 2002, 110), that "nonviolence is neither maimed nor weak," but all-powerful (Gandhi 2002, 106) and "infinitely greater than and superior to brute force" (Gandhi 2002, 115).

"Our weak, unmanly, social concepts of good and evil and their tremendous ascendancy over body and soul have finally made all bodies

and souls weak and have broken the independent, autonomous, unconstrained people, the pillars of a *strong* civilisation," Nietzsche lamented in
Daybreak (Nietzsche 1881, §163). He maintained that it was not the
strongest people, evil people, beasts of prey who were the ruination of the
strong. It was those who were the weakest, those weakened by illness,
those who were casualties, crushed, shattered to begin with, the weakest
who most undermine life among people, who poison and jeopardize people's confidence in life, in human beings, and in themselves in the most
dangerous way. It is they who constitute the greatest danger to healthy
people (Nietzsche 1887, III §14).

In *On the Genealogy of Morals*, Nietzsche placed the blame for bringing
about this execrable reversal of values squarely on the Jews. According to
his theories, the Jews achieved mastery over their enemies and their conquerors by daring to reverse their values totally and with dreadful consistency. It was a fact, he maintained, that with its vengeance and its reversal
of all values, Israel had so far triumphed over all other ideals, and time and
time again over all nobler ideals.

The Jews then sustained this reversal with tenacity by affirming that
only wretched, poor, powerless, humble people were good, that only suffering, needy, sick, ugly people were godly, blessed by God, that for them
alone was there bliss, while in comparison noble, powerful people were
accursed, execrated, damned for all time as evil, cruel, lascivious, rapacious,
godless. For Nietzsche, this reversal of values, which he considered monstrous and immeasurably disastrous, constituted a most fundamental declaration of war and initiated the slave revolt in morals that slowly achieved
victory. He said that one was obliged to face the facts: "the people—the
slaves, the plebes, the herd triumphed. . . . The lords were disposed of; the
morals of the common man triumphed. . . . Unquestionably, this poisoning was successful (Nietzsche 1887, I §§7–9).

Nietzsche explains how "out the trunk of the tree of vengeance and
hatred, of Jewish hatred,—of the deepest and most sublime, ideal producing, value transforming hatred, the likes of which has never been seen upon
this earth, grew something just as inimitable, a *new love*, the deepest and
most sublime of all kinds of love . . ." (Nietzsche 1887, I §8). He saw
Jesus, the gospel of love incarnate, the "redeemer" bringing bliss and victory to poor, sick, sinful people, as being "temptation in its most sinister
and irresistible form, the temptation and the dead end road to precisely
those Jewish values and reforming of ideals" (Nietzsche 1887, I §8).
Nietzsche asked whether any more dangerous bait could be contrived that
equaled "the enticing, enthralling, stunning, corrupting power of that
symbol of the holy cross, of that ghastly paradox of a God on the cross, of
that mystery of one unconceivable, final, most extreme, cruelty and self-
crucifixion of God *for the salvation of people*" (Nietzsche 1887, I §8).

Surely Nietzsche protested much too much. If, as it appears on the surface, weakness is really weak, powerlessness is really powerless, then what is the problem? The weak and powerless could not possibly have ever taken actual power in the first place. How did they triumph against all odds? Why then combat them in such passionate terms, or combat them at all, unless, to use Arthur Danto's words, "the theory concealed behind all this were correct, how the weak should have prevailed over the strong, disarming them in some manner as to get them to behave like the weak" (Danto, 172).

Torturing People's Consciences

In *Explaining Hitler*, Rosenbaum (Rosenbaum, 299–318) studies George Steiner's *The Portage to San Cristóbal of A.H.* (Steiner 1981), a work in which an imaginary, surviving Hitler presents a darker version of Great Rabbi Jacob Kaplan's thesis that the real source of Nazi anti-Semitism is to be found in the Jewish espousal of values of fraternity, justice, equality, universal kinship that are inimical to racism (Kaplan 1952, 11–12; 211–13).

At the end of Steiner's work, voicing ideas recalling those of Nietzsche and Freud, Hitler declares that not just the Germans, but the whole world, millions had found in him "the plain mirror of their needs and appetites" (Rosenbaum, 309). The whole world, this fictional Hitler says, wanted to eradicate the Jews because they had invented the conscience and left people guilty serfs tortured by expectations that they could never satisfy. Steiner's Hitler summarizes these expectations as the triple "blackmail of transcendence" exercised upon humanity by Moses with his Ten Commandments, by Jesus with his Sermon on the Mount, and by Karl Marx with his demands for social justice, who had effectively tortured humankind with their demands of conscience, love, and justice.

"What," Rosenbaum quotes Steiner's Hitler, "were our camps compared to *that*? Ask of man to be more than he is, hold before his tired eyes an image of altruism, of compassion, of self-denial which only the saint or the madman can touch, and you stretch him on the rack. Till his soul bursts. What can be crueler than the Jew's addiction to the ideal? . . . Three times the Jew has pressed on us the blackmail of transcendence. Three times he has infected our blood and brains with the bacillus of perfection" (Rosenbaum, 309).

In *Explaining Hitler*, Steiner explains that his hypothesis is that "our invention of God, of Jesus, our invention of Marxist utopia, has left humanity so uncertain inwardly that it is trying to banish its own bad conscience" (Rosenbaum, 316). He admits to believing that over the long run the torture of conscience is worse than even the torture in the concentration camps for "to feel yourself at fault probably builds up unbearable hatreds, *self*-hatreds. To feel yourself found out" (Rosenbaum, 316).

To Rosenbaum's question as to whether it was wrong to ask people to be better than themselves, Steiner replies: "No. . . . But they hate you for it. We hate no one as deeply as somebody who says we've got to do better and keeps saying it and rubbing it in, just rubbing our nose in our own failing. Oh boy! Who do we hate most? Those who have been generous to us in a moment of weakness, those who have seen us in abject need? And when we end up doing well, we will do anything not to look them in the eye again" (Rosenbaum, 313).

Conclusion

In Part One, I examined *theories* about evil. In Part Two, I studied *real manifestations* of evil. Part Three has been devoted to going from reality to theory. The partisans of nonviolent responses to evil of Part Three have aimed to eradicate precisely the kinds of evils depicted in Part Two and beautified, glorified, and idealized in Part One. They have dared to argue with their words and lives that seemingly unrealistic theories of noncooperation with evil are more deeply rooted in the deepest realities about evil and people than is normally suspected or has yet been fully elucidated. They have taught how it is that one is to understand this intelligence in practical, concrete, real terms. Their theories are formulated and their actions undertaken in terms so completely diametrically opposed to those of Part One as to indicate that both parties are actually facing quite the same phenomenon, but from opposite angles.

Sigmund Freud painted human existence as the theater of a kind of warfare where human beings are caught between destructive forces and *eros*, which is at work to preserve union and harmony. Mocking any nonviolent effort to contain it, destruction implacably carves its inroads, to use Freud's words, it "tramples in blind fury on all that comes in its way, as though there were to be no future and no peace among men after it is over" (Freud 1915, 65).

In 1930, Freud concluded his "Civilization and its Discontents" with the observation that human beings had so mastered the forces of nature that with their help they could easily utterly exterminate one another. He then adds that it is now to be expected that the other 'Heavenly Power', *eros*, "will make an effort to assert himself in the struggle with his equally immortal adversary," the power of death, aggression and destruction. "But," Freud asks, "who can foresee with what success and with what result?" (Freud 1930, 340)

The pertinence of Freud's question hangs on the assumption that goodness and evil are in some sense fairly matched, or that there is no greater power that can be appealed to that outperforms destruction and *eros*. The theorists and practitioners of nonviolent responses to evil studied here have maintained, however, that evil is always, and inevitably, too unintelligent, shortsighted, even blind, to hold sway for long; that a powerful force of goodness and justice that pierces through illusions to get to the reality of situations and to transform them does indeed exist; that, though it may often find itself strenuously repressed on all sides, there is an inherent urge for peace, goodness, justice, abiding love, freedom, unselfish love, forgiveness, hope, light, life, joy, generosity; that, in some people, genuine, not feigned or inculcated, revulsion at violence and destruction stands closer to nature; that one can conquer hate by love, untruth by truth, violence by self-suffering. Dedicated partisans of nonviolence have been willing to give their lives, and frequently actually have, to make those things clear.

That being so, more than Freud's observations do, a description of a battlefield experience by Ernst Jünger aptly depicted the forces with which partisans of nonviolent responses to evil see themselves to be contending. In a flight of lyricism, Jünger portrayed the landscape of a World War I battleground as a place of "two mighty forces of nature locked in conflict," where "moments of another kind when the deep discord and even deeper unity of this landscape came more clearly to one's mind. It was strange, for example, to hear at night the cry of partridges from the waste fields, or at dawn the careless song of the lark as it rose high above the trenches. Did it not seem then," he asks, "that life itself was speaking out of the confidence of its savage and visionary heart, knowing very well that in its more secret and essential depths it had nothing to fear from even the deadliest of wars, and going its way quite unaffected by the superficial interchange of peace and war?" (Jünger 1929, x–xi).

The alternative forces to which partisans of nonviolence would appeal are far more powerful than destructive power is and play on a deeper understanding of human realities than it does. They are not explicable in terms of Freud's god *eros*. In Martin Luther King's case, it was *agape*, which he defines as the "understanding, creative, redemptive good will for all," which "Biblical theologians would call the overflowing love of God that seeks nothing in return working in the minds of people" (King 1958, 31–32), that stood at the center of his fight against evil. *Agape*, he explained, "means loving people, "not because they are lovable, not because they do things that attract us, but because God loves them . . . we love the person who does the evil even while hating the deed that the person does" (King 1958, 32), ideas that Freud found incomprehensible. By his own admission, *eros* is selfish.

Nonviolent work to uproot evil assumes that however obvious it is that evil makes its inroads, and although the battle may be fierce at times, the odds are overwhelmingly stacked against evil and it ultimately loses. Just as there may be but a thin layer of civilization, so there is but a thin layer of destruction, which leaves root systems intact so that what appeared so easy to snuff out inevitably grows again. The universe is constantly at work repairing what is going wrong and has scored countless impressive victories. It remains overwhelmingly magnificently wondrous and beautiful. Love, goodness, life, creation, peace have to be primary or there would be nothing for hatred, evil, death, and destruction try to undo. They would have undone it all eons ago. The flowers of evil ultimately wilt and die, a dream carries them away.

Paradoxically, studying the theories of evil of people like Hitler and Nietzsche in conjunction with those of partisans of nonviolence, we find affirmations of the strength of weakness, the power of powerlessness, the violence of nonviolence, the reality of spiritual forces. It is no accident that that veteran of the underclass Hitler and that sickly Nietzsche were as lucid about the puissance of powerlessness, the might of weakness, the force of nonviolence, the potency of spiritual forces as those who have dared to shout the unbearable secret that weakness is powerful.

In theory and on paper, ideas about violent responses to evil all too often seem to win hands down. People take a derisive attitude toward declarations that nonviolence, unarmed truth, and unconditional love can limn the true and ultimate structure of a living reality, can undermine the entire existing order of the world, can engineer a complete transformation of the established structure of life, can uproot evil, can easily conquer hate by love, untruth by truth, violence by self-suffering, can have the final word in reality.

Upon inspection, one finds that the theories of partisans of nonviolence are not as crazy as they sound, but are often rooted in experimentation and stand validated by experience. After all, it has actually been recognized since time immemorial that peacefully preaching peace is violent, humility is daring, meekness is bold, gentleness is terrifying. As Goss has pointed out "Dreamers aren't dangerous. Most advocates of non-violence have done time in prisons, in camps, and almost all the great non-violent people have been assassinated, like Jesus. That's no accident" (Houver, 2).

Piercing veils of illusion, especially those of those with illusions of power, has always been a dangerous business. So let us conclude this study of the roots and flowers of evil by using Nietzsche's words: "Thus paradox stands against paradox! The truth cannot be on both sides: and is it in general on one of them? Put it to the test" (Nietzsche 1881, §163).

Bibliography

Actes du Colloque Jean Goss. Paris, 30 octobre 1993 (Printed at the Gutenberg Lycée, Illkirch, 1995).

Aly, Götz. 1994a. "Medicine against the Useless." In Aly, Chroust, and Pross, pp. 22–98.

———. 1994b. "Pure and Tainted Progress." In Aly, Chroust, and Pross, pp. 156–237.

Aly, Götz, Peter Chroust, and Christian Pross. 1994. *Cleansing the Fatherland: Nazi Medicine and Racial Hygiene.* Trans. Belinda Cooper. Baltimore: Johns Hopkins Press.

Anderson, George M. 2000. *With Christ in Prison.* New York: Fordham University Press.

Ansell-Pearson, Keith. 1994. *An Introduction to Nietzsche as Political Thinker: The Perfect Nihilist.* Cambridge UK: Cambridge University Press.

Antelme, Robert. 1957. *L'Espèce humaine, récit.* Paris: Gallimard.

———. 1996. *Textes inédits, sur l'Espèce humaine: Essais et Témoignages.* Paris: Gallimard.

Appel, Frederick. 1999. *Nietzsche contra Democracy.* Ithaca: Cornell University Press.

Arendt, Hannah. 1963. *Eichmann in Jerusalem: A Report on the Banality of Evil.* New York: Penguin 1992.

Aries, Paul. 1997. *Le Retour du Diable: Satanisme, Exorcisme, Extrême droite.* Villeurbanne: Editions Golias.

Aschheim, Steven. 1992. *The Nietzsche Legacy in Germany 1890–1990.* Berkeley: University of California Press.

Assoun, Paul-Laurent. 1980. *Freud et Nietzsche.* Paris: Presses Universitaires de France.

Aussaresses, Paul. 2001. *Services spéciaux, Algérie 1955–1957.* n.p.: Perrin.

Bäumler, Alfred. 1931. *Nietzsche der Philosoph und Politiker.* Leipzig: Reclam.

Bataille, Georges. 1957. *La littérature et le mal.* Paris: Gallimard.

Baudelaire, Charles. 1832-66, *Correspondance I–II.* Paris: Bernard Grasset, 1966.

———. 1846. "Promethée delivré." In Baudelaire 1980, pp. 443–45.

———. 1851. "Pierre Dupont." In Baudelaire 1980, pp. 532–36.

———. 1855a. "Puisque réalisme il y a." In Baudelaire 1980, pp. 464–66.

———. 1855b. "Exposition universelle 1855." In Baudelaire 1980, pp. 722–35.

221

———. 1855-57. "Edgar Poe, sa vie et ses œuvres: Notes nouvelles sur Edgar Poe." In Baudelaire 1980, pp. 575–600.

———. 1857. *Les Fleurs du mal et autres poèmes.* Paris: Garnier-Flammarion, 1964.

———. 1857b. "Les Drames et les romans honnêtes." In Baudelaire 1980, pp. 455–58.

———. 1859. "Théophile Gautier." In Baudelaire 1980, pp. 492–507.

———. 1860. *Les Paradis artificiels.* Paris: Garnier-Flammarion, 1966.

———. 1861. "Richard Wagner et Tannhäuser à Paris." In Baudelaire 1980, pp. 849–72.

———. 1863. "Le peintre de la vie moderne." In Baudelaire 1980, pp. 790–815.

———. 1869. *Le Spleen de Paris (Petits Poèmes en Prose): La Fanfarlo.* Paris: Garnier-Flammarion, 1987.

———. 1949. *Journaux Intimes, Fusées, Mon cœur mis à nu: carnet.* Paris: José Corti.

———.1975-76. *Œuvres Complètes I– II* (Edition Pléiade). Paris: Gallimard.

———. 1980. *Œuvres Complètes.* Paris: Editions Robert Laffont.

Beaugé, Florence. 2001. "L'accablante confession du Général Aussaresses sur la torture en Algérie." *Le Monde,* May 3.

Beckenhaupt, D. 1931. *Nietzsche und das gegenwärtige Geistesleben.* Leipzig: Heitz & Co.

Becker, Josef and Ruth, eds. 1983. *Hitlers Machtergreifung 1933: Vom Machantritt Hitlers 30. Januar 1933 bis zur Besiegelung des Einparteienstaates 14. Juli, 1933.* Munich: Deutscher Taschenbuch Verlag.

ben Cheikh, Ghaleb. "Fondements théologiques de la non-violence dans l'islam." In Bovy 2001, pp. 151–54.

Benjamin, Walter. 1974. *Charles Baudelaire: Un poète lyrique à l'apogée du capitalisme.* Paris: Payot.

Bergman, Ingmar. 1987. *The Magic Lantern.* Trans. Joan Tate. London: Penguin.

Bernadac, Christian. 1978. *Le Mystère Otto Rahn (Le Graal et Montségur): Du Catharisme au Nazisme.* Paris: Editions France-Empire.

Bertrand, Louis. 1914. "Nietzsche et la guerre." In *Nietzsche 1892–1914,* pp. 291–306. Paris: Maisonneuve et Larose, 1998.

Beschet, Paul. 1989. *Mission en Thuringe: Au temps du nazisme.* Paris: Editions Ouvrières.

Bianquis, Geneviève. 1929. *Nietzsche en France: L'influence de Nietzsche sur la pensée française.* Paris: Alcan.

Blin, Georges. 1948. *Le sadisme de Baudelaire.* Paris: Corti.

Bohrer, K. H. "Le présent absolu." *Du temps et du mal.* Paris: Maison des Sciences de l'Homme.

Bonner, Elena. 1986. *Alone Together: The Harrowing Story of Elena Bonner and Andrei Sakharov's Internal Exile in the Soviet Union.* New York: Vintage, 1988.

Bonner, Elena. 1992. *Mothers and Daughters.* New York: Alfred Knopf.

Borman, William. 1986. *Gandhi and Non-Violence.* Albany: State University of New York Press.

Bovy, Marie-Pierre, ed. 2001. *Gandhi: l'héritage: La non-violence défie toutes lesi, formes d'exclusion et d'oppression à l'Est comme à l'Ouest, au Nord comme au Sud.* Nantes: Siloë.

Bourlet, Joachim. 2001. "Hollande: les protestations accélèrent les deportations." *Histoire du Christianisme* (7 May): pp. 86–87.

Brustein, William. 1996. *The Logic of Evil: The Social Origins of the Nazi Party 1925–1933*. New Haven: Yale University Press.

Bullock, Alan. 1952. *Hitler: A Study in Tyranny*. London: Odhams Press Limited.

Bush, William. 1999. *To Quell the Terror: The True Story of the Carmelite Martyrs of Compiègne*. Washington D.C.: ICS Publications.

Carus, Paul. 1900. *The History of the Devil and the Idea of Evil*. New York: Random House, 1996.

Cary, Stephen. *The Intrepid Quaker: One Man's Quest for Peace: Memoirs, Speeches, and Writings of Stephen G. Cary*. Edited by A. Anderson and J. Coleman. Wallingford, PA: Pendle Hill Publications, 2003.

Cavaillès, Jean. 1932a. "Un mouvement de jeunesse en Allemagne." *Philosophia Scientiae* 3, no. 1 (1998): 1–21.

———. 1932b. "L'Allemagne et le Reichstag." *Philosophia Scientiae* 3, no. 1 (1998): 23–35.

———. 1933. "Crise du protestantisme allemande. *Philosophia Scientiae* 3, no. 1 (1998): 37–47.

———. 1934a. "Le conflit à l'intérieur du protestantisme allemande. *Philosophia Scientiae* 3, no. 1 (1998): 49–54.

———. 1934b. "La crise de l'église protestante allemande. *Philosophia Scientiae* 3, no. 1 (1998): 55–62.

Cerbelaud, Dominique. 1997. *Le Diable*. Paris: Editions de l'Atelier.

Chestov, Leon. 1925. *L'idée de bien chez Tolstoi et Nietzsche*. Paris: Editions du Siècle.

Claverie, Pierre. 1996. *Lettres et messages d'Algérie*. Paris: Karthala.

Cohn, Norman. 1996. *Warrant for Genocide: The Myth of the Jewish World Conspiracy and the Protocols of the Elders of Zion*. London: Serif. (Orig. pub. 1967.)

Cojean, Annick. 2002. "Chers Parents, Mikhaïl Gorbatchev." *Le Monde*, August 18-19.

Clark, Maudemarie. 1990. *Nietzsche on Truth and Philosophy*. Cambridge UK: Cambridge University Press.

Corngold, Stanley, and Geoffrey Waite. 2002. "A Question of Responsibility: Nietzsche with Hölderlin at War, 1914–1946." In Golomb and Wistrich, pp. 196–214.

Crépon, Pierre. 1991. *Les Religions et la Guerre*. Paris: Albin Michel.

Danto, Arthur. 1965. *Nietzsche as Philosopher*. New York, Columbia University Press, 1980.

de Chergé, Christian. 1997. *L'invincible espérance*. Paris: Bayard.

de Gaultier, Jules. 1926. *Nietzsche*. Paris: Delpeuch.

Delbanco, Andrew. 1995. *The Death of Satan: How Americans Have Lost the Sense of Evil*. New York: Farrar, Strauss and Giroux.

Delorme, Christian. 2001. "L'Algérie entre intégrismes et résistance passive de 1991 à 1998." In Bovy, pp. 131–34.

Dillard, Contre-Amiral. 1947. *La vie et la mort du R. P. Dillard*. Paris: Les Œuvres Françaises.

Döblin, Alfred. 1961. *Berlin Alexanderplatz.* Otten: Walter Verlag.

Doyle, Arthur Conan. 1890. "The Science of Deduction." *The Sign of Four.* London: Spencer Blackett.

Dummett, Michael. 1973. *Frege: Philosophy of Language,* London: Duckworth.

Euripides. 1998. *The Bacchae.* London: Nick Hern Books.

Faitelson, Alex. 1999. *Courage dans la tourmente en Lituanie 1941–1945: Mémoires du ghetto de Kovno.* Trans. Eve Line Blum-Cherchevsky. Paris: L'Harmattan. (Originally published in English as *Heroism and Bravery in Lithuania 1941–1945.* New York: Gefen Books, 1997.)

Farin, Michel. 1998. *Résistance et pardon: Maïti Girtanner.* Paris: Presses du Louvre.

Ferrières, Gabrielle. 1950. *Jean Cavaillès: Un philosophe dans la guerre 1903–1944.* Paris: Seuil, 1982.

Finnegan, William. 1998. *Cold New World: Growing Up in a Harder Country.* New York: Random House.

Fondane, Benjamin. 1947. *Baudelaire et l'expérience du gouffre.* Paris: Seghers.

Fraenkel, Heinrich, and Roger Manvell. 1989. *Goebbels: Der Verführer.* 2nd ed. Munich: Wilhelm Heyne Verlag.

Frege, Gottlob. 1924. "Diary: Written by Professor Dr Gottlob Frege in the Time from 10 March to 9 April 1924." Ed. G. Gabriel and W. Kienzler. *Inquiry* 39: 303–42.

Freud, Sigmund. 1908. "'Civilized' Sexual Morality and Modern Nervous Illness." In Freud 1985, pp. 33–55.

———. 1915. "Thoughts for the Times on War on Death." In Freud 1985, pp. 57–89.

———. 1921. "Group Psychology and the Analysis of the Ego." In Freud 1985, pp. 91–178.

———. 1927. "The Future of an Illusion." In Freud 1985, pp. 179–241.

———. 1930. "Civilization and its Discontents." In Freud 1985, pp. 243–340.

———. 1933. "Why War?" In Freud 1985, pp. 345–62.

———. 1974. *Cocaine Papers.* New York: Stonehill.

———. 1985. *Civilization, Society and Religion, Group Psychology, Civilization and its Discontents and Other Works.* Trans. James Strachey. London: Penguin.

Friedländer, Saül. 1998. *Nazi Germany and the Jews, the Years of Persecution (1933–1939).* New York: Perennial.

Gandhi, Mohandas. 1927-29. *Autobiography, or The Story of My Experiments with Truth.* London: Penguin, 1982.

———. 2002. *Essential Writings.* Ed. John Dear. Maryknoll, NY: Orbis Books.

Garaudy, Roger. 1995. *Mythes fondateurs de l'Etat d'Israel.* Paris: Samzidat.

Gates, Robert M. 1996. *From the Shadows: The Ultimate Insider's Story of Five Presidents and How They Won the Cold War.* New York: Simon and Schuster.

Gill, Anton. 1993. *A Dance between the Flames: Berlin Between the Wars.* London: Abacus.

Gilman, Sander, ed. 1987. *Conversations with Nietzsche: A Life in the Words of His Contemporaries.* Trans. David Parent. New York: Oxford University Press.

Ginzburg, Eugenia. 1967. *Journey into the Whirlwind.* San Diego: Harvest.

Golomb, Jacob, ed. 1997. *Nietzsche and Jewish Culture.* London: Routledge.

Golomb, Jacob, and Robert S. Wistrich, eds. 2002. *Nietzsche, Godfather of Fascism? On the Uses and Abuse of a Philosophy*. Princeton: Princeton University Press.

Goodrick-Clarke, Nicholas. 1985. *The Occult Roots of Nazism: Secret Aryan Cults and their Influence on Nazi Ideology*. New York: I. B. Tauris.

———. 1998. *Hitler's Priestess: Savitri Devi, the Hindu-Aryan Myth, and Neo-Nazism*. New York: New York University Press.

Gorbachev, Mikhail. 2000. *On My County and the World*. New York: Columbia University Press.

Gorska, M. Teresa, and M. Noela Wojtatowicz. 2000. *Blessed Martyrs of Nowogrodek*. Trans. M. Rita Kathryn Sperka. Chicago: Congregation of the Sisters of the Holy Family of Nazareth.

Goss-Mayr, Hildegard. 1998. *Oser le combat non-violent: aux côtés de Jean Goss*. Trans. from the German by Paul Kessler. Paris: Cerf.

Groethuysen, Bernard. 1926. *Introduction à la pensée philosophique allemande depuis Nietzsche*. Paris: Stock.

Hallen, Barry. 2000. *The Good, the Bad and the Beautiful: Discourse about Values in Yoruba Culture*. Bloomington: Indiana University Press.

Harrington, Anne. 1996. *Reenchanted Science: Holism in German Culture from Wilhelm II to Hitler*. Princeton: Princeton University Press.

Hasselbach, Ingo, and Winfried Bonengel. 1995. *Die Abrechung: Ein Neonazi Steigt Aus*. Berlin: Aufbau Taschenbuch Verlag.

Hayden, Deborah. 2003. *Pox: Genius, Madness, and the Mysteries of Syphilis*. New York: Basic Books.

Hersey, George. 1988. *The Evolution of Allure*. Cambridge, MA: MIT Press.

Hillesum, Etty. 1986. *Une vie bouleversée, suivi de Lettres de Westerbork*. Paris: Seuil.

Hitler, Adolf. 1926. *Mein Kampf*. Trans. Ralph Manheim. Boston: Houghton and Mifflin, 1971.

———. 1941-44. *Hitler's Table Talk 1941–44*. London: Weidenfeld and Nicolson, 1973.

Hoess, Rudolf. 1947. *Commandant of Auschwitz: The Authentic Confessions of a Mass Murderer*. Trans. Constantine Fitzgibbon. London: Pan Books, 1959.

Hollingdale, R. J. 1996. "The Hero as Outsider." In Magnus and Higgins, pp. 71–89.

Holub, Robert C. 2002. "The Elisabeth Legend: The Cleansing of Nietzsche and the Sullying of His Sister." In Golomb and Wistrich, pp. 215–35.

Houver, Gérard. 1981. *A Non-Violent Lifestyle: Conversations with Jean and Hildegard Goss*. Trans. Richard Bateman. London: Marshall Morgan and Scott Lamp Press.

Husserl, Edmund. 1898/99. "Aus der Einleitung der Vorlesung 'Erkenntnistheorie und Hauptpunkte der Metaphysik.'" In *Allgemeine Erkenntnistheorie, Vorlesung 1902/03*, pp. 223–55. Dordrecht: Kluwer, 2001.

Isherwood, Christopher. 1935. *The Berlin Stories: Last of Mr Norris, Goodbye Berlin*. New York: New Directions, 1972.

Jaspers, Karl. 1997. *Nietzsche: An Introduction to the Understanding of his Philosophical Activity*. Baltimore: Johns Hopkins Press.

Johnson, James Weldon. 1912. *The Autobiography of an Ex-Colored Man.* New York: Dover, 1995.

Jünger, Ernst. 1929. *The Storm of Steel.* New York: Howard Fertig, 1996.

————. 1930. *Copse 125: A Chronicle from the Trench Warfare of 1918.* New York: Howard Fertig, 2003.

Jung, Carl. 1910. "A Letter to Freud." In Jung 1995, pp. 25–26.

————. 1945. "After the Catastrophe." In Jung 1995, pp. 181–99.

————. 1946. "The Fight with the Shadow." In Jung 1995, pp. 174–80.

————. 1995. *Jung on Evil.* Ed. Murray Stein. London: Routledge.

Kammerer, Jean. 1995. *Mémoire en liberté: La barraque des prêtres à Dachau.* Paris: Brépols.

Kaplan, Francis. 1990. *Marx antisémite?* Paris: Imago.

Kaplan, Jacob. 1952. *Les Temps d'épreuve.* Paris: Minuit.

————. 1984. *N'oublie pas.* Paris: Stock.

————. 1995. *Justice pour la foi juive: Dialogue avec Pierre Pierrard.* Paris: Cerf.

Kaufmann, Walter. 1956. *Nietzsche: Philosopher, Psychologist, Antichrist.* New York: Meridian.

Kershaw, Ian. 1995. *Hitler 1889–1939: Hubris.* London: Penguin.

Khadda, Naget. 2001. "La symbolique de la violence dans l'imaginaire collectif algérien." In Bovy, pp. 143–50.

King, Martin Luther. 1956. "Our Struggle." In King 1992, pp. 4–13.

————. 1957, "Facing the Challenge of a New Age." In King 1992, pp. 14–28.

————. 1958. "The Power of Nonviolence." In King 1992, pp. 29–33.

————. 1959a. "My Trip to the Land of Gandhi." In King 1992, pp. 39–48.

————. 1959b. "The Social Organization of Nonviolence." In King 1992, pp. 49–53.

————. 1960a. "Pilgrimage to Nonviolence." In King 1992, pp. 55–62.

————. 1960b. "The Rising Tide of Racial Consciousness." In King 1992, pp. 64–72.

————. 1961. "The Time for Freedom Has Come." In King 1992, pp. 74–82.

————. 1963a. "Letter from Birmingham Jail." In King 1992, pp. 83–100.

————. 1963b. "I Have a Dream." In King 1992, pp. 101–6.

————. 1963c. "Eulogy for the Martyred Children." In King 1992, pp. 115–18.

————. 1964. "Nobel Prize Acceptance Speech." In King 1992, pp. 107–11.

————. 1965. "Our God is Marching on!" In King 1992, pp. 119–24.

————. 1966. "Nonviolence: The Only Road to Freedom." In King 1992, pp. 125–34.

————. 1967a. "A Time to Break Silence." In King 1992, pp. 135–52.

————. 1967b. "Where Do We Go From Here?" In King 1992, pp. 169–79.

————. 1968a. "The Drum Major Instinct." In King 1992, pp. 180–92.

————. 1968b. "I See the Promised Land." In King 1992, pp. 193–203.

————. 1992. *I Have a Dream: Writings and Speeches That Changed the World.* Ed. James Melvin. Washington. San Francisco: Harper.

Köhler, Joachim. 2002. *Zarathustra's Secret: The Interior Life of Friedrich Nietzsche.* Trans. Ronald Taylor. New Haven: Yale University Press.

Kogon, Eugen. 1946. *Der SS Staat: Das System der deutschen Konzentrationslager.* Frankfurt am Main: Europaïsche Verlagsanstalt.

Kreiser, Lothar. 2001. *Gottlob Frege: Leben—Werk—Zeit.* Hamburg: Felix Meiner Verlag.

La Mère Marie de Jésus, Fondatrice des Petites-Sœurs de l'Assomption: gardes-malades des pauvres à domicile. 1931. Paris: La Bonne Presse.

Lampert, Laurence. 1993. *Nietzsche and Modern Times.* New Haven: Yale University Press.

Lang, Berel. 2002. "Misinterpretation as the Author's Responsibility (Nietzsche's fascism, for instance)." In Golomb and Wistrich, pp. 47–65.

———. 2000. *Holocaust Representation: Art within the Limits of History and Ethics.* Baltimore: Johns Hopkins Press.

———. 1990. *Act and Idealism in the Nazi Genocide.* Chicago: University of Chicago Press.

Lannay, J. C. 1952. *Nietzsche, ou l'histoire d'un égocentrisme athée.* Paris: Desclée de Brouwer.

Lanzmann, Claude. 2001. *Sobibor, 14 octobre 1943, 16 heures.* Evreux: Cahiers du cinéma.

Leaman, Oliver. 1995. *Evil and Suffering in Jewish Philosophy.* Cambridge UK: Cambridge University Press.

Leiter, Brian. 2002. *Nietzsche on Morality.* London: Routledge.

Lichtenberger, Henri. 1904. *La philosophie de Nietzsche.* Paris: Alcan.

Londres, Albert. 1929. *Le Juif errant est arrivé.* Paris: Le Serpent à Plumes, 1998.

Magnus, Bernd. 1997. "Holocaust Child: Reflections on the Banality of Evil." *Philosophy Today*, Suppl, pp. 8–18.

Magnus, Bernd, and Kathleen Higgins, eds. 1996. *The Cambridge Companion to Nietzsche.* New York: Cambridge University Press.

Maldamé, Jean-Michel. 2001. *Le scandale du mal, une question posée à Dieu.* Paris: Cerf.

Mann, Thomas. 1941. *Appels aux Allemands 1940–45.* Paris: Editions Balland, 1985.

———. 1947. *Doctor Faustus.* Trans. T. T. Lowe-Porter. London: Penguin, 1968.

May, Simon N. 2002. *Nietzsche's Ethics and his War on 'Morality.'* Oxford: Clarendon.

Mazauric, Claude, ed. 1989. *Robespierre.* Paris: Messidor.

McNamara, Robert S. 1995. *In Retrospect: The Tragedy and Lessons of Vietnam.* New York: Random House.

Maritain, Jacques. 1963. *Dieu et la permission du mal.* Paris: Desclée de Brouwer.

Mencken, Henry L. 1908. *Friedrich Nietzsche.* London: T. Fisher Unwin.

Mennecke, Friedrich. 1941-44. "Selected Letters of Doctor Friedrich Mennecke." Ed. P. Chroust. In Aly, Chroust and Pross, pp. 238–95.

Michelet, Edmond. 1955. *Rue de la Liberté: Dachau 1943–1945.* Paris: Seuil.

Monier, Frédéric. 1998. *Le complot dans la République: Stratégies du secret de Boulanger à la Cagoule.* Paris: Editions la Découverte.

Monk, Ray. 1990. *Ludwig Wittgenstein: The Duty of Genius.* London: J. Cape.

———. 1996. *Bertrand Russell: The Spirit of Solitude 1872-1921.* New York: The Free Press.

Mullisch, Harry. 1961. "L'horreur et sa représentation (28.5.1961)." In *L'Affaire 40/61*, 137–47. Trans. from Dutch into French by Mireille Cohendy. Paris: Gallimard.

Müller-Lauter, Wolfgang. 2002. "Experiences with Nietzsche." In Golomb and Wistrich, pp. 66–89.

Münch, Maurus. 1977. *Prêtres allemands à Dachau.* Amiens: Fraternité Saint-Benoît.

Neiman, Susan. 2002. *Evil in Modern Thought: An Alternative History of Philosophy.* Princeton: Princeton University Press.

New York Times Archives 1851-1995. On-line at http://pqasb.pgarchives.com/ nytimes.

Nietzsche, Friedrich. 1872. (The Birth of Tragedy) *Die Geburt der Tragödie, Oder: Griechenthum und Pessimismus.* Stuttgart: Philipp Reclam jun., 1993.

———. 1878. (Human, All Too Human) *Menschliches allzu Menschliches: Ein Buch für Freie Geister.* Frankfurt: Insel Verlag.

———.1880. (The Wanderer and His Shadow) *Der Wanderer und sein Schatten.* In Nietzsche 1878, pp. 445–585.

———. 1881. (Daybreak) *Morgenröte: Gedanken über die moralischen Vorurteile.* Stuttgart: Alfred Kröner Verlag, 1952.

———. 1883-85. *Thus Spoke Zarathustra.* In Nietzsche 1954, pp. 115–439.

———. 1886. (Beyond Good and Evil) *Jenseits von Gute und Böse: Vorspiel einer Philosophie der Zukunft.* In Nietzsche 1984, pp. 9–211.

———. 1887. (On the Genealogy of Morals) *Zur Genealogie der Moral: Eine Streitschrift.* In Nietzsche 1984, pp. 211–363.

———. 1888. "The Antichrist: Attempt at a Critique of Christianity." In Nietzsche 1954, 568–656.

———. 1954. *The Portable Nietzsche.* Ed. and trans. Walter Kaufmann. New York: Viking Press.

———. 1984. *Jenseits von Gute und Böse, mit der Streitschrift Zur Genealogie der Moral.* Frankfurt: Insel Verlag.

Nordau, Max. 1993. *Degeneration.* Lincoln: University of Nebraska Press.

Owen, David. 1995. *Nietzsche, Politics and Modernity.* London: Sage.

Padfield, Peter. 1990. *Himmler: Reichsführer-SS.* London: Macmillan.

Philonenko, Alexis. 1998. *Nietzsche 1892–1914.* Paris: Maisonneuve et Larose.

Picard, Max. 1945. *Hitler in uns selbst.* Zurich: Rentsch.

Pichois, Claude, and Jean Ziegler. 1996. *Charles Baudelaire.* Paris: Fayard.

Picon, Gaétan. 1998. *Nietzsche: La vérité de la vie intense.* Paris: Hachette.

Piketty, Guillaume, ed. 1998. *Pierre Brossolette: Résistance (1927–1943).* Paris: Odile Jacob.

Pius XI and Joseph Goebbels. 1937. *Le dernier avertissement, Pie XI: encyclique Mit brennender Sorge, Goebbels: Dernier avertissement aux catholiques allemands.* Paris: Editions Romillat, 1994.

Pius XII. 1939-1944. *Die Briefe Pius XII. an die deutschen Bischöfe 1939–1944.* Mainz: Matthias Grünewald-Verlag, 1966.

Pius XII. 1942. *Papal Documents on Mary.* Ed. W. J. Doheny and J. P. Kelly. Milwaukee: The Bruce Publishing Co., 1954.

Pois, Robert. 1986. *National Socialism and the Religion of Nature.* Beckenham: Croom Helm Ltd.

Poliakov, Léon. 1987. *Le Mythe Aryen: Essai sur les sources du racisme et des nationalismes.* Brussels: Editions Complexe, 1971.

Porché, François. 1944. *Baudelaire: Histoire d'une âme*. Paris: Flammarion.

Pross, Christian. 1994. "Introduction." In Aly, Chroust, and Pross, pp. 1–21.

Rauschning, Hermann. 1940. *The Voice of Destruction*. New York: Putnam and Sons.

Reichel, Peter. 1993. *La fascination du nazisme*. Paris: Odile Jacob.

Reid, Constance. 1986. *Hilbert-Courant*. New York: Springer Verlag.

Rhodes, James. 1980. *The Hitler Movement: A Modern Millenarian Revolution*. Stanford: Stanford University Press.

Robespierre, Maximilien de. 1794a. "Sur les principes de morale politique qui doivent guider la Convention dans l'administration intérieure de la République (17 pluviôse an II/5 février 1794)." In Mazauric, pp. 297–305.

———. 1794b. "Sur les principes de morale politique qui doivent guider la Convention dans l'administration intérieure de la République (18 floréal an II/7 mai 1794)." In Mazauric, pp. 306–31.

Robinson, Dave. 1999. *Nietzsche and Postmodernism*. New York: Totem.

Rorty, Richard. 1989. *Contingency, Irony, and Solidarity*. Cambridge: Cambridge University Press.

Rosenbaum, Ron. 1998. *Explaining Hitler: The Search for the Origins of his Evil*. London: Macmillan.

Rovan, Joseph. 1999. *Mémoires d'un Français qui se souvient d'avoir été Allemand*. Paris: Seuil.

Russell, Bertrand. 1896. *German Social Democracy*. Nottingham: Spokesman Books.

———. 1968. *The Autobiography of Bertrand Russell, 1914–1944*. Vol. 2. London: Allen and Unwin.

Russell, Jeffrey Burton. 1986. *Mephistopheles: The Devil in the Modern World*. Ithaca: Columbia University Press.

Safranski; Rüdiger. 1994. *Heidegger et son temps*. Trans. from the German by Isabelle Kalinowski. Paris: Grasset.

Sakharov, Andrei. 1968. *Progress, Coexistence, and Intellectual Freedom*. New York: Norton.

Salaquarda, Jörg. 1996. "Nietzsche and the Judaeo-Christian Tradition." In Magnus and Higgins, pp. 90–118.

Santaniello, Weaver. 1994. *Nietzsche, God and the Jews: His Critique of Judeo-Christianity in Relation to the Nazi Myth*. Albany: SUNY Press.

———. 1997. "A Post-Holocaust Re-examination of Nietzsche and the Jews: Vis-à-vis Christendom and Nazism." In Golomb, pp. 21–55.

Satan. 1948. Paris: Desclée de Brouwer & Cie.

Schacht, Richard. 1995. *Making Sense of Nietzsche: Reflections Timely and Untimely*. Urbana: University of Illinois Press.

———. 2001. *Nietzsche's Postmoralism*. Cambridge UK: Cambridge University Press.

Schacht, Richard, ed. 1994. *Nietzsche, Genealogy, Morality: Essays on Nietzsche's Genealogy of Morals*. Berkeley: University of California Press.

Schwarzfuchs, Simon. 1998. *Aux prises avec Vichy: Histoire politique des Juifs de France (1940–1944)*. Paris: Calmann-Lévy.

Sereny, Gitta. 1974. *Into That Darkness: An Examination of Conscience*. New York: Vintage.

———. 1995. *Albert Speer: His Battle with the Truth*. New York: Vintage.

Serman, William. 1986. *La commune de Paris (1871)*. Paris: Fayard.

Siegel, Ronald K. 1994. *Whispers: The Voices of Paranoia*. London: Touchstone.

Simon, Albert. 2000. *Dieu à Buchenwald*. Paris: Editions de l'ouvrier.

Sleinis, E. E. 1994. *Nietzsche's Revaluation of Values: A Study in Strategies*. Urbana: University of Illinois.

Smith, Barry, and Adam Morton, eds. 2002. *Evil*. Special issue, *The Monist*, vol. 85, no. 2 (April).

Sommet, Jacques. 1987. *L'honneur de la liberté*. Paris: Centurion.

———. 1990. *Passion des hommes et pardon de Dieu*. Paris: Centurion.

Sommet, Jacques, and Albert Longchamp. 1995. *L'Acte de Mémoire: 50 ans après la déportation*. Paris: Editions de l'Atelier.

Sommet, Jacques, et. al. n.d. *Conflits & Réconciliation*. Revue Vie Chrétienne, no. 266, suppl.

Stein, Edith. 1934. "II. 2 Love for Love, III. 1 Love of the Cross." Accessed at www.karmel.at/ics/edith/stein_13.html.

———. 1999. *Source cachée, œuvres spirituelles*. Paris: Cerf.

Steiner, George. 1967. *Language and Silence: Essays on Language, Literature and the Inhuman*. New York: Atheneum.

Steiner, George. 1975. *After Babel: Aspects of Language and Translation*. New York: Oxford University Press.

———. 1999. *The Portage to San Cristóbal of A.H.* Chicago: University of Chicago Press.

Strong, Tracy B. 1996. "Nietzsche's Political Misappropriation." In Magnus and Higgins, 119–47.

Szafran, Maurice. 1994. *Simone Veil, Destin*. Paris: Flammarion.

Tazerout, M. 1946. *Critique de l'éducation allemande*. Paris: Nouvelles Editions Latines.

Tazerout, M. 1946. *L'éducation vitaliste*. Paris: Nouvelles Editions Latines.

Thomas, Laurence Mordekhai. 1993. *Vessels of Evil: American Slavery and the Holocaust*. Philadelphia: Temple University Press.

Thoreau, Henry David. 1984. *Civil Disobedience, and Reading*. London: Penguin.

Toland, John. 1976. *Adolf Hitler*. New York: Doubleday & Company.

Tolstoy, Leo. 1879. "A Confession." In Tolstoy 1987, pp. 19–80.

———. 1893. "Religion and Morality." In Tolstoy 1987, pp. 131–50.

———. 1902. "What is Religion and of What Does its Essence Consist?" In Tolstoy 1987, pp. 81–128.

———. 1908. "The Law of Love and the Law of Violence." In Tolstoy 1987, pp. 151–290.

———. 1987. *A Confession and Other Religious Writings*. Trans. and introduction by Jane Kentish. London: Penguin.

Traversac, Behja. 2001. "La genèse de la violence en Algérie." In Bovy, pp. 135–42.

Trotsky, Leon. 1936. "Their Morals and Ours." *The New International* 4, no. 6 (June).

―――. 1937. "Thermidor and Anti-Semitism." *The New International* (May 1941).

Vermeil, Edmond. 1939. *Doctrinnaires de la évolution allemande 1918–1938.* Paris: F. Scrolot.

La Violence: Une force à convertir. Christus 48, no. 192 (October 2001).

Verneaux, Roger. 1956. *Problèmes et mystères du mal.* Paris: Tegui.

Von Gumppenberg, Hans. 1921. *Philosophie und Okkultismus.* Munich: Rösl & Cie.

Von Hassell, Ulrich. 1978. *Diaries, 1938–1944: The Story of the Forces Against Hitler Inside Germany.* New York: AMS Press.

Voss, Hermann. 1932-42. "The Posen Diaries of the Anatomist Herman Voss." In Aly, Chroust, and Pross, pp. 99–155.

Walz, Georges, ed. 1932. *La vie de Frédéric Nietzsche d'après sa correspondance.* Paris: Roeder.

Warren, Mark. 1988. *Nietzsche and Political Thought.* Cambridge, MA: MIT Press.

Weinrich, Max. 1999. *Hitler's Professors: The Part of Scholarship in Germany's Crimes Against the Jewish People.* New Haven: Yale University Press. (Orig. pub. 1946.)

Westernhagen, Curt von. 1936. *Nietzsche, Juden, Antijuden.* Weimar: A. Duncker.

Wistrich, Robert S. 2002. "Between the Cross and the Swastika: A Nietzschean Perspective." In Golomb and Wistrich, pp. 144–69.

Würth, Johannes. 1992. *Priester im Dritten Reich: Erinnerungen eines Pfarrers.* Stein am Rhein: Christiana-Verlag.

Yovel, Yirimiyahu. 1998. *Dark Riddle: Hegel, Nietzsche, and the Jews.* University Park, PA: Pennsylvania University Press.

Zweig, Stefan. 1964. *The World of Yesterday.* Lincoln: University of Nebraska Press.

Index

233

Model ~~Fund~~ of Short-long -
                        floating

- Low prefno yielding > 5
   but want b more
   Thinks they're getting dear
        on a week/two
   - Short t-term repo
        CD's at 2%
   - MTA - NY Bond
        triple tax-free